Fact File

An All-American Animal

Black Bear
(Ursus americanus)

There are between 16,000 and 24,000 American black bears in California's mountains and forests. These beautiful animals can be over 6 feet in length and weigh 200 pounds or more. The California brown bear, the state symbol, disappeared 80 years ago.

In autumn, black bears spend some 20 hours a day hunting and eating. They are building the fat that will keep them alive when they hibernate.

HOUGHTON MIFFLIN

California Science

4

HOUGHTON MIFFLIN   BOSTON

Program Authors

William Badders
Director of the Cleveland Mathematics and
Science Partnership
Cleveland Municipal School District, Cleveland, Ohio

Douglas Carnine, Ph.D.
Professor of Education
University of Oregon, Eugene, Oregon

James Feliciani
Supervisor of Instructional Media and Technology
Land O' Lakes, Florida

Bobby Jeanpierre, Ph.D.
Assistant Professor, Science Education
University of Central Florida, Orlando, Florida

Carolyn Sumners, Ph.D.
Director of Astronomy and Physical Sciences
Houston Museum of Natural Science, Houston, Texas

Catherine Valentino
Author-in-Residence
Houghton Mifflin, West Kingston, Rhode Island

Primary Grade Consultant

Kathleen B. Horstmeyer
Past President SEPA
Carefree, Arizona

Content Consultants
See Teacher's Edition for a complete list.

California Teacher Reviewers

Robert Aikman
Cunningham Elementary
Turlock, California

Christine Anderson
Rock Creek Elementary
Rocklin, California

Dan M. Anthony
Berry Elementary
San Diego, California

Patricia Babb
Cypress Elementary
Tulare, California

Ann Balfour
Lang Ranch Elementary
Thousand Oaks, California

Colleen Briner-Schmidt
Conejo Elementary
Thousand Oaks, California

Mary Brouse
Panama Buena Vista Union
School District
Bakersfield, California

Monica Carabay
Four Creeks Elementary
Visalia, California

Printed in the U.S.A.

ISBN-13: 978-0-618-68618-6
ISBN-10: 0-618-68618-5

Science Content Standards for California Public Schools reproduced by permission, California Department of Education, CDE Press, 1430 N Street, Suite 3207, Sacramento, CA 95814.

4 5 6 7 8 9-CRK-15 14 13 12 11 10 09 08

California

California Teacher Reviewers (cont'd.)

Sheri Chu
Vineyard Elementary
Ontario, California

Teena Collins
Frank D. Parent Elementary
Inglewood, California

Gary Comstock
Cole Elementary
Clovis, California

Jenny Dickinson
Bijou Community School
South Lake Tahoe, California

Cheryl Dultz
Kingswood Elementary
Citrus Heights, California

Tom East
Mountain View Elementary
Fresno, California

Sharon Ferguson
Fort Washington Elementary
Fresno, California

Robbin Ferrell
Hawthorne Elementary
Ontario, California

Mike Freedman
Alta-Dutch Flat Elementary
Alta, California

Linda Gadis-Honaker
Banyan Elementary
Alta Loma, California

Lisa Gomez
Marshall James Elementary
Modesto, California

Lisa Green
Jordan Elementary
Orange, California

Carey Iannuzzo
Fitzgerald Elementary
Rialto, California

Teresa Lorentz
Banta Elementary
Tracy, California

Christine Luellig
Henderson Elementary
Barstow, California

Peggy MacArthur
Montevideo Elementary
San Ramon, California

Jeffrey McPherson
Parkview Elementary
Garden Grove, California

Susan Moore
Lang Ranch Elementary
Thousand Oaks, California

William Neddersen
Tustin Unified School District
Tustin, California

Josette Perrie
Plaza Vista School
Irvine, California

Lisa Pulliam
Alcott Elementary
Pomona, California

Jennifer Ramirez
Skyline North Elementary
Barstow, California

Nancy Scali
Arroyo Elementary
Ontario, California

Janet Sugimoto
Sunset Lane School
Fullerton, California

Laura Valencia
Kingsley Elementary
Montclair, California

Sally Van Wagner
Antelope Creek Elementary
Rocklin, California

Jenny Wade
Stockton Unified School District
Stockton, California

Judy Williams
Price Elementary
Anaheim, California

Karen Yamamoto
Westmore Oaks Elementary
West Sacramento, California

Contents

UNIT A
Ecosystems

Big Idea All organisms need energy and matter to live and grow. Living organisms depend on one another and their environment for survival.

Horned lizard

Activities

Mojave Desert

Contents

UNIT B
Energy and Matter in Ecosystems

Big Idea All organisms need energy and matter to live and grow. Living organisms depend on one another and on their environment for survival.

American painted
lady butterfly

Activities

Yosemite National Park

Contents

UNIT C
The Solid Earth

Big Idea The properties of rocks and minerals reflect the processes that formed them. Waves, wind, water, and ice shape and reshape Earth's land surface.

Activities

Death Valley

Contents

Activities

Golden Gate Bridge, San Francisco

Using Your Textbook

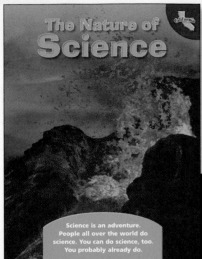

Science is an adventure. People all over the world do science. You can do science, too. You probably already do.

The Nature of Science

In the front of your book, you will be introduced to scientists and to ways of investigating science.

Every unit in your book has two or more chapters.

EARTH UNIT C SCIENCE

The Solid Earth

Stalactites forming in caves

Big Idea!

The properties of rocks and minerals reflect the processes that formed them. Waves, wind, water, and ice shape and reshape Earth's land surface.

153

Independent Books are books you can read on your own.

Big Idea! tells you the part of your **California Science Standards** that connects the Main Ideas of each lesson.

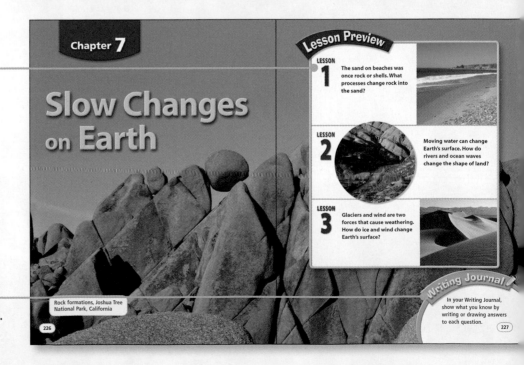

Chapter 7

Slow Changes on Earth

Rock formations, Joshua Tree National Park, California

226

Lesson Preview

LESSON 1 The sand on beaches was once rock or shells. What processes change rock into the sand?

LESSON 2 Moving water can change Earth's surface. How do rivers and ocean waves change the shape of land?

LESSON 3 Glaciers and wind are two forces that cause weathering. How do ice and wind change Earth's surface?

Writing Journal

In your Writing Journal, show what you know by writing or drawing answers to each question.

227

Lesson Preview gives information and asks questions about each lesson.

Writing Journal tells you to write or draw answers to the questions.

Vocabulary Preview

introduces important science terms, with pictures, and vocabulary skills.

California Science Standards are identified for each chapter.

Every lesson in your book has two parts.
Lesson Part 1: Directed Inquiry

Building Background gives you science facts and information.

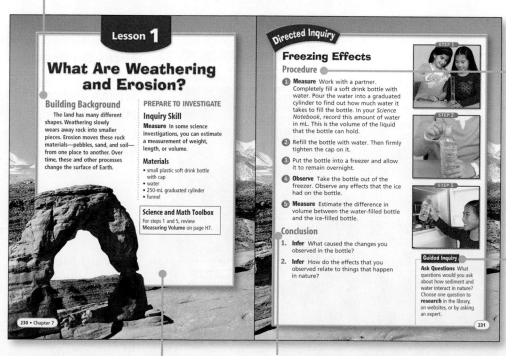

Procedure lists the steps you will follow to conduct your Investigation.

Guided Inquiry lets you take your investigation further.

California Science Standards appear in blue throughout each lesson.

Conclusion guides you in thinking about your investigation.

Lesson Part 2: Learn by Reading

Vocabulary lists the new science words that you will learn.

Main Idea tells you what is important.

Reading Skill helps you understand and organize information as you read.

Lesson Wrap-Up

Visual Summary shows you different ways to summarize what you've read.

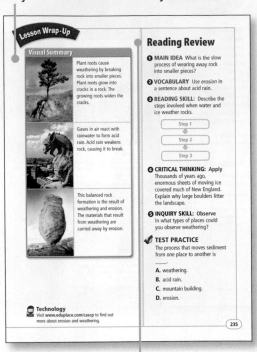

Reading Review lets you check your understanding after you read.

Focus On

Focus On lets you learn more about a key concept in a chapter.

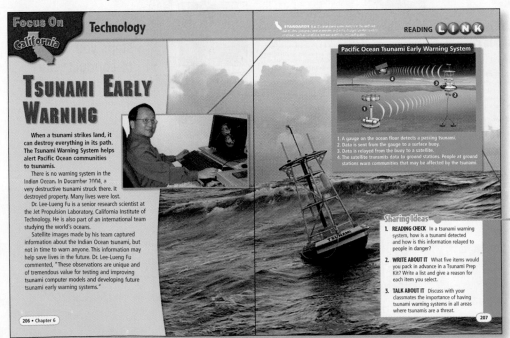

Focus On types include: History of Science, Technology, Primary Source, Literature, and Readers' Theater.

Sharing Ideas has you check your understanding and write and talk about what you have learned.

Extreme Science

Compares and contrasts interesting science information.

Writing Journal provides writing guidance for the Extreme Science lesson.

Links and Careers/People in Science

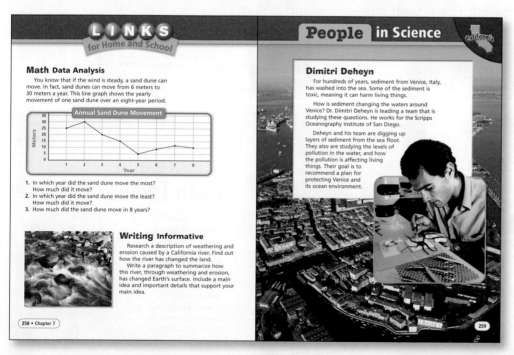

Links connects science to other subject areas.

Careers/People in Science tells you about the work of real scientists.

Chapter and Unit Review and Test Practice

Helps you to know you are on track with learning California science standards.

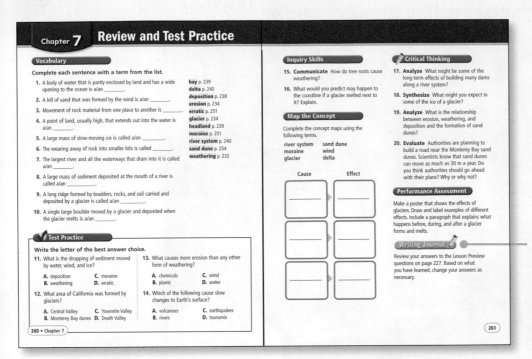

Chapter 7 — Review and Test Practice

Vocabulary

Complete each sentence with a term from the list.

1. A body of water that is partly enclosed by land and has a wide opening to the ocean is a/an _____.
2. A hill of sand that was formed by the wind is a/an _____.
3. Movement of rock material from one place to another is _____.
4. A point of land, usually high, that extends out into the water is a/an _____.
5. A large mass of slow-moving ice is called a/an _____.
6. The wearing away of rock into smaller bits is called _____.
7. The largest river and all the waterways that drain into it is called a/an _____.
8. A large mass of sediment deposited at the mouth of a river is called a/an _____.
9. A long ridge formed by boulders, rocks, and soil carried and deposited by a glacier is called a/an _____.
10. A single large boulder moved by a glacier and deposited when the glacier melts is a/an _____.

bay p. 239
delta p. 240
deposition p. 238
erosion p. 234
erratic p. 251
glacier p. 234
headland p. 239
moraine p. 251
river system p. 240
sand dune p. 254
weathering p. 232

Test Practice

Write the letter of the best answer choice.

11. What is the dropping of sediment moved by water, wind, and ice?
   A. deposition   C. moraine
   B. weathering   D. erratic

12. What area of California was formed by glaciers?
   A. Central Valley   C. Yosemite Valley
   B. Monterey Bay dunes   D. Death Valley

13. What causes more erosion than any other form of weathering?
   A. chemicals   C. wind
   B. plants   D. water

14. Which of the following cause slow changes to Earth's surface?
   A. volcanoes   C. earthquakes
   B. rivers   D. tsunamis

260 • Chapter 7

Inquiry Skills

15. **Communicate** How do tree roots cause weathering?

16. What would you predict may happen to the coastline if a glacier melted next to it? Explain.

Map the Concept

Complete the concept maps using the following terms.

river system   sand dune
moraine   wind
glacier   delta

Cause → Effect

Critical Thinking

17. **Analyze** What might be some of the long-term effects of building many dams along a river system?

18. **Synthesize** What might you expect in some of the ice of a glacier?

19. **Analyze** What is the relationship between erosion, weathering, and deposition and the formation of sand dunes?

20. **Evaluate** Authorities are planning to build a road near the Monterey Bay sand dunes. Scientists know that sand dunes can move as much as 30 m a year. Do you think authorities should go ahead with their plans? Why or why not?

Performance Assessment

Make a poster that shows the effects of glaciers. Draw and label examples of different effects. Include a paragraph that explains what happens before, during, and after a glacier forms and melts.

Writing Journal

Review your answers to the Lesson Preview questions on page 227. Based on what you have learned, change your answers as necessary.

261

Writing Journal instructs you to review the questions you answered at the start of the chapter.

Unit Wrap-Up

Learn more about science using the **Discover More** question. Also find a link to a simulation on the EduPlace web site.

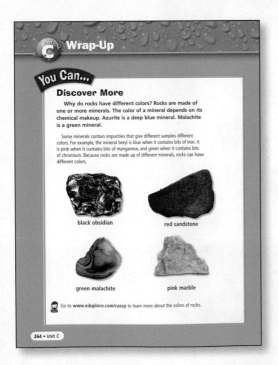

Unit C Wrap-Up

You Can...

Discover More

Why do rocks have different colors? Rocks are made of one or more minerals. The color of a mineral depends on its chemical makeup. Azurite is a deep blue mineral. Malachite is a green mineral.

Some minerals contain impurities that give different samples different colors. For example, the mineral beryl is blue when it contains bits of iron. It is pink when it contains bits of manganese, and green when it contains bits of chromium. Because rocks are made up of different minerals, rocks can have different colors.

black obsidian   red sandstone

green malachite   pink marble

Go to www.eduplace.com/cascp to learn more about the colors of rocks.

264 • Unit C

References

The back of your book includes sections you will refer to again and again.

Index

Biodegradable material, 136   Compass, 306, 317, 344   Competition

Glossary

bay (bay) A body of water that is partly enclosed by land and has a wide

Health and Fitness Handbook

Science and Math Toolbox

Science and Math Toolbox

Using a Hand Lens H2
Making a Bar Graph H3
Using a Calculator H4
Finding an Average H5
Using a Tape Measure or Ruler H6
Measuring Volume H7
Using a Thermometer H8
Using a Balance H9
Making a Chart to Organize Data H10
Reading a Circle Graph H11
Measuring Elapsed Time H12
Measurements H14

Start with Your Standards

Your California Science Standards

Welcome to the adventure of science!

Many famous scientists and inventors have lived and worked in California. Someday, you could be one, too!

Your science standards tell you what you should know by the end of Grade 4. They also tell what you should be able to do when you investigate and experiment. When you use your science book, you will find the standards printed next to each section of the lesson and chapter.

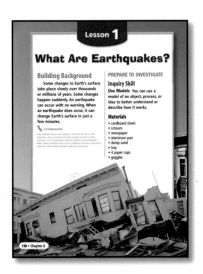

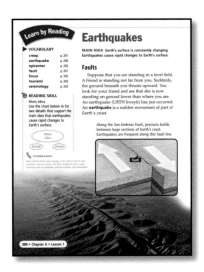

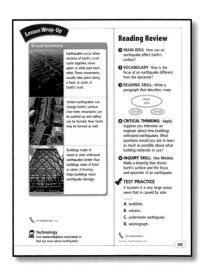

Houghton Mifflin Science will lead you to mastering your standards. Along the way, you will ask questions, do hands-on investigations, think critically, and read what scientists have discovered about how the world works. You will also get to know real people who do science every day.

How Families Can Help

- Get to know the California Science Content Standards on the pages that follow. If you want to learn more about science education, you can find the Science Framework for California Public Schools online at **www.cde.ca.gov/ci/**

- Relate the science of the standards to activities at home such as cooking, gardening, and playing sports.

- Get to know your child's science textbook, encouraging him or her to use the table of contents, index, and glossary. Point out the importance of titles and headings as a means to finding the information needed.

- Help your child choose library books to read about science, nature, inventors, and scientists. You can use the Recommended Literature for Math & Science online database at **www.cde.ca.gov/ci/sc/ll/**

- Find opportunities for your child to use numbers and mathematics skills and to measure and to estimate measurements, such as when planning a trip.

- Encourage your child to do experiments and enter science fairs.

Mount Shasta

Science Content Standards

These Science Content Standards are learning goals that you will achieve by the end of fourth grade. Below each standard is the unit or chapter in this book where that standard is taught. In that unit and chapter, there are many opportunities to master the standard—by doing investigations, reading, writing, speaking, and drawing concept maps.

Physical Sciences

Electricity and magnetism are related effects that have many useful applications in everyday life. As a basis for understanding this concept:
Unit D: Electricity and Magnetism

1.a. *Students know* how to design and build simple series and parallel circuits by using components such as wires, batteries, and bulbs.
Chapter 8: Electricity

1.b. *Students know* how to build a simple compass and use it to detect magnetic effects, including Earth's magnetic field.
Chapter 9: Magnetism and Electromagnets

1.c. *Students know* electric currents produce magnetic fields and know how to build a simple electromagnet.
Chapter 9: Magnetism and Electromagnets

1.d. *Students know* the role of electromagnets in the construction of electric motors, electric generators, and simple devices, such as doorbells and earphones.
Chapter 9: Magnetism and Electromagnets

1.e. *Students know* electrically charged objects attract or repel each other.
Chapter 8: Electricity

1.f. *Students know* that magnets have two poles (north and south) and that like poles repel each other while unlike poles attract each other.
Chapter 9: Magnetism and Electromagnets

1.g. *Students know* electrical energy can be converted to heat, light, and motion.
Chapter 8: Electricity
Chapter 9: Magnetism and Electromagnets

Life Sciences

All organisms need energy and matter to live and grow. As a basis for understanding this concept:
Unit A: Ecosystems
Unit B: Energy and Matter in Ecosystems

California red-legged frog

2.a. *Students know* plants are the primary source of matter and energy entering most food chains.
Chapter 3: Energy in Ecosystems

2.b. *Students know* producers and consumers (herbivores, carnivores, omnivores, and decomposers) are related in food chains and food webs and may compete with each other for resources in an ecosystem.
Chapter 2: Interactions of Living Things
Chapter 3: Energy in Ecosystems
Chapter 4: Matter in Ecosystems

2.c. *Students know* decomposers, including many fungi, insects, and microorganisms, recycle matter from dead plants and animals.
Chapter 4: Matter in Ecosystems

Set 3 Life Sciences

Living organisms depend on one another and on their environment for survival. As a basis for understanding this concept:
Unit A: Ecosystems
Unit B: Energy and Matter in Ecosystems

3.a. *Students know* ecosystems can be characterized by their living and nonliving components.
Chapter 1: Parts of Ecosystems

3.b. *Students know* that in any particular environment, some kinds of plants and animals survive well, some survive less well, and some cannot survive at all.
Chapter 1: Parts of Ecosystems
Chapter 2: Interactions of Living Things
Chapter 4: Matter in Ecosystems

3.c. *Students know* many plants depend on animals for pollination and seed dispersal, and animals depend on plants for food and shelter.
Chapter 2: Interactions of Living Things

3.d. *Students know* that most microorganisms do not cause disease and that many are beneficial.
Chapter 3: Energy in Ecosystems
Chapter 4: Matter in Ecosystems

Anza-Borrego Desert State Park

California

Set 4 — Earth Sciences (Rocks and Minerals)

The properties of rocks and minerals reflect the processes that formed them. As a basis for understanding this concept:
Unit C: The Solid Earth

4.a. *Students know* how to differentiate among igneous, sedimentary, and metamorphic rocks by referring to their properties and methods of formation (the rock cycle).
Chapter 5: Rocks and Minerals

4.b. *Students know* how to identify common rock-forming minerals (including quartz, calcite, feldspar, mica, and hornblende) and ore minerals by using a table of diagnostic properties.
Chapter 5: Rocks and Minerals

Set 5 — Earth Sciences (Waves, Wind, Water, and Ice)

Waves, wind, water, and ice shape and reshape Earth's land surface. As a basis for understanding this concept:
Unit C: The Solid Earth

Mono Lake

5.a. *Students know* some changes in the earth are due to slow processes, such as erosion, and some changes are due to rapid processes, such as landslides, volcanic eruptions, and earthquakes.
Chapter 6: Rapid Changes on Earth
Chapter 7: Slow Changes on Earth

5.b. *Students know* natural processes, including freezing and thawing and the growth of roots, cause rocks to break down into smaller pieces.
Chapter 7: Slow Changes on Earth

5.c. *Students know* moving water erodes landforms, reshaping the land by taking it away from some places and depositing it as pebbles, sand, silt, and mud in other places (weathering, transport, and deposition).
Chapter 7: Slow Changes on Earth

Set 6

Investigation and Experimentation

Scientific progress is made by asking meaningful questions and conducting careful investigations. As a basis for understanding this concept and addressing the content in the other three strands, students should develop their own questions and perform investigations. Students will:

Directed Inquiry and Guided Inquiry investigations in every lesson

6.a. Differentiate observation from inference (interpretation) and know scientists' explanations come partly from what they observe and partly from how they interpret their observations.
Directed Inquiry and Guided Inquiry investigations

6.b. Measure and estimate the weight, length, or volume of objects.
Directed Inquiry and Guided Inquiry investigations

6.c. Formulate and justify predictions based on cause-and-effect relationships.
Directed Inquiry and Guided Inquiry investigations

6.d. Conduct multiple trials to test a prediction and draw conclusions about the relationships between predictions and results.
Directed Inquiry and Guided Inquiry investigations

6.e. Construct and interpret graphs from measurements.
Directed Inquiry and Guided Inquiry investigations

6.f. Follow a set of written instructions for a scientific investigation.
Directed Inquiry and Guided Inquiry investigations

The Nature of Science

Science is an adventure.
People all over the world do
science. You can do science, too.
You probably already do.

Big Idea

Scientific progress is made by asking meaningful questions and conducting careful investigations.

Start With Your Standards

STANDARD SET 6. Investigation and Experimentation

6. Scientific progress is made by asking meaningful questions and conducting careful investigations. As a basis for understanding this concept and addressing the content in the other three strands, students should develop their own questions and perform investigations. Students will:

6.a. Differentiate observation from inference (interpretation) and know scientists' explanations come partly from what they observe and partly from how they interpret their observations.

6.b. Measure and estimate the weight, length, or volume of objects.

6.c. Formulate and justify predictions based on cause-and-effect relationships.

6.d. Conduct multiple trials to test a prediction and draw conclusions about the relationships between predictions and results.

6.e. Construct and interpret graphs from measurements.

6.f. Follow a set of written instructions for a scientific investigation.

The Nature of Science

Do What Scientists Do

Meet Patrick Chuang, a professor of Earth Sciences at the University of California Santa Cruz. He investigates clouds.

As Dr. Chuang could tell you, water enters the atmosphere as an invisible gas called water vapor. When the gas cools, it condenses to form tiny water droplets. These make up clouds.

Just how tiny are the water droplets? And how many droplets make up a cloud? Dr. Chuang asked questions like these. To find the answers, he helped invent a tool to measure and count cloud droplets.

The tool is a machine that beams laser light through a cloud, then measures how the light scatters. The **data**, or information collected, show the size, speed, and number of droplets.

This airplane is outfitted to carry scientific experiments into the atmosphere.

A typical size for droplets is 20 micrometers. That's about one fourth the width of a human hair! About one million of these droplets combine to form a single raindrop.

Dr. Chuang studies his data to learn more about how rain forms. He hopes to predict how Earth's rainfall might change in the future.

Scientists interpret their observations.

Scientists can learn much by observing nature with their eyes, ears, and other senses. Yet some objects are too large or too small to observe easily. Many events happen too slowly or too quickly.

For his droplet-measuring tool, Dr. Chuang relied on laser light—something he could observe and measure. Then he interpreted his observations to draw conclusions about clouds.

The laser machine rides attached to the plane's wing.

Think Like a Scientist

The ways scientists ask and answer questions about the world around them is called **scientific inquiry.** Scientific inquiry requires certain attitudes, or ways of thinking. To think like a scientist you have to be:

- curious and ask a lot of questions.

- careful when investigating and experimenting.

- able to keep an open mind. That means you listen to the ideas of others.

- open to changing what you think when your investigation results surprise you.

- willing to question what other people tell you.

Tides are changes in the level of the ocean that occur each day. What causes tides?

Use Critical Thinking

When you think critically you make decisions about what others tell you or what you read. Is what you heard or read fact or opinion? A *fact* can be checked to make sure it is true. An *opinion* is what you think about the facts.

Did anyone ever tell you how something works that you found hard to believe? When you ask, "What facts back up your idea?" you are thinking critically. Critical thinkers question scientific statements.

Tides seem to rise and fall at different times each day. I wonder what causes tides to keep changing that way?

I read that tides are caused by the pull of the Moon's gravity on Earth's oceans. The level of the oceans keeps rising and falling as the Moon and Earth move into different positions.

Science Inquiry

Using scientific inquiry helps you understand the world around you. For example, suppose you collect a sample of water from the ocean and put it in the freezer over night.

Observe The next day, you notice that the ocean water is not completely frozen. You also notice that ice cubes in the freezer are frozen solid.

Ask a Question When you think about what you saw, heard, or read, you may have questions.

Hypothesis Think about facts you already know. Do you have an idea about the answer? Write it down. That is your hypothesis.

Experiment Plan a test that will tell if the hypothesis is true or not. List the materials and tools you will need. Write the steps you will follow. Make sure that you keep all conditions the same except the one you are testing. That condition is called the *variable*.

Conclusion What do your results tell you? Do they support your hypothesis or show it to be false?

Describe your experiment with enough detail that others can repeat it. Communicate your results and conclusion.

My Salt Water Experiment

Observe It seems that ocean water does not freeze at the same temperature as plain water. Ocean water is salty.

Ask a question How does salt affect the freezing point of water?

Hypothesis Plain water will freeze before salt water because it has a higher freezing point than salt water.

Experiment I will put labeled containers of the same amount of salt water and plain water in a freezer. I will check on the containers every 3 minutes. I will record in which container the water freezes first.

Conclusion Plain water turns to ice before salt water. The results support my hypothesis. Plain water has a higher freezing point than salt water.

Inquiry Process

Here is a process that some scientists follow to answer questions and make new discoveries.

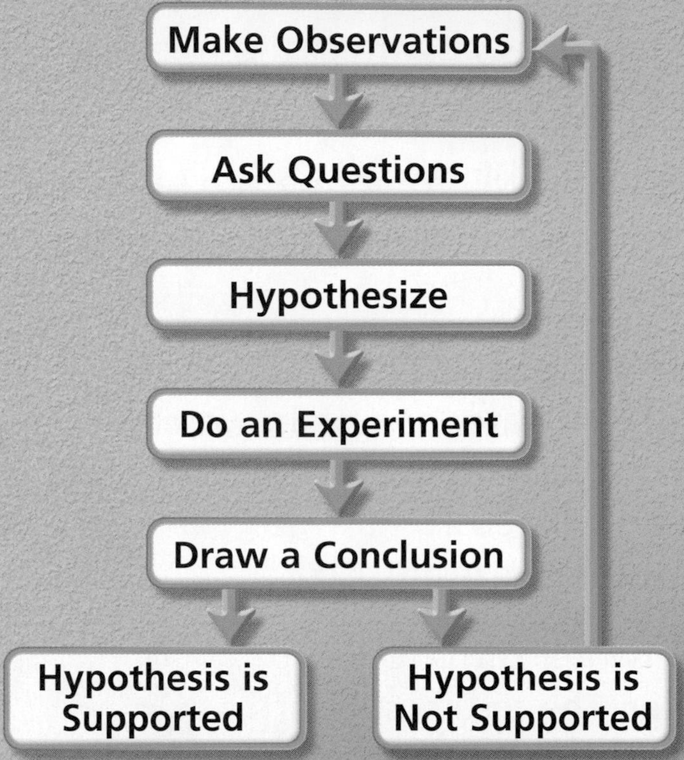

```
            Make Observations ◄──┐
                 │               │
            Ask Questions        │
                 │               │
             Hypothesize         │
                 │               │
           Do an Experiment      │
                 │               │
           Draw a Conclusion     │
              │       │          │
     Hypothesis is   Hypothesis is
      Supported      Not Supported ──┘
```

Science Inquiry Skills

You'll use many of these inquiry skills when you investigate and experiment.

- Ask Questions
- Observe
- Compare
- Classify
- Predict
- Measure

- Hypothesize
- Use Variables
- Experiment
- Use Models
- Communicate
- Use Numbers

- Record Data
- Analyze Data
- Infer
- Collaborate
- Research

STANDARDS
Formulate and justify predictions based on cause-and-effect relationships.
Follow a set of written instructions for a scientific investigation.

Try It Yourself!

Experiment With an Energy Sphere

When you touch both metal strips of the Energy Sphere, the sphere lights. This works with two people—as long as they are in contact with one another.

1 What questions do you have about the Energy Sphere?

2 How would you find out the answers?

3 Write your experiment plan and predict what will happen using the words *cause* and *effect*.

Be an Inventor

Alberto Behar's interest in space led him to a career in space engineering. At a NASA lab in California, Dr. Behar helped to invent a new kind of Martian rover. Called the tumbleweed, it looks more like a giant beach ball than a vehicle. It moves when the wind blows it.

The idea for the tumbleweed came about by accident. During a test of a rover with large inflatable wheels, one of the wheels fell off. The wind blew the wheel several kilometers before someone caught it. The idea of a wind-blown rover was born.

The tumbleweed has performed very well in tests on Earth. Dr. Behar thinks it may soon be used to explore the surface of Mars.

"When I was about seven or eight, I wanted to be an astronaut. I checked out all of the books on space I could at the library..."

What Is Technology?

The tools people make and the things they build with tools are all **technology.** A toy car is technology. So is a race car.

Scientists use technology, too. For example, a laser beam can be used to make very precise measurements. Scientists also use microscopes to see things they cannot see with just their eyes.

Many technologies make the world a better place to live. But sometimes a technology that solves one problem can cause other problems. For example, farmers use fertilizer to increase the yields of their crops. But fertilizer can be carried by rain water into lakes and streams where it can harm fish and other living things.

A Better Idea

"I wish I had a better way to _____." How would you fill in the blank? Everyone wishes they could find a way to do their jobs more easily or have more fun. Inventors try to make those wishes come true. Inventing or improving an invention requires time and patience.

George Hansburg patented the pogo stick in 1919. It was a Y-shaped metal stick with two foot rests and a spring. Today's pogo sticks are not much different.

Pogo Stick

spring

foot rest

How to Be a Good Inventor

1. **Identify a problem.** It may be a problem at school, at home, or in your community.

2. **List ways to solve the problem.** Sometimes the solution is a new tool. Other times it may be a new way of doing an old job or activity.

3. **Choose the best solution.** Decide which idea you predict will work best. Think about which one you can carry out.

4. **Make a sample.** A sample, called a *prototype,* is the first try. Your idea may need many materials or none at all. Choose measuring tools that will help your design work better.

5. **Try out your invention.** Use your prototype, or ask someone else to try it. Keep a record of how it works and what problems you find. The more times you try it, the more information you will have.

6. **Improve your invention.** Use what you learned to make your design work better. Draw or write about the changes you make and why you made them.

7. **Share your invention.** Show your invention to others. Explain how it works. Tell how it makes an activity easier or more fun. If it did not work as well as you wanted, tell why.

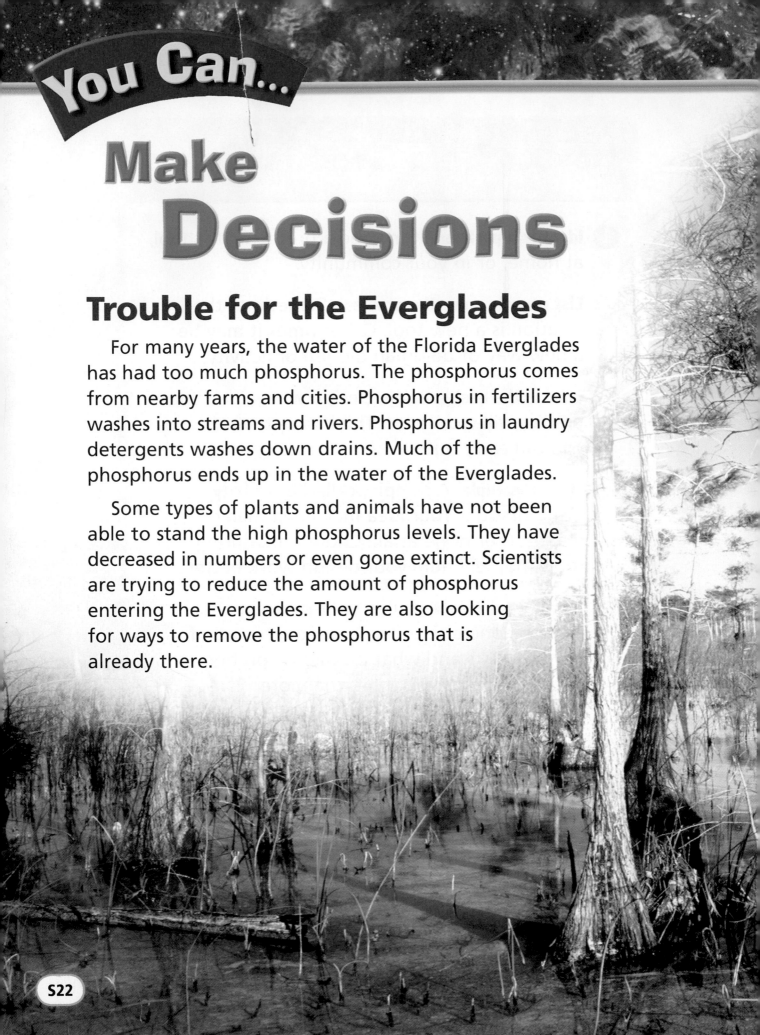

Make Decisions

Trouble for the Everglades

For many years, the water of the Florida Everglades has had too much phosphorus. The phosphorus comes from nearby farms and cities. Phosphorus in fertilizers washes into streams and rivers. Phosphorus in laundry detergents washes down drains. Much of the phosphorus ends up in the water of the Everglades.

Some types of plants and animals have not been able to stand the high phosphorus levels. They have decreased in numbers or even gone extinct. Scientists are trying to reduce the amount of phosphorus entering the Everglades. They are also looking for ways to remove the phosphorus that is already there.

Deciding What to Do

What methods are best to help lower phosphorus levels in the water of the Everglades?

Here's how to make your decision about the phosphorus problem. You can use the same steps to help solve problems in your home, in your school, and in your community.

Learn → Learn about the problem. Take the time needed to get the facts. You could talk to an expert, read a science book, or explore a web site.

List → Make a list of actions you could take. Add actions other people could take.

Decide → Think about each action on your list. Decide which choice is the best one for you or your community.

Share → Communicate your decision to others.

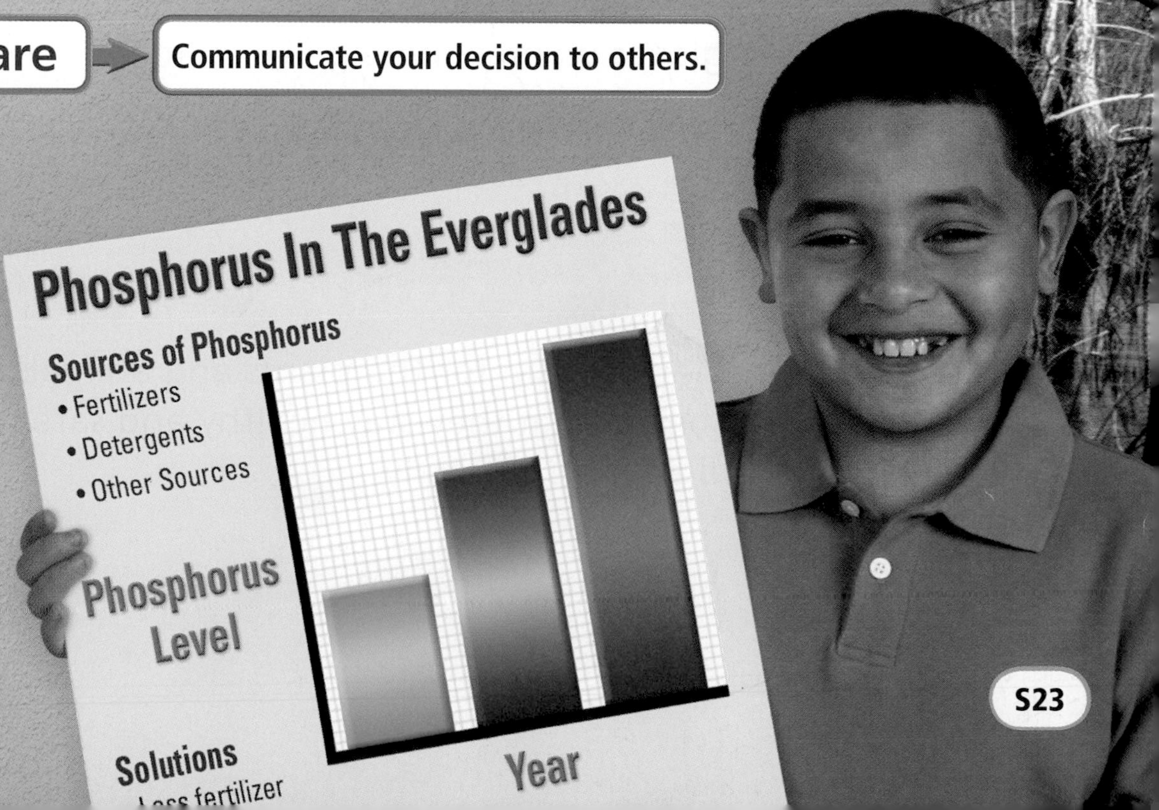

Phosphorus In The Everglades

Sources of Phosphorus
- Fertilizers
- Detergents
- Other Sources

Phosphorus Level

Year

Solutions
Less fertilizer

Science Safety

☑ Know the safety rules of your school and classroom and follow them.

☑ Read and follow the safety tips in each Investigation activity.

☑ When you plan your own investigations, write down how to keep safe.

☑ Know how to clean up and put away science materials. Keep your work area clean and tell your teacher about spills right away.

☑ Know how to safely plug in electrical devices.

☑ Wear safety goggles when your teacher tells you.

☑ Unless your teacher tells you to, never put any science materials in or near your ears, eyes, or mouth.

☑ Wear gloves when handling live animals.

☑ Wash your hands when your investigation is done.

Caring for Living Things

☑ Learn how to care for the plants and animals in your classroom so that they stay healthy and safe. Learn how to hold animals carefully.

Special growths on lupine roots add nitrogen to the soil, which makes the soil healthier.

Mountain lions find shelter in thick brush or caves.

LIFE **UNIT A** SCIENCE

Ecosystems

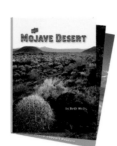

Sea lions in California kelp forest

Yosemite National Park

The tallest peak of The Three Brothers
mountain range is called Eagle's Peak

LIFE UNIT A SCIENCE

Ecosystems

California Connection

Visit www.eduplace.com/cascp to find out about California water and land ecosystems.

All organisms need energy and matter to live and grow. Living organisms depend on one another and their environment for survival.

Chapter 1

Parts of Ecosystems

Caribou, Denali National Park, Alaska

LESSON 1

Barnacles and seaweed survive by clinging to rocks. What other nonliving things help living things survive?

LESSON 2

Living things can only grow when their needs are met. What do most plants need?

LESSON 3

A tropical rainforest is one type of ecosystem. What are some other types of land ecosystems?

LESSON 4

Rivers, lakes, and tidal pools are water ecosystems. What do these water ecosystems provide to water birds?

Writing Journal

In your Writing Journal, show what you know by writing or drawing answers to each question.

Vocabulary Preview

Vocabulary

Glossary

Vocabulary Skill

Prefix/Suffix

ecosystem

The prefix *eco-* means "environment." The word *system* means "many parts working together to form a complete whole." Say each part of the word alone. Then say both parts together.

chaparral

An ecosystem where winters are wet and mild, but summers are extremely hot and dry.

taiga

A fairly dry ecosystem of the far north with very cold, long winters and short, cool summers.

rainforest

An ecosystem with a lot of rain all year round.

desert
A dry ecosystem with sandy soil.

Start with Your Standards

Standard Set 3. Life Sciences

3.a. *Students know* ecosystems can be characterized by their living and nonliving components.

3.b. *Students know* that in any particular environment, some kinds of plants and animals survive well, some survive less well, and some cannot survive at all.

Standard Set 6. Investigation and Experimentation standards covered in this chapter: 6.a., 6.c.

What Are Nonliving Parts of Ecosystems?

Building Background

Think about all the things found in and around a river. Do you think of living things, such as frogs, fish, or dragonflies? Perhaps you think of air and water. Air and water are nonliving things. Every ecosystem has living and nonliving parts. Without the nonliving parts, living things could not survive.

PREPARE TO INVESTIGATE

Inquiry Skill

Compare When you compare objects or events, you observe how they are alike and how they are different.

Materials

- plastic container (terrarium) with lid
- metric ruler
- gravel
- rocks
- potting soil
- dish of water
- hand lens
- goggles

Science and Math Toolbox

For step 1, review **Using a Hand Lens** on page H2.

Life Support

Procedure

1. **Observe** Use a hand lens to examine the gravel, soil, rocks, and water. These are all nonliving things.

2. **Measure** Fill a plastic container with a layer of gravel about 2 centimeters deep. Then add a layer of soil about 5 centimeters deep on top of the gravel. Use a ruler to measure. **Safety:** Wear goggles when adding gravel and soil to the container.

3. Place rocks and a shallow dish of water in the container. Put the lid on.

4. **Record Data** In your *Science Notebook*, list all the nonliving things in the container. Include those things you can see and any that you know are there but cannot see. Make a drawing of each thing you see. Label your drawings.

Conclusion

1. **Compare** Compare your list with another student's list. How are they similar? How are they different?

2. **Infer** What types of plants and animals do you think could live in your jar? What observations did you make that would support your inference?

3. **Predict** How would these living things interact with the nonliving things in the jar?

STEP 2

STEP 3

STEP 4

Nonliving Things

rock

Guided Inquiry

Ask Questions What questions do you have about the living and nonliving things you would find in a California tide pool? What are some ways you could **research** answers to your questions?

Learn by Reading

VOCABULARY

ecosystem   p. 8

READING SKILL

Classify

Use a chart to show the nonliving parts of a desert ecosystem and a polar ecosystem.

Group	Group

Nonliving Things in Ecosystems

MAIN IDEA Nonliving parts of an ecosystem, such as water, air, and sunlight, help living things meet their basic needs.

Ecosystems and Nonliving Things

Look out the window and you'll see an ecosystem (EE koh sihs tuhm). An **ecosystem** is made up of all the living and nonliving things that interact in an area. Nonliving things in ecosystems can include water, air, soil, and light.

Living things need nonliving things to meet their basic needs. Most plants need soil to grow. Both plants and animals depend on sunlight. Plants need sunlight to make food. Some plants and animals can survive only in warm temperatures. Others grow better in shade provided by trees, such as those found in a forest. Shade protects living things from direct sunlight and high temperatures.

The nonliving things in different ecosystems vary. For example, both a forest and an icy polar region have water, sunlight, soil, and air. However, the temperature of those nonliving things are quite different. These differences in nonliving things determine what can live in each ecosystem.

CLASSIFY What are some nonliving parts of an ecosystem?

Express Lab

Activity Card 1
Identify Nonliving Objects

A Forest Ecosystem

Light Nearly all plants need light to make food.

Air Both plants and animals need air to carry out their life processes.

Water A stream provides needed water for some of the animals and plants in the forest.

Shade Some organisms thrive in the shade offered by trees.

Soil Soil on the forest floor provides plants with the support and nutrients they need to grow.

Different Ecosystems

Each ecosystem has its own set of nonliving parts, which include light, water, temperature, and soil. These conditions determine the kinds of living things that are able to survive in that ecosystem. A living thing can survive only where its needs are met.

A Polar Ecosystem

All the soil on a polar ice sheet is covered by ice. Temperatures are very low. During half of the year there is little or no sunlight.
Even in this harsh place, there are animals that are able to survive and meet their needs. Polar bears are among them. With layers of fat and thick fur, these animals are able to keep warm. For food polar bears hunt animals that live in ocean water under and around the ice.

A Desert Ecosystem

In a desert ecosystem, daytime temperatures are very high. There is very little rainfall. The soil is sandy and has few nutrients. Desert plants and animals are adapted to these conditions. For example, the saltbush plant sends its roots deep into the ground to collect water. Many desert animals are active only at night when temperatures are lower.

CLASSIFY What conditions would you find in a polar ecosystem?

Visual Summary

Ecosystems are made up of living and nonliving things. Nonliving things include water, soil, rocks, and light.

Different ecosystems have different light, soil, water, and temperature conditions.

The light, soil, water, and temperature conditions in an ecosystem determine which plants and animals can live there.

Technology

Visit **www.eduplace.com/cascp** to find out more about the nonliving parts of ecosystems.

Reading Review

❶ MAIN IDEA How do some of the nonliving parts of an ecosystem help a plant or animal meet its basic needs?

❷ VOCABULARY Use *ecosystem* in a sentence about a desert.

❸ READING SKILL: Use a chart to show living and nonliving parts of a polar ecosystem.

Group	Group

❹ CRITICAL THINKING:
Analyze What is the relationship between living and nonliving parts of an ecosystem?

❺ INQUIRY SKILL: Compare Identify and compare all the nonliving parts of the forest ecosystem shown on page 9.

✓ TEST PRACTICE
The nonliving parts of an ecosystem _____.

A. are the same in every ecosystem.

B. determine which plants and animals can live in that ecosystem.

C. include animals and plants.

D. do not interact with the living parts of an ecosystem.

What Are Living Parts of Ecosystems?

Building Background

Every ecosystem is home to its own set of plants and animals and its own set of nonliving parts. This bristlecone pine tree, for example, lives in a hot, dry area. This ecosystem provides all the food, water, and sunlight the tree needs.

PREPARE TO INVESTIGATE

Inquiry Skill

Research When you do research, you learn more about a subject by looking in books, searching the Internet, or asking science experts.

Materials

- resource materials
- plastic container (terrarium) from Directed Inquiry, page 7
- grass and moss plants
- earthworms
- crickets
- apple slices
- cotton balls

Science and Math Toolbox

For step 1, review **Making a Chart to Organize Data** on page H10.

Right at Home

Procedure

1 **Research** In your *Science Notebook*, make a chart like the one shown. Use resource materials provided by your teacher to help you complete the Basic Needs column.

Living Thing	Basic Needs	How It Meets Needs
grass		
moss		
worm		
cricket		

2 **Experiment** Use the container from the Lesson 1 Directed Inquiry. Plant grass and moss plants firmly in the soil. Place a few earthworms and crickets in the container along with an apple slice. Change the water in the dish and add cotton balls to it. Then replace the lid. You have made a terrarium (tuh RAIR ee uhm), or a model of an ecosystem. Put it in sunlight.

3 **Observe** Several times a day, observe the living things to see how they meet their needs. Record your observations. Change the water and cotton balls and add apple slices when necessary.

Conclusion

1. **Compare** Exchange charts with another student. How are your data similar? How are they different?

2. **Predict** Choose one of the nonliving things in your terrarium. If this nonliving thing were removed, what effect would this have on the living things? Would each living thing still be able to meet its basic needs? Explain your answer.

Guided Inquiry

Experiment Plan an experiment to find out how an animal in a nearby ecosystem meets its needs. With your teacher's permission, **observe** the animal outside.

VOCABULARY

community	p. 16
energy	p. 14
environment	p. 16
organism	p. 14
oxygen	p. 14
population	p. 16
reproduce	p. 15
temperate zone	p. 16

READING SKILL

Cause and Effect
Use the chart to show the effect that nonliving parts of an ecosystem have on the living things in that ecosystem.

Cause → Effect

▲ Bats find shelter in caves.

Living Things in Ecosystems

MAIN IDEA Living things depend on nonliving things to meet their basic needs. Different plants and animals meet their needs in different ecosystems.

Traits of Living Things

What do plants, animals, and all other organisms need to survive? An **organism** (AWR guh nihz uhm) is a living thing. All organisms have similar basic needs.

Energy Moving, growing, and breathing all require energy (EHN ur jee). **Energy** is the ability to cause change. All organisms need a source of energy. Plants use energy from sunlight to make food. Animals get energy by eating plants or other animals.

Nutrients Nutrients are materials in food and soil that organisms need for energy and for growth.

Air Air is a mixture of gases. One of the gases in air is **oxygen** (AHK sih juhn). Most living things need oxygen to survive. When plants make food they give off oxygen.

Shelter All animals need a place to live. An animal's home may give it shelter and provide it with protection from other animals. Some animals use plants for shelter.

Water Living things are made mostly of water. In fact, more than three-fourths of your blood is water. Most living things can live for only a short time without water.

How is a bat different from a stuffed animal? The bat is alive and carries out life processes. A life process is a function that an organism performs to stay alive and reproduce (re pruh DOOS). Organisms **reproduce** by making more organisms of their own kind.

⏲ **CAUSE AND EFFECT** **Explain why organisms must meet their basic needs.**

Life Processes

Life Process		What It Means
Take in nutrients		Organisms take in materials like air, sunlight, water, and nutrients.
Grow and develop		Organisms use energy to grow and develop.
Release energy		Organisms release energy from food.
React to their surroundings		When a plant bends toward the light, it is reacting to its surroundings. All living things react to changes in their surroundings.
Give off wastes		Plants give off oxygen as a waste product of making food. Animals give off carbon dioxide and other wastes.
Reproduce		All living things have the ability to reproduce. This means that they can produce offspring, or young, like themselves.

Communities and Populations

Recall that ecosystems are made up of all living and nonliving things in an area. The forest shown here is one kind of ecosystem. It is found in a temperate (TEHM pur iht) zone. A **temperate zone** is an area of the Earth where the temperature rarely gets very hot or very cold. In this temperate forest ecosystem, many different organisms live and each carry out their life processes. That's because the nonliving conditions here allow many kinds of plants and animals to meet their basic needs.

An organism will survive only in an environment (ehn VY ruhn muhnt) that meets its needs. An **environment** is everything that surrounds and affects an organism.

All the organisms in an ecosystem make up a **community** (kuh MYOO nih tee). Within a community, there are different populations (pahp yuh LAY shunz) of living things. A **population** is all the members of one kind of plant or animal in a community. So all the white-tailed deer in the forest community make up one animal population. All the trillium in the forest make up one plant population.

CAUSE AND EFFECT Explain why a temperate forest ecosystem can support so many kinds of plants and animals.

Deer rely on grasses and tree leaves for food.

Express Lab

Activity Card 2
Experience Life Processes

A Forest Ecosystem

Warblers use forest trees for shelter.

Beavers use trees to build lodges for shelter.

Trillium plants grow best in shady areas with damp soils.

Conditions in Ecosystems

A terrarium is a model ecosystem. In a terrarium, living parts in the model interact with each other and with nonliving parts. Different parts of the model have slightly different conditions. In the terrarium shown, the rock and twigs under the heat lamp are dry and warm. The soil under the ferns is moist and cool. Like the terrarium, large ecosystems have conditions that vary in different areas. Organisms live where the conditions best meet their needs.

In the ocean, conditions vary in a coral reef ecosystem. Some organisms meet their needs at the top of the reef, near the water's surface. Others live in deeper water. The reef is made of living and nonliving parts of tiny coral animals. Many corals produce a hard outer casing. When they die, their stony casing remains. Over time new coral animals grow on the casings, forming the reef.

CAUSE AND EFFECT How can conditions within the same terrarium model ecosystem be different?

Model Ecosystem

ferns growing in soil

lizards getting heat from lamp

Visual Summary

Different plants and animals meet their needs in different ecosystems. The nonliving and living things in an ecosystem help organisms to carry out life processes.

All the different populations of plants and animals living in one area make up a community. The community is supported by the nonliving conditions of that ecosystem.

Different areas of an ecosystem have different conditions. Organisms live in the conditions that best meet their needs.

Reading Review

1 MAIN IDEA How do living things in an ecosystem interact?

2 VOCABULARY Define the term *environment*.

3 READING SKILL: What might happen if all the trees in a forest ecosystem were cut down? Use a graphic organizer for your answer.

Cause → Effect

4 CRITICAL THINKING: Apply Describe an ecosystem in which conditions are slightly different in different areas of the ecosystem.

5 INQUIRY SKILL: Research Use resource materials to research a rainforest ecosystem. Why do so few plants grow on the rainforest floor?

 TEST PRACTICE

A community is made up of _____.

A. all the organisms in an ecosystem.

B. all the nonliving things in an ecosystem.

C. all the organisms and nonliving things in an ecosystem.

D. all the members of one kind of plant or animal.

Technology
Visit **www.eduplace.com/cascp** to read more about plants and animals in different ecosystems.

What Are Some Land Ecosystems?

Building Background

Every ecosystem on Earth has its own set of plants and animals. The environment of each land ecosystem provides the organisms that live there with the things they need to survive. This colorful bird, for example, lives in the trees of the Amazon rainforest. The rainforest provides all the food, water, and shelter the bird needs.

PREPARE TO INVESTIGATE

Inquiry Skill

Analyze Data When you analyze data, you look for patterns to help you predict, infer, and draw conclusions.

Materials

- hand lens
- 1 piece of string

Science and Math Toolbox

For step 3, review **Using a Hand Lens** on page H2.

Observe Ecosystems

Procedure

1. **Record Data** In your *Science Notebook* make a chart like the one shown.

2. **Experiment** Take a short walk outdoors with your teacher and classmates. Lay your string along the ground in a place where you can kneel down. **Safety:** Watch out for any sharp objects on the ground.

3. **Observe** With your hand lens very close to the string, observe all the living and nonliving things along the entire length of your string.

4. **Record Data** Record your observations in your *Science Notebook*. Make a note about the nonliving conditions where you did your observations. For example, was the area sunny or shady?

Conclusion

1. **Analyze Data** Exchange charts with another student. How did the nonliving conditions of the area affect what could live there?

2. **Predict** Explain why your chart was similar to or different from your classmate's chart. Predict whether the organisms listed on your chart could live in the conditions listed on your classmate's chart.

STEP 1

Living Things	Nonliving Things

STEP 2

STEP 3

Guided Inquiry

Ask Questions Imagine your favorite California land ecosystem. Make a list of questions about the nonliving and living parts of that ecosystem. **Research** answers to your questions in the library.

Land Ecosystems

VOCABULARY

chaparral   p. 25
desert   p. 24
rainforest   p. 22
taiga   p. 26

READING SKILL

Main Idea and Details
Use the chart to show two details that support the idea that ecosystems are different from one another because of their nonliving conditions.

MAIN IDEA The nonliving conditions of each land ecosystem help determine which plants and animals can survive there.

Tropical Rainforest

A **rainforest** (RAYN fawr ihst) is an ecosystem where it rains a lot. Tropical rainforests are located near Earth's equator. It is quite warm all year and there is plenty of sunshine.

Tropical rainforests burst with life. Thousands upon thousands of species of plants and animals meet their needs in tropical rainforests around the world. These organisms thrive in the abundant sunlight, rain, and warm temperatures. Because tropical rainforests are home to so many plants, they produce a lot of Earth's oxygen.

The canopy of a tropical rainforest is the area at the tops of tall, full-grown trees. In a South American rainforest, trees such as the Kapok tree make up the canopy. Birds, monkeys, tree frogs, and many other organisms meet their needs in the canopy. Other organisms live in the understory, the shady area beneath the tree tops. Young trees and bushes make up the understory. Still other organisms live on the forest floor, which is very shady. These organisms include ferns, shrubs, vines, and animals such as jaguars.

Light, water, shelter, and temperature are different in the canopy, in the understory, and on the forest floor.

MAIN IDEA AND DETAILS Why do rainforests have so many kinds of plants and animals?

Tropical Rainforest Ecosystem

Canopy Many organisms live in the sunny, lush, rainforest canopy. Full-grown trees thrive in the sunlight. Many animals find food and shelter here.

harpy eagle

sloth

kapok tree

howler monkey

Understory The cocoa tree lives in the understory. It gets some dappled sunlight from above.

cocoa tree

jaguar

tapir

poison arrow frog

Forest Floor Some plants and animals live where shelter, water, and shade are abundant.

bromeliad

leaf-cutter ants

hercules beetle

23

roadrunner

desert tortoise

▲ The Mojave Desert in California is an ecosystem where plants and animals survive in harsh conditions.

Desert

A **desert** (DEH zurt) is a dry ecosystem with sandy soil. In some deserts, it might rain just once a year. In some rainforests, though, it rains nearly every day! In most desert ecosystems, daytime temperatures are very high. The soil has few nutrients.

Deserts are found all over the world. They exist in the American West, Africa, the Middle East, Asia, South America, and Australia. All of these deserts are similar because they all have plenty of sunlight, high temperatures, little rain, and soil with few nutrients. They are different because they support different plant and animal communities. All desert organisms are able to live in harsh desert conditions. But each desert has its own unique set of plants and animals. For example, plants and animals that live in the deserts of Australia are different from those living in California's Mojave Desert.

Chaparral

California is home to some of Earth's chaparral (shap ur AL) ecosystems. A **chaparral** ecosystem has wet, mild winters but extremely hot, dry summers.

Wildfires are common. Lightning strikes can ignite chaparral plants. Some of these plants actually need fire. Their seeds can only open and grow after a fire. Plants of the chaparral include shrubby, fire-resistant oaks, pines, and brush.

Animals of the chaparral include the cactus wren, scrub jay, gopher snake, and coast horned lizard. These animals can live for a long time in very dry conditions. The animals need the chaparral plants for water, food, and shelter.

Chaparral ecosystems are found in South America, Eurasia, Africa, and Australia. California's chaparral ecosystem is the only chaparral in North America.

MAIN IDEA AND DETAILS Explain why fire is important to chaparral ecosystems.

This chaparral ecosystem is in Mount Diablo State Park, California. ▼

scrub jay

horned lizard

25

Taiga

Taiga (TY guh) ecosystems are very cold. Winters are extremely long, cold, and severe. Summers are short and cool. Taiga ecosystems are fairly dry, with most moisture falling in the form of snow.

The most common trees in the taiga are pines, firs, and spruce trees. These trees are known as evergreens because they remain green all year. The leaves of these trees are thin, waxy needles that help keep in water. The needles also resist freezing temperatures.

These trees are well adapted to the nonliving conditions of the taiga. They are different from trees found in rainforests. Animals of the taiga include moose, deer, and wolves.

Taiga ecosystems are found across all of the northern parts of North America and Eurasia. They contain many trees. These trees are an important source of oxygen.

MAIN IDEA AND DETAILS Why do pine tree needles need to keep in water and resist freezing temperatures?

▼ **This taiga ecosystem is in Alaska.**

moose

Express Lab

Activity Card 3
Observe Ecosystems

Lesson Wrap-Up

Visual Summary

Nonliving conditions help determine what plants and animals can survive in an ecosystem. These conditions include rainfall, temperature, and sunlight.

Different land ecosystems have different nonliving conditions. For example, temperatures sometimes may be very warm and sometimes very cold, such as in some desert ecosystems.

Every ecosystem has its own set of animals and plants and nonliving conditions. The environment of each land ecosystem provides the organisms that live there with the things they need to survive.

Technology
Visit **www.eduplace.com/cascp** to find out more about Earth's land ecosystems.

Reading Review

❶ MAIN IDEA Explain why a Brazil nut tree probably could not live in a chaparral ecosystem.

❷ VOCABULARY Explain the difference between a desert and a chaparral.

❸ READING SKILL Why do trees of taiga ecosystems have thin, waxy leaves?

❹ CRITICAL THINKING: Synthesize Explain this statement: "In some ways, all ecosystems on Earth are alike, even deserts and rainforests."

❺ INQUIRY SKILL: Analyze Data White-tailed deer are present in more than one type of ecosystem. Explain why this is possible.

 TEST PRACTICE

Fire is a normal part of the chaparral ecosystem because ____.

A. it is very dry.

B. it is very hot.

C. lightning strikes are common.

D. all of the above.

27

Read this selection from *Midnight Fox* about a boy searching for the den of a black fox. Then compare it to a table from *Crafty Canines*. The table gives information about five other kinds of foxes.

The Midnight Fox

By Betsy Byars

Tom spies a fox in a woody area. Suddenly, he is caught up with tracking this mysterious fox.

For the past two weeks I had been practically tearing the woods apart looking for the den of the black fox. I had poked under rocks and logs and stuck sticks in rotted trees, and it was a wonder that some animal had not come storming out....

After a while I looked across the creek and I saw a hollow where there was a small clearing. There was an outcropping of rocks behind the clearing and an old log slanted against the rocks. Soft grass sloped down to the creek bank.

I don't know how long I sat there—I usually forgot about my watch when I was in the woods—but it was a long time. I was just sitting, not expecting anything or waiting for anything. And the black fox came through the bushes.

She...gave a small yapping bark, and at once, out of a hole beneath rocks came a baby fox.

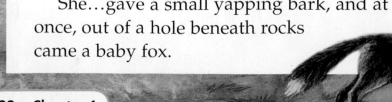

Crafty Canines: Coyotes, Foxes, and Wolves
by Phyllis J. Perry

There are twenty species of foxes. Climate and terrain influence where a fox lives. Most of the time, a fox makes its den in an empty rabbit hole or other burrow. If there are no burrows, a fox might dig one.

Fox	Habitat
Red Fox	Open fields and woodlands in Asia, Europe, the Middle East, Canada, and throughout the United States
Kit Fox	Deserts of the southwestern United States, northern Mexico, and Baja, California
Bat-Eared Fox	Open grasslands and semideserts of eastern and northern Africa, and from Southern Angola and Zimbabwe to South Africa
Crab-Eating Fox	Woodlands and savannahs of Columbia, Venezuela, Brazil, Guyana, Suriname, eastern Peru, Bolivia, Paraguay, Argentina, and Uruguay
Arctic Fox	Along the coast of Greenland and in the northern sections of Canada, Alaska, Iceland, Scandinavia, and Siberia

Sharing Ideas

1. **READING CHECK** In *The Midnight Fox*, where does Tom discover the baby fox?

2. **WRITE ABOUT IT** Make a chart comparing and contrasting the habitat of the Arctic fox and the habitat described in *The Midnight Fox*.

3. **TALK ABOUT IT** Discuss the living and nonliving parts of the ecosystem described in *The Midnight Fox*.

What Are Some Water Ecosystems?

Building Background

Earth is sometimes called "The Ocean Planet." Most of Earth's surface is covered by water. From the open ocean, to coral reefs, to rivers and lakes, the nonliving conditions of Earth's water ecosystems help determine which plants and animals can live there. These tropical fish for example, get everything they need to survive from the coral reef where they live.

PREPARE TO INVESTIGATE

Inquiry Skill

Infer When you infer, you use facts you know and observations you have made to draw a conclusion.

Materials

- plastic aquarium
- metric ruler
- gravel
- rocks
- water
- snails
- aquatic plants
- goggles

Science and Math Toolbox

For step 2, review **Making a Chart to Organize Data,** on page H10.

Water World

Procedure

1. **Observe** Examine the nonliving gravel, rocks, and water. Observe the living snails and aquatic plants.

2. **Hypothesize** In your *Science Notebook,* make a chart like the one shown. After you observe the snail, write down your best idea about how the snail meets its needs.

3. **Measure** Fill a container with a layer of gravel about 2 cm deep. Use a ruler to measure. Then add a few rocks. **Safety:** Wear goggles when adding gravel and rocks to the container.

4. Slowly pour the water into the bowl. Carefully insert an aquatic plant into the gravel. Gently add one snail to the water's surface. Place your aquarium in daylight, but out of direct sunlight.

5. **Predict** Where do you think the snail will go? Will it float on the water's surface, sink to the bottom, or move somewhere else? Write your predictions in your *Science Notebook.*

Conclusion

1. **Hypothesize** What would happen to the organisms if you removed the water from the container?

2. **Infer** What food do you think the snail will find to eat? How is this related to where the snail goes?

STEP 2

Observation	Hypothesis

STEP 3

STEP 5

Guided Inquiry

Experiment In one week **observe** your aquarium. Observe it again in two weeks. Write down where the snail is located each time. Use your observations to explain the location of the snail.

Water Ecosystems

MAIN IDEA The different nonliving conditions of each water ecosystem help determine what organisms can survive there.

Saltwater Ecosystems

Ocean ecosystems have areas with different nonliving conditions. Depending on the tide, the shoreline is covered by salt water or exposed to air and sunlight. Shoreline plants and animals live with these changes. For example, clams attach themselves to rocks with sticky threads so waves cannot pull them out to sea. Just beyond the shoreline is the coastal ocean. California's coastal ocean is home to great underwater forests of giant kelp—a tall, brown seaweed. Otters and other animals live among the swaying kelp fronds.

VOCABULARY

coral reef   p. 33

READING SKILL

Compare and Contrast
As you read use the chart below to compare saltwater and freshwater ecosystems.

Compare	Contrast

Shoreline Zone

Sea stars and anemones, such as those shown here, live in the constantly changing shoreline zone.

Coastal Ocean

In some coastal ocean areas fish and other marine life live in coral reefs.

A **coral** (KOR uhl) **reef** is a type of ecosystem found in warm, tropical salt water and built on a structure of coral deposits. Coral reefs are found throughout the world near Earth's equator. Corals are tiny animals that grow only in the warm, sunlit water of coastal oceans. Some corals make a hard, stony casing that they leave behind when they die. These casings build the structure of the reef, which grows larger over time. Coral reefs are home to a rich community of plants and animals.

Away from the coastal ocean is the open ocean. Algae are plantlike organisms, and most are single-celled. So many algae cover the surface of Earth's oceans that algae produce most of the Earth's oxygen. They also provide food for many ocean animals.

Sunlight does not reach very far down into the open ocean. So most of the ocean is very dark and very cold. Organisms that live here are able to survive in these conditions. Some fish make their own light, just as lightning bugs do. The light helps the fish hunt for food.

COMPARE AND CONTRAST Compare the nonliving conditions of the open ocean to those of a coral reef.

Open Ocean

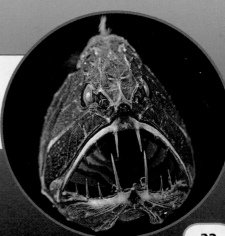

Dolphins, whales, and jellies spend much of their time near the surface in open ocean zones.

Huge schools of herring, tuna, and other fish live in the middle depths of the open ocean.

Fangtooth fish and other creatures have adapted to the cold, dark, deepest parts of the ocean.

Freshwater Ecosystems

Other bodies of water are made up of fresh water. These ecosystems include streams, rivers, ponds, lakes, and wetlands.

Streams and rivers have water that flows. Near the beginning of a river, the current is usually fast and the water is clear. Trout and other fast-swimming fish live in this area. Farther downstream, the current slows. Plants are able to take root. Beavers and waterfowl live here.

As the river flows, it picks up mud and silt. Near the end of the river, the water drops these sediments and becomes murky. Catfish and carp may live in these dark waters.

Ponds and lakes are made of still water. Some ponds are small and may disappear during dry spells. Some lakes, such as the Great Lakes, are very large.

Deep ponds and lakes have three different areas. Algae, plants, insects, and fish most often live near the sunlit, warm surface. Farther down, the water is cooler, but some sunlight gets through. Plankton, tiny organisms that live in water, are found in this area. Fish and other larger animals eat plankton.

In even deeper water, it is dark and cold. Other organisms survive here. Some of these organisms live off of the dead plants and animals that float down from above.

COMPARE AND CONTRAST Compare three types of freshwater ecosystems.

Fresh water lakes such as this one are home to many kinds of organisms. ▼

kingfisher

Express Lab

Activity Card 4
Draw the Ocean

Visual Summary

Water ecosystems are different from each other because their nonliving conditions are different. Different water ecosystems have different kinds of plants and animals.

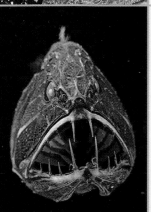

Oceans cover most of Earth's surface. Saltwater ecosystems include coral reefs, shorelines, the coastal ocean, and the open ocean. Oceans are home to a great variety of plants and animals.

Freshwater ecosystems include ponds, lakes, rivers, streams, and wetlands. Each of these is unique—and is home to its own set of organisms. Nonliving conditions in each are different than other freshwater ecosystems.

Reading Review

❶ MAIN IDEA Explain why different water ecosystems are home to different communities of plants and animals.

❷ VOCABULARY Use the term *coral reef* in a sentence about the ocean.

❸ READING SKILL: Use a chart to compare freshwater and saltwater ecosystems. Summarize their differences.

Compare	Contrast

❹ CRITICAL THINKING: Evaluate Which water ecosystem on Earth is the biggest? Hint: it is very cold, mostly dark, and very deep.

❺ INQUIRY SKILL: Infer If the oceans were to become much warmer, how might this affect the shoreline?

 TEST PRACTICE

Unlike freshwater ecosystems, saltwater ecosystems are _____.

A. salty.   **C.** sunny.

B. dry.   **D.** full of life.

Technology

Visit **www.eduplace.com/cascp** to find our more about Earth's water ecosystems.

Life Under Ice

Brrrrr! This Antarctic jelly lives in some of the coldest water on Earth. Without his protective suit, the diver would freeze in minutes. But the cold is no problem for the jelly. Some plants and animals do very well in extreme environments.

"Jellyfish" are not actually fish. They are invertebrates: animals that get along fine without a spine. The Antarctic jelly shown here is a giant. Its bell (the bowl shape at the top) can be as big as a kitchen table! Its tentacles can reach over 9 meters (30 ft) long. That's longer than most houses are tall! Jellies use their long tentacles to sting and catch their food.

Since jellies meet their needs in the ocean, they rely on ocean currents. Though some can move on their own, most jellies depend on the ocean's currents to move them around and bring them food.

This tropical jelly needs very warm water to survive. It would quickly die in the Antarctic jelly's environment.

Most jellies simply float wherever the ocean currents take them. Others, like this Antarctic jelly, can move through the water by expanding and contracting their bells

Writing Journal

In your writing journal, compare the environment of the Antarctic waters with other water ecosystems.

Math Negative Numbers

The amount of rainfall in the world's deserts can be as little as 0.25 cm (0.1 in.) per year. More than 250 cm (100 in.) can fall in the rainforest in a year. In deserts such as the Mojave and Sonoran deserts in California, average temperatures can range between 38°C (100.4°F) during the day and −4°C (25°F) at night.

1. What multiple of the desert rainfall occurs in the rainforest?

2. Use the thermometer to find the difference between the temperature of 38°C and −4°C .

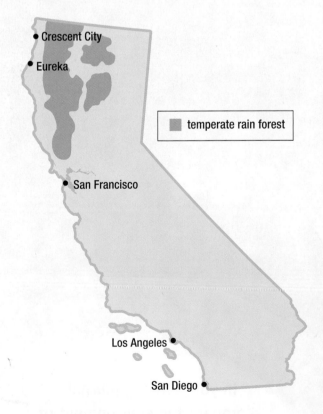

temperate rain forest

Writing Summarize

Use the Internet or the library to learn about a plant or an animal that lives in a temperate rainforest in California. The map shows the region you will be researching.

Find out how the temperate rainforest meets that organism's needs. Summarize what you learned in one paragraph. Include an explanation of the word *temperate*. Then, based on your summary, write a paragraph explaining whether or not you think that organism would survive in a tropical rainforest. Cite reasons that come from information in your summary paragraph.

Landscaper

Have you ever passed a golf course and noticed the beautiful green grass and neatly trimmed shrubs? Professional landscapers have been busy. Landscapers keep lawns healthy, bushes pruned, and flowers blooming. Landscapers also maintain the grounds at athletic stadiums, office parks, college campuses, botanical gardens, and homes.

What It Takes!

- A high-school diploma
- Curiosity about all kinds of plants
- The physical strength to maintain landscapes

Park Ranger

Park rangers work in city, state, and national parks all across the country. They help protect wildlife, rescue lost hikers, and educate the public about nature and conservation. They also patrol trails and study wildlife behavior.

What It Takes!

- A degree in history, geography, natural science, or other field
- Volunteer work or internship in a park

Vocabulary

Complete each sentence with a term from the list.

1. Animals get their _____ from eating plants or other animals.

2. All of the organisms of an ecosystem make up a/an _____.

3. Wildfires help some plant seeds open in a/an _____.

4. All the members of one kind of plant or animal in a community make up a/an _____.

5. An area where it rarely gets very hot or very cold is a/an _____.

6. Everything that surrounds an organism is the _____ it lives in.

7. Because moose and wolves can survive in a very cold, dry environment, they are often found in _____ ecosystems.

8. One life process is to make more of one's own kind, or _____.

9. An ecosystem found in warm, tropical saltwater and built on a structure of coral deposits is a/an _____.

10. An ecosystem with a lot of rain, plenty of sunshine, and warm temperatures is a tropical _____.

chaparral p. 25
community p. 16
coral reef p. 33
desert p. 24
ecosystem p. 8
energy p. 14
environment p. 16
organism p. 14
oxygen p. 14
population p. 16
rainforest p. 22
reproduce p. 14
taiga p. 26
temperate zone p. 16

Test Practice

Write the letter of the best answer choice.

11. An ecosystem is made up of _____.

   A. plants.
   B. all the living and nonliving things that interact in an area.
   C. all the nonliving things in an area.
   D. animals.

12. To survive, all plants, animals, and other organisms need _____.

   A. water.
   B. energy.
   C. air.
   D. all of the above.

13. Nonliving conditions in a desert are _____.

   A. cold and wet most of the time.
   B. extremely hot, sunny, and dry all year.
   C. usually very dry and cold.
   D. rainy and warm.

14. A tropical rainforest has different organisms than a taiga ecosystem because _____.

   A. its nonliving conditions are different.
   B. it has more rain.
   C. it is much warmer.
   D. all of the above.

15. **Compare** How are an open ocean ecosystem and a deep lake ecosystem alike? How are they different?

16. You are raising earthworms in a glass tank. When the tank is covered with a dark cloth for a while, you often find the worms on top of the soil near the food. Predict the best time of day to observe earthworms in their natural habitat.

Map the Concept

Use the terms from the following list to complete the concept map.

animals   plants
sunlight   water
temperature   other organisms
air

Nonliving Parts of an Ecosystem	Living Parts of an Ecosystem

Critical Thinking

17. **Apply** What could happen to a chaparral ecosystem if fires were never allowed to burn?

18. **Synthesize** Identify some of the nonliving things in an ocean ecosystem. Then describe some of the conditions of your favorite ocean ecosystem.

19. **Evaluate** What might you say to someone who told you that shelter is not an important part of an ecosystem?

20. **Analyze** Explain the difference between an ecosystem and a community.

Performance Assessment

Build an Ecosystem
Imagine that you can create your own land or water ecosystem. What would the nonliving conditions (sunlight, temperature, rainfall) be? What living and nonliving things would be found in the ecosystem? How would the living things rely on the nonliving conditions? Make a drawing of your ecosystem. Label all the living and nonliving things. Compare your ecosystem with those of other students. How are they similar? How are they different? Why do you think they are different?

Writing Journal

Review your answers to the Lesson Preview questions on page 3. Change your answers as needed, based on what you have learned.

Chapter 2

Interactions of Living Things

Cheetahs chasing a bat-eared fox

LESSON 1

A redwood shades a fern, a bird eats a berry, and a bee buzzes from one flower to another. How do plants and animals depend on each other?

LESSON 2

The Canadian lynx's big feet act like snowshoes. The white-spotted fur of a young deer helps it hide. Organisms live and survive in different ways. Are some more successful than others?

LESSON 3

A raccoon is one organism that eats frogs. Snakes eat frogs too. In what other ways do organisms compete with each other for resources?

Writing Journal

In your Writing Journal, show what you know by writing or drawing answers to each question.

Vocabulary Preview

Vocabulary

Glossary

Vocabulary Skill

Sentence Context
adaptation

Look for clues in the following sentence to help you understand the meaning of the word *adaptation*.

A dolphin's blowhole is an adaptation that allows it to live in the ocean.

camouflage
The coloring or other physical appearance of an animal that helps it blend in with its surroundings.

prey
Any animal that is hunted for food by a predator.

seed dispersal
The scattering or carrying away of seeds from the plant that produced them.

predator
An animal that hunts other animals for food.

Standard Sets 2, 3. Life Sciences

2.b. *Students know* producers and consumers (herbivores, carnivores, omnivores, and decomposers) are related in food chains and food webs and may compete with each other for resources in an ecosystem.

3.b. *Students know* that in any particular environment, some kinds of plants and animals survive well, some survive less well, and some cannot survive at all.

3.c. *Students know* many plants depend on animals for pollination and seed dispersal, and animals depend on plants for food and shelter.

Standard Set 6. Investigation and Experimentation standards covered in this chapter: 6.b., 6.d.

How Do Organisms Depend on Each Other?

Building Background

In all ecosystems, animals depend on plants for food and shelter. Plants depend on animals, too. This hummingbird is sipping the sugary nectar it needs to survive. The hummingbird helps the flower reproduce and spread its seeds.

PREPARE TO INVESTIGATE

Inquiry Skill

Use Models You can use a model of an object, process, or idea to better understand or describe how it works.

Materials

- cotton balls
- masking tape
- red clay or modeling compound
- small beads
- paper circles from a hole-puncher
- construction paper
- scissors

Dispersing Seeds

Procedure

1. **Collaborate** Work with a partner. With your teacher's help, gather a few of each of the supplies provided.

2. **Observe** Look at your supplies with your partner. Imagine that the small beads and the paper circles are seeds. All the other materials can be used to make coverings for the seeds that will help the seeds disperse, or be scattered somewhere else.

3. **Hypothesize** How could you use these items to make different models of seeds with coverings? Decide how your seed models will work. How could you make a model that would float on the wind? What would a model of a seed that an animal would want to eat look like? How could you make a seed model that would stick to fur as a burr would?

4. **Make Models** Use your supplies to make at least three different seed models.

5. **Communicate** Show your seed models to the rest of the class. Observe other students' models.

Conclusion

1. **Infer** If your models were real seeds, how would they work?

2. **Predict** For each of your models, predict how the seed might be dispersed. Explain your answer.

STEP 2

STEP 3

STEP 4

Guided Inquiry

Ask Questions Get a variety of real seeds from your teacher. Write a list of questions about how those seeds are dispersed by animals. **Research** answers to your questions in the library or on the Internet.

READING SKILL

Main Idea and Details
Use a chart to show details that support the idea that animals depend on one another.

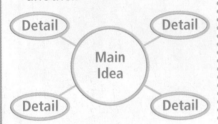

Interactions of Living Things

MAIN IDEA Living things in an ecosystem depend on one another for basic needs such as food, shelter, and protection.

Interdependence

The living things found in an ecosystem are interdependent (ihn tur dih PEHN duhnt). This means that living things depend on each other to meet their needs. You know that many animals depend on plants for food. But organisms depend on each other for other things, too.

Plants can be a source of shelter for animals. In turn, animals can provide protection for plants. The swollen thorn acacia tree and a type of stinging ant are interdependent. The ants live in the hollowed-out bulbs that are at the base of the thorns. They feed on a sugary liquid that is found in the tree's leaves.

As the ants use the tree for shelter and food, the tree benefits, too. When another kind of animal starts grazing on the tree, the ants swarm and sting the animal, driving it away.

◄ A colony of stinging ants makes its home in the swollen thorn acacia tree.

There is another example of interdependence that occurs in the Pacific Ocean. The sea anemone (uh NEHM uh nee) is an animal that lives on the ocean floor. It uses its poisonous tentacles to capture fish and other animals. But one type of fish is not in danger from the anemone. In fact, this fish, called a clown fish, makes its home right there among the tentacles.

Some scientists think that the clown fish has a coating on its body that protects it from the anemone's sting. In its home, the clown fish is safe from its own enemies. They stay away from the poisonous tentacles of the anemone. The anemone benefits from the clown fish, too. The fish keeps the anemone's tentacles clean by eating scraps of food that cling to them.

In Africa, a similar relationship exists between the Nile crocodile and a bird called the Egyptian plover. The crocodile allows the bird into its mouth. There the bird eats leeches attached to the crocodile's gums. Both animals benefit. The bird gets a meal. The crocodile gets its teeth cleaned.

MAIN IDEA **How are the clown fish and the sea anemone interdependent?**

◀ **The clown fish makes its home among the protective tentacles of the sea anemone.**

The Egyptian plover cleans the crocodile's teeth while getting a meal. ▶

49

Relationships in Ecosystems

Every living thing has a role to play within its ecosystem. You can think of this as the particular job an organism does in its environment.

Plants play the role of producer (pruh DOO sur). A **producer** is an organism that makes its own food. The food that plants make is used for energy by organisms that eat the plants. All organisms need energy.

Plants use energy from sunlight to make food. In turn, plants use energy from the food they make to grow and to produce offspring. Some of the food is stored in the leaves, stems, and roots of a plant.

When an animal eats a plant, energy in the plant is transferred to the animal. Animals are consumers (kuhn SOO murz). A **consumer** gets energy by eating plants, or by eating other animals that eat plants. Consumers use this energy to live.

In the end, all the consumers in an ecosystem depend on producers for food. Without producers, the other organisms in an ecosystem could not survive.

great horned owl

black-tail deer

Trees and other plants are producers. Producers use the energy in sunlight to make food.

Anna's hummingbird

Trees provide shelter for animals and other plants.

redwood trees

ferns

western gray squirrel

Animals are consumers. Consumers rely on producers, or other animals that eat producers, for food.

Shelter is another basic need of living things. It is often met with the help of other organisms. For example, squirrels and many kinds of birds make their homes among the branches of trees. There, hidden in the leaves, the nests of these animals are protected from the hot sun. They are also protected from hungry animals.

Trees provide shelter and protection for plants, too. For example, some plants grow best in moist, shady conditions. Plants such as ferns and mosses might find shelter at the base of a tree.

Some animals' homes may become shelter for other animals. Woodchucks make their homes by digging tunnels deep under the soil. But when the woodchuck leaves, animals such as skunks and rabbits may move in.

Hermit crabs also find shelter in homes built by other animals. Hermit crabs do not have a hard shell of their own. They use the shells that snails leave behind for shelter.

MAIN IDEA What is the relationship between producers and consumers?

Express Lab

Activity Card 5
Draw Some Seeds

Pollinators and Seed Dispersal

In an ecosystem, some living things help other living things carry out reproduction (ree pruh DUHK shuhn). Reproduction is the life process of having offspring. It is another basic need of living things.

Many plants reproduce by making seeds. For a plant to make seeds, pollen (PAHL uhn) must be moved from one part of a flower to another, or from one flower to another. How does pollen move? Wind and water can carry pollen, but so can animals such as insects or birds. An animal that helps plants make seeds by moving pollen is called a **pollinator** (PAHL uh nay tur).

Pollinators feed on the pollen and nectar they find on flowers. As they feed, they carry pollen from flower to flower. When pollen touches the right part of the flower, seeds begin to form.

Some plants depend on animals to carry their seeds to new places where they can grow. **Seed dispersal** (dih SPUR suhl) is the scattering or carrying away of seeds from the plant that produced them. Some plant seeds are carried by the wind. For example, dandelion seeds fly away when you blow on them.

Other plant seeds get caught in the fur of animals. These seeds may be carried great distances from the parent plant before falling off and beginning to grow.

Some plants produce seeds that develop inside of fruit. Animals eat the fruit and either drop the seeds or deposit them in their waste. If conditions are favorable, the seeds will grow in their new location.

MAIN IDEA How do plants depend on animals to reproduce?

Insects and birds help pollinate flowers and disperse seeds.

Visual Summary

Living things in an ecosystem are interdependent.

Animals depend on plants for food and sometimes for shelter.

Many plants depend on animals to help them reproduce and disperse seeds.

Reading Review

❶ MAIN IDEA Name two ways that an animal might depend on a plant.

❷ VOCABULARY Use the terms *producer* and *consumer* in a sentence.

❸ READING SKILL: What main idea is illustrated by the interaction of the stinging ant and the acacia tree?

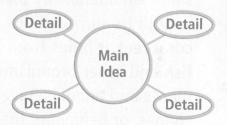

❹ CRITICAL THINKING: Apply Name one example of interdependence between an animal and a plant in a local ecosystem.

❺ INQUIRY SKILL: Use Models Using what you learned by making models of seeds, predict how the seeds of a blueberry plant would be dispersed.

✔ TEST PRACTICE

All animals in an ecosystem depend on _____.

A. producers.   **C.** pollinators.

B. consumers.   **D.** seeds.

Technology
Visit **www.eduplace.com/cascp** to do more research on interdependence.

How Are Organisms Adapted to Survive?

Building Background

Believe it or not, this delicate-looking creature is a lettuce sea slug—an animal! By blending in with its surroundings on the coral reef, it hides from hungry fish and other organisms. Many plants and animals have colors, shapes, or behaviors that help them survive in their environment. If their environment changes, then organisms may adapt.

PREPARE TO INVESTIGATE

Inquiry Skill

Observe It is important to know the difference between what you observe using your senses and tools and what you think about those observations.

Materials

- black construction paper
- small index card
- clock or watch
- masking tape
- mealworms
- plastic jars
- scissors

Science and Math Toolbox

For step 5, review **Measuring Elapsed Time** on page H12.

A Mealworm Home

Procedure

1 **Collaborate** Work with a partner. Use black construction paper to cover the outside of a plastic jar as shown.

STEP 1

2 Cut a square of black paper that is slightly larger than the opening of the jar. Position the square over the opening of the jar. Leaving a space, tape the square in place as shown.

3 Use an index card to lift a mealworm and place it in an uncovered plastic jar. **Safety:** Handle mealworms gently.

STEP 2

4 **Observe** With your partner, use masking tape to join together the openings of the two jars. Place the joined jars on their side in a well-lit area.

5 **Predict** Every 10 minutes for the next half hour, observe and record the location of your mealworm. After your second observation, predict where the mealworm will move to.

STEP 3

Conclusion

1. **Experiment** Repeat this experiment several more times to test your prediction. What conclusion can you draw about how your results and predictions are related?

2. **Infer** Based on your observations, what can you conclude about the type of environment a mealworm prefers? Why do you think this is?

Guided Inquiry

Experiment First **predict** how the mealworm would move if it was placed in the covered jar first. Then plan an experiment to test your prediction. Get your teacher's permission to carry it out.

Adaptations of Living Things

VOCABULARY

adaptation   p. 56
camouflage   p. 58
habitat   p. 56
hibernate   p. 59
mimicry   p. 59
predator   p. 56
prey   p. 56
species   p. 56

READING SKILL

Problem-Solution
Use a chart to show how a plant or animal adaptation solves a problem.

Problem	Solution

MAIN IDEA To survive, plants and animals must be adapted to their environment. Their adaptations help organisms obtain food, hide from other animals, and generally survive the conditions of their environment.

Plant and Animal Adaptations

Sharks live in water, cactuses grow in dry deserts. It's clear that different plants and animals survive in different environments. The place where a plant or animal lives is called its **habitat** (HAB ih tat). The ocean is a dolphin's habitat. The habitat of a toucan is the rainforest.

Plants and animals have adaptations (ad ap TAY shunhnz) that help them survive. An **adaptation** can be a physical feature or a behavior that helps a plant or animal survive.

Any given adaptation is present in all individuals of a given type of organism. For example, every wood duck on Earth has sharp claws to help it grip tree branches. Wood ducks, as a species (SPEE sheez) are adapted to live in wooded areas near lakes and ponds. A **species** is a group of organisms that produces organisms of the same kind.

Some animals are adapted to hunt and eat other animals. **Predators** (PREH deh turz) are animals that hunt other animals for food. **Prey** (PRAY) is any animal that is hunted for food by a predator.

PROBLEM AND SOLUTION Give an example of how an animal adaptation solves a problem.

Forest

The aye aye has large eyes that help it see at night. The aye aye's third finger is very long and thin. It uses it for digging food out of trees.

Rainforest

Water that stays on leaves can cause disease. The leaves of many rainforest plants have pointed ends that allow rainwater to drip off.

Desert

Light-colored fur helps the jackrabbit blend into its surroundings. Its large ears help it keep cool in the desert by giving off heat.

Tundra

The musk ox's habitat is covered with snow much of the year. How might the musk ox's thick fur help it survive?

Physical Adaptations

Have you ever seen an animal that looked so much like its surroundings that you almost didn't notice it? Such an animal has an adaptation called camouflage (KAM uh flahzh). **Camouflage** is the coloring, marking, or other physical appearance of an animal that helps it blend in with its surroundings.

Animals use camouflage to hide from both predators and prey. The camouflage of the lettuce sea slug on page 54 helps it hide from ocean predators. A Bengal tiger is a predator that uses camouflage. Its stripes help the tiger blend with the tall grass where it hunts at dawn and dusk. Its prey does not see the tiger approach.

Many insects protect themselves by using mimicry (MIHM ih kree). **Mimicry** is an adaptation that allows an animal to protect itself by looking like another kind of animal or like a plant. The South American owl butterfly has large spots on its wings that look like the eyes of an owl. These spots scare away birds that might want to eat the butterfly.

A predator can fool its prey by looking like something that is not a threat. For example, a leafy sea dragon looks like a clump of seaweed. Small sea animals get caught when they get close to this "seaweed."

🎯 **PROBLEM AND SOLUTION** **How does mimicry help an animal to survive?**

The South American owl butterfly uses mimicry to scare away birds. ▼

A young deer's light brown fur and white spots look like patches of sunlight and shade. ▼

Behavior

Behavior, as well as appearance, can help a predator as it hunts its prey. Humpback whales blow circles of bubbles around schools of fish. The fish cannot escape from the circle and become easy prey for the whales. Wolves and other animals hunt in groups. The group surrounds the prey so it cannot easily escape.

Behavior also helps prey survive. Rabbits run in a zig-zag pattern, which helps them dodge predators. Zebras use their hooves and teeth to defend themselves.

In some environments, winter brings freezing temperatures and snow. Animals such as bats, frogs, and chipmunks have an adaptation that helps them survive the cold winter. They **hibernate** (HY bur nayt), or go into a deep sleep, during which they use very little energy and usually do not need to eat. In this deep sleep, the animals' heartbeat and breathing rate slow down.

PROBLEM AND SOLUTION What are two examples of adaptations that help animals hunt?

▲ The kangaroo rat survives in the desert by staying in its burrow during the heat of the day.

This archer fish catches insects by shooting them down with a strong jet of water. ▶

Surviving Change

What happens to an animal or plant when its habitat changes? Imagine a population of deer with young fawns. If all the trees in their forest home were suddenly cut down, their habitat would change dramatically. Organisms rely on their habitat to provide everything they need to survive.

If an organism's habitat changes, the organism may or may not meet its basic needs. Some plants and animals survive better than others when their habitats change.

Some species have adaptations that have helped them survive changes in their habitats. These species include peregrine falcons, red-tailed hawks, and pigeons. In their natural habitats, these birds make nests in hollows on the sides of cliffs, or high in mature trees. Now these species are found nesting on high window ledges and roof overhangs in cities and towns across the United States.

Raccoons are also well adapted to survive changes in their natural habitats. Their natural habitats include wooded areas near ponds and streams. They also survive well in cities and towns. They search garbage cans for food and use city sewers to hide. Some have even gone into people's houses in search of something to eat!

◀ A peregrine falcon perches among the skyscrapers of downtown Los Angeles.

Giant pandas need bamboo to survive. ▶

Many species, however, are less able to meet all their basic needs when their habitat changes. Organisms adapted to live in very specific habitats, for example, have difficulty meeting their needs if that habitat changes.

Giant pandas eat almost nothing but bamboo. They cannot survive without it. But their strict diet—an adaptation to eat only bamboo—is putting them at risk.

Bamboo forests in the mountains of central China have been cut down. Without bamboo forests, giant pandas cannot survive in the wild. The Chinese government and environmental groups are working to preserve the giant panda's habitat.

Koalas are one of Australia's most familiar and adored animals. Koalas live in the scattered, dry eucalyptus forests of Eastern Australia. They prefer eating only a few of the hundreds of kinds of eucalyptus there. But, like the bamboo forests, eucalyptus woodlands are vanishing. It is thought that 80 percent of the koala's original habitat has been destroyed. The destruction of habitat and food sources puts the koalas in serious danger of disappearing, too.

PROBLEM AND SOLUTION Propose a solution to the koala's problem.

▲ Koalas eat only a few kinds of eucalyptus.

Express Lab

Activity Card 6
Make a Habitat

Carolina parakeet

passenger pigeon

▲ The loss of their forest habitat and overhunting led to the extinction of Carolina parakeets and passenger pigeons.

Extinction

What would happen to giant pandas if their habitat totally disappeared? Unless there were individuals living in zoos, they would become extinct (ihk STIHNKT). **Extinction** is when all members of a species die out. Any species can become extinct when the species is unable to adapt to change.

The first European settlers in America were amazed to see giant flocks of passenger pigeons. Some flocks could darken the sky for minutes on end. These birds needed huge areas of forest to survive. But over time, the forests were cut down.

Passenger pigeon populations grew smaller. Then, about a hundred years ago, the remaining birds were hunted to extinction. Carolina parakeets suffered a fate similar to the passenger pigeon.

The habitat of ivory-billed woodpeckers was the forests that once covered most of the southern United States. By the 1930s much of the birds' habitat had been cut down. Until recently, these birds were thought to be extinct. But some scientists are convinced that an ivory-billed woodpecker was seen in Arkansas in 2004.

Habitat destruction continues to be one of the biggest threats to species all over the world.

PROBLEM AND SOLUTION How could people help lower the risk of extinction for many plants and animals?

The male ivory-billed woodpecker has a red crest ▼

Visual Summary

Plants and animals have adaptations that help them meet their needs for food, air, water, and shelter. These adaptations can be physical features or behaviors.

When an organism's habitat changes, it may or may not be able to be able to meet its needs. Some plants and animals are better able to survive changes in their habitats than others.

If a species is unable to adapt to changes in its habitat, or the habitat disappears, the species may become extinct.

Technology
Visit **www.eduplace.com/cascp** to find out more about adaptations.

Reading Review

❶ MAIN IDEA Why do organisms have adaptations?

❷ VOCABULARY Use the term *adaptation* in a sentence.

❸ READING SKILL: What is a solution for saving the giant panda from extinction?

Problem	Solution

❹ CRITICAL THINKING: **Synthesize** Explain how mimicry makes it difficult for some prey to be found by predators.

❺ INQUIRY SKILL: **Observe** Look at an ant or other insect. What features of the ant or other insect help it survive? Describe this adaptation.

✔ TEST PRACTICE

A young spotted deer is able to avoid predators by using _____.

A. mimicry.

B. camouflage.

C. hibernation.

D. changes in behavior.

Master of Disguise

Can a blob of seaweed grin? No, you're looking at a goosefish. This flat, shaggy fish has the perfect camouflage that helps it survive in its ocean-floor habitat. It can hide from predators. It can also *be* a predator by blending in with its surroundings.

The goosefish attracts prey with another adaptation. Attached to a spike on its head is something that looks like a worm. When other fish come near this wiggling bait, the goosefish gulps them down in a flash!

This master of disguise makes survival as a "blob of seaweed" look like a big-mouthed snap!

Can You Find Me?

Bugs beware! The goldenrod spider turns itself yellow or white to match its flowery hunting ground.

Hey! Some of those leaves have legs! You can see them, but predators and prey of this praying mantis usually can't.

Writing Journal

Describe in your writing journal a physical adaptation that would help an animal survive in an extreme desert.

How Do Organisms Compete?

Building Background

How many wolves can live in a forest? The answer depends on the size of the forest and the amount of food it provides for the wolves. Wolves must also compete with other animals for food, water, and shelter. In any population—of wolves, trees, birds, or people—population size is limited by things like food, water, and living space.

PREPARE TO INVESTIGATE

Inquiry Skill

Hypothesize If you think you know why something that you observe happens, you can make a hypothesis, or an educated guess, about it.

Materials

- measuring cup
- 3 plastic cups
- 32 lima bean seeds
- soil
- water
- marker
- goggles

Limits to Growth

Procedure

1. **Collaborate** Work with a partner. Label three cups *A*, *B*, and *C*. Fill each cup with soil. Each cup should contain about the same amount of soil. **Safety:** Wear goggles.

2. **Use Variables** Place 2 seeds in cup *A*. Place 10 seeds in cup *B*. Place 20 seeds in cup *C*.

3. **Measure** Measure and pour 25 mL of water into each cup.

4. Place all three cups in a sunny spot. In your *Science Notebook*, make a chart like the one shown for each cup.

5. Over the next three weeks, water the cups when the soil is dry. Make sure each cup receives the same amount of sunlight.

6. **Record Data** Two times each week, measure the height of the lima bean seedlings. Record the data.

Conclusion

1. **Hypothesize** What differences did you observe in the growing seeds? What do you think caused these differences?

2. **Use Variables** How would your answer to question 1 change if you did not use the same amount of water for each cup in step 5? For example, what if cup *A* was well watered but cups *B* and *C* were not?

STEP 1

STEP 2

STEP 4

Cup _____		
Date	Height	Observations

Guided Inquiry

Experiment What would happen if, in step 2, you put half the number of lima beans in each cup. **Predict** the results. Then do the experiment and graph your results.

READING SKILL

Cause and Effect
Use the chart to show
why plants and animals
compete.

Cause → Effect

In a temperate forest,
raccoons, snakes, and
shore birds compete with
each other to eat wood
frogs and their eggs. ▼

Competing for Resources

MAIN IDEA Food, air, water, and living space are
limited in any ecosystem. To survive, organisms
compete for these resources.

Competing for Food and Water

To survive, every organism needs water, air,
food, and living space. Organisms often compete
for these resources (ree sor sehz). A **resource**
is something found in nature that is useful to
organisms. Resources are always limited. In a
pond ecosystem, for example, wood frogs are
food for animals such as raccoons, snakes, and
birds. If there are not enough frogs, animals that
rely on them for food may not survive.

raccoon

snake

shore bird

wood frog

Competing for Living Space

Living space is another limited resource. Just as plants and animals compete for food and water, they also compete for space. If plants are too crowded some will die. This competition for space limits population size.

Many birds raise their young in colonies on protected beaches or on cliffs. Birds may be squeezed so close together that one nest begins where another ends. Birds that cannot find nesting sites in the protected colony may be forced to raise their young in more exposed nesting areas. They and their young will be more at risk of being eaten by predators.

Tropical rainforests are full of shrubs, bushes, and trees that compete for space in the sun. Many plants have adaptations that allow them to reach for sunlight. Some

▲ Murre birds live in crowded colonies.

have long, hanging roots that extend from the canopy to the soil far below. Others have roots that tap into material in and around tree trunks and branches. Still others have no roots at all, and can get the nutrients they need from the air and water around them.

CAUSE AND EFFECT What would happen if all the wood frogs in a pond died?

Express Lab

Activity Card 7
Model Competition for Food

A Balanced Ecosystem

In any ecosystem, populations are always changing. Old animals die and new ones take their place. When a tree falls, plants that thrive in sunlight begin to grow. In a balanced ecosystem, there are enough resources for all its living things.

In a healthy ecosystem, the populations of predators and prey are balanced. But sometimes this balance can be upset. One real-life example occurred on Isle Royale, in Lake Superior.

Moose first arrived on the island around 1900. They may have walked across an ice bridge. When they arrived, the moose had no predators and plenty of plants to eat.

Within 30 years, the moose population skyrocketed. Then it fell sharply. Why? Their food had grown scarce.

Wolves, predators of moose, came to the island in 1950. The moose population dropped, and the wolf population grew. After a time, wolf numbers dropped. Not enough moose remained to support all the wolves. With fewer wolves, the moose population rose again. Now in balance, the populations of these two species continue to rise and fall.

CAUSE AND EFFECT How might a decrease in predators affect prey?

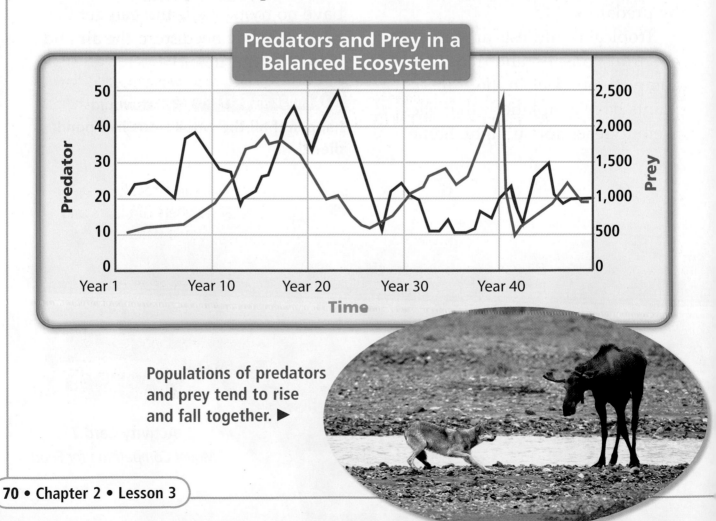

Predators and Prey in a Balanced Ecosystem

Populations of predators and prey tend to rise and fall together. ▶

Lesson Wrap-Up

Visual Summary

Organisms in every ecosystem compete with each other in order to meet their basic needs.

In every ecosystem, resources are limited. Resources include food and water, as well as living space.

A balanced ecosystem has enough resources to meet the needs of all its living things.

Technology
Visit **www.eduplace.com/cascp** to find out more about how organisms compete for resources.

Reading Review

❶ MAIN IDEA Why do plants and animals compete for resources?

❷ VOCABULARY Define *resource*.

❸ READING SKILL: Explain why limited resources force organisms to compete.

❹ CRITICAL THINKING: Apply Does your classroom have unlimited resources? Explain.

❺ INQUIRY SKILL: Hypothesize In a pond ecosystem, suppose that the population of raccoons rises. What do you think will happen to the populations of wood frogs and other predators of wood frogs?

 TEST PRACTICE

A tropical rainforest has far greater numbers of plants and animals than a desert because ____.

A. it has more resources.

B. it has more sunlight.

C. it has less sand.

D. trees offer plenty of shelter to other plants and animals.

COMPUTER "LIFE"

To compete for resources, an organism must be alive. Right? Not necessarily, claim scientists at California Institute of Technology. If you aren't alive but you are competing for resources, then what are you?

The scientists, along with their colleagues, wrote a computer code. In some ways the code acts like a living organism, including using resources as living things do. But the resources it uses are digital bits of information, namely 0s and 1s.

The scientists hope that what they learn about digital "life forms" will help explain how organisms on Earth compete. For this reason they made more than one code. The codes competed with each other for resources.

It turned out that some codes were better able to get their "food" than were others. When the scientists changed the conditions in the digital environment, the digital codes even adapted to the changes.

Dr. Christoph Adami used computer models to study competition. ▶

Computer model showing competition among digital "life forms."

The poppies in this California field are very successful in competing for resources.

Sharing Ideas

1. **READING CHECK** Why are some people calling the computer codes a "digital life form"?

2. **WRITE ABOUT IT** Tell why studying competition on a computer model would be helpful. What would be some drawbacks of doing so?

3. **TALK ABOUT IT** Do you think digital codes are alive? Why or why not?

73

southern sea otter

giant moa

LINKS
for Home and School

Math Link Exact Numbers and Estimates

Southern sea otters live in kelp forests off the coast of central California. They eat purple sea urchins, which eat kelp. The urchins could harm the kelp forest ecosystem if they became too plentiful. So the sea otters play an important role in limiting their numbers.

In the early 1700s, southern sea otters numbered in the hundreds of thousands. By the late 1800s, fur hunters had made them almost extinct. In 2002, scientists counted 2,139 southern sea otters.

1. Is hundreds of thousands an exact number or an estimate?

2. Is 2,139 an exact number or an estimate?

3. About how many years did it take for the sea otters to be hunted almost to extinction?

Writing Narrative

Select one animal that has become extinct within the last 200 years. You can choose an animal that you learned about in this chapter or research to find another choice, such as the giant moa shown here. Write a short report that gives reasons why the animal you selected became extinct. Include any historical background that can help explain the animal's extinction.

Alejandro Acevedo-Gutiérrez

Dolphins "round up" their food! They herd small fish into a tightly spinning "bait ball," and then take turns attacking for a bite.

This is just one of the behaviors that Californian Alejandro Acevedo-Gutiérrez learned about when he was studying marine biology. Understanding how marine animals interact with each other helps scientists know what conditions these animals need to survive.

While he was studying, Acevedo-Gutiérrez was part of a team that made the IMAX movie called "Dolphins." He hopes that watching these graceful animals will inspire young people to think about a career in science.

Alejandro Acevedo-Gutiérrez, marine biologist.

Vocabulary

Complete each sentence with a term from the list.

1. An animal that carries pollen from one flower to another is a/an _____.

2. The scattering of seeds is called _____.

3. Coloring or marking that helps an animal blend into its surroundings is its _____.

4. The place where a plant or animal lives is called its _____.

5. The state when all members of a species die out is called _____.

6. One animal's prey may be another animal's _____, an animal that hunts other animals for food.

7. An organism that makes its own food is a/an _____.

8. A group of organisms that produces organisms of the same kind is a/an _____.

9. An insect that looks like a leaf is using _____ for protection.

10. An organism that eats plants or other animals that eat plants is a/an _____.

adaptation p. 56
camouflage p. 58
consumer p. 50
extinction p. 62
habitat p. 56
hibernate p. 59
mimicry p. 58
pollinator p. 52
predator p. 56
prey p. 56
producer p. 50
resource p. 68
seed dispersal p. 52
species p. 56

Test Practice

Write the letter of the best answer choice.

11. All organisms on Earth have adaptations to help them _____.

    A. breathe through a blowhole.
    B. meet their needs and stay alive.
    C. look like other animals.
    D. avoid competition.

12. An eagle eating a snake is a predator, but a frog being eaten by a snake is the snake's _____.

    A. predator.   **C.** pollinator.
    B. producer.   **D.** prey.

13. When certain bats, bears, raccoons, and chipmunks go into a deep sleep during the cold winter, they _____.

    A. die.   **C.** hibernate.
    B. dream about summer. **D.** eat.

14. Something found in nature that is useful to organisms and helps them survive is a/an _____.

    A. pollinator.   **C.** adaptation.
    B. species.   **D.** resource.

15. Hypothesize What do you think would happen to the moose population on Isle Royale if the wolves were to be removed? Support your hypothesis with what you know.

16. How can measuring help you investigate how well plants are surviving in their environment?

Map the Concept

Use the examples below to fill in the concept map.

young spotted deer
mountain ash berries
redwood tree
wood frog
owl butterfly
hibernating bats
sea anemone
dandelion seeds

Producers	Consumers

Critical Thinking

17. Apply You observe that a brown duck has made a nest in the brown reeds along the edges of a pond. How does the duck depend on plants?

18. Synthesize Choose an ecosystem. Use what you know to explain how plants and animals in this ecosystem depend on one another.

19. Analyze How can an animal be both a predator and prey?

20. Evaluate A columnist in your local newspaper writes that animals and plants do not have adaptations. How would you respond?

Performance Assessment

Urban Renewal
Redesign the town you live in so that it can meet the needs of your community, while also protecting the resources of a nearby natural ecosystem. Recall that a balanced ecosystem is one in which there are enough resources for *all* its living things. You can make drawings, write plans, or make proposals. Be as specific as possible.

Consider buildings, roads, transportation, housing, education, and community events. How would your plans affect organisms and populations in the ecosystem?

Writing Journal

Review your answers to the Lesson Preview questions on page 43. As needed, change your answers based on what you have learned.

Write the letter of the best answer choice.

1. Which California ecosystem contains shrubs adapted to fire?
   A. the open ocean
   B. chaparral
   C. marine tidal pools
   D. taiga

2. Which of the following is NOT an example of interdependence?
   A. Ants feed on acacia tree and keep other animals from eating the tree.
   B. A bird cleans a crocodile's teeth by eating bits of food in between them.
   C. A bird builds a nest in the branches of a very large tree using some twigs from the tree.
   D. The clown fish lives in a sea anemone and cleans bits of food from the anemone's tentacles.

3. Nonliving parts of ecosystems that living things require include _____.
   A. water.
   B. space or shelter.
   C. food.
   D. all of these.

4. Which of the following is an example of camouflage?
   A. color of the leaves of a maple tree
   B. size of a jackrabbit's ears
   C. pattern of stripes of a Bengal tiger's fur
   D. thickness of the fur of a musk ox

5. Which seed does a bird disperse?

   A.

   B.

   C.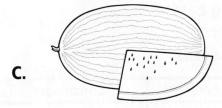

   D.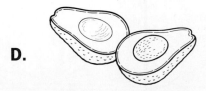

6. Which ecosystem is likely to have the most number of plants?
   A. desert
   B. chaparral
   C. rainforest
   D. none of the above

7. Which water ecosystem has the fewest nutrients?

    A. coastal zone

    B. open ocean

    C. shoreline

    D. coral reef

8. Which is an example of mimicry?

A.

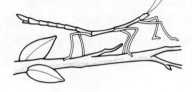

B.

C.

D.

Answer the following in complete sentences.

9. Make a hypothesis about why the California condor is a critically endangered species.

10. Explain how a lack of predators can throw an ecosystem out of balance.

You Can...

Discover More

Most bats sleep during the day and are active at night. An insect-eating bat uses an adaptation called echolocation to find the food it needs to survive. To echolocate, the bat uses its ears and its ability to make high-pitched sounds.

The bat constantly sends out high-pitched sounds. The sounds bounce off objects, such as trees, houses, and flying insects. The sounds return from the objects as echoes. The bat uses its highly sensitive hearing to interpret the echoes. The bat can tell from the echo the exact location and even the size and speed of an object. That's a handy ability to have when hunting flying insects in the dark.

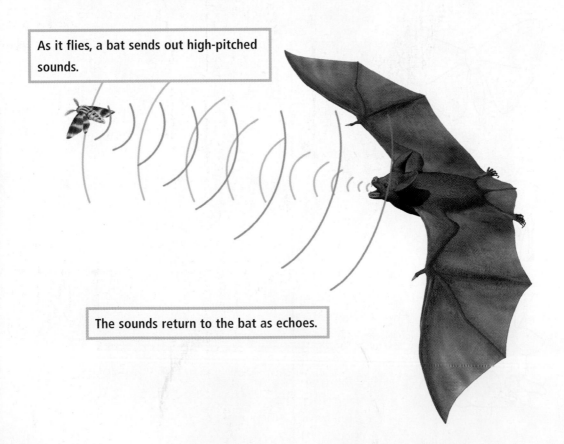

As it flies, a bat sends out high-pitched sounds.

The sounds return to the bat as echoes.

 Simulations Go to www.eduplace.com/cascp to explore how echolocation helps insect-eating bats find food to survive.

Energy and Matter in Ecosystems

California Connection

Visit www.eduplace.com/cascp to find out more about energy and matter in California ecosystems.

Joshua Tree National Park

This unique monolith was probably shaped by wind blowing small pieces of sand over the rock for thousands of years.

Painted Lady butterflies have taste sensors on their legs.

Scott's orioles make their nests from dried grasses and animal hair.

LIFE · UNIT B · SCIENCE

Energy and Matter in Ecosystems

Wildflowers, Anza-Borrego Desert, California

California Big Idea!

All organisms need energy and matter to live and grow.

Living organisms depend on one another and on their environment for survival.

Chapter 3

Energy in Ecosystems

Endangered green sea turtle and reef fish

LESSON

1

It moves from the Sun, to plants, to animals that eat plants, and to animals that eat other animals. What is it that goes from the Sun through this chain of living things?

LESSON

2

Every ecosystem is a complex web of relationships among different kinds of organisms. What animals might compete with each other to eat this grasshopper?

LESSON

3

A very small organism may help a large organism survive. What are some examples of this?

Writing Journal

In your Writing Journal, show what you know by writing or drawing answers to each question.

83

Vocabulary Preview

Vocabulary

Glossary

Vocabulary Skill

Word Root

omnivore

Knowing some Latin roots can help you understand the meaning of *omnivore*. The word parts *omni–* and *–vore* come from Latin words. The Latin word *omnis* means "all" or "every" and *vorare* (vo RAH ray) means "to devour." *Omnivore* means "eats everything." Try using Latin roots to understand the meanings of *carnivore* and *herbivore*. The Latin word *carnis* means "flesh" and *herba* means "plant."

carnivore
An animal that eats only other animals.

omnivore
An animal that eats both plants and animals.

microorganism
A tiny living thing that can be seen only with a microscope.

herbivore

An animal that eats only plants.

Start with Your Standards

Standard Sets 2., 3. Life Sciences

2.a. *Students know* plants are the primary source of matter and energy entering most food chains.

2.b. *Students know* producers and consumers (herbivores, carnivores, omnivores, and decomposers) are related in food chains and food webs and may compete with each other for resources in an ecosystem.

3.d. *Students know* that most microorganisms do not cause disease and that many are beneficial.

Standard Set 6. Investigation and Experimentation covered in this chapter: 6.a., 6.c., 6.f.

What Are Food Chains?

Building Background

Corn plants use the Sun's energy to grow. You eat corn for its taste and for the energy it contains. A salmon gets energy from the smaller fish it eats. You, or a hawk if it gets there first, get energy from the salmon. You or the hawk, the salmon, the small fish, and the corn are parts of food chains.

PREPARE TO INVESTIGATE

Inquiry Skill

Ask Questions You ask questions to find out how or why something that you observe happens. Questions can lead to scientific investigations.

Materials

- goggles
- disposable gloves
- owl pellet
- paper towel
- tweezers
- toothpick
- hand lens

Science and Math Toolbox

For steps 1 and 3, review **Using a Hand Lens** on page H2.

What Owls Eat

Procedure

1. **Observe** Spread out a paper towel on your work surface. Use tweezers to place an owl pellet on the paper towel. An owl pellet is made up of the undigested food of an owl. Use a hand lens to observe it. **Safety:** Wear goggles and disposable gloves.

2. **Record Data** In your *Science Notebook*, make a chart like the one shown. Record what you observe using the hand lens.

3. Use tweezers and a toothpick to gently pull apart the pellet into small pieces. Look at each piece through the hand lens. Record your observations in your chart.

4. **Classify** Group similar items when you find them. In your *Science Notebook*, list categories for the types of things you have found. **Safety:** Wash your hands thoroughly when you finish the activity.

Conclusion

1. **Classify** What items did you find? How did you group them? What observations support your way of grouping the items?

2. **Infer** Based on your observations, in what kind of ecosystem do you think an owl lives?

3. **Ask Questions** Write a list of questions you have about what other organisms live in an owl's ecosystem.

STEP 1

STEP 2

Description of Item	Drawing

STEP 3

Guided Inquiry

Experiment Ask your teacher to help you find and use a microscope. **Observe** the objects that you found in the owl pellet. What did you learn about what owls can and cannot digest?

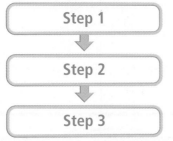

Food Chains

MAIN IDEA In an ecosystem, energy flows from the Sun to producers and from producers to consumers.

Energy from the Sun

All living things need energy to survive. They get that energy from food. Some animals eat plants. Some animals eat other animals that eat plants.

Plants do not eat food. Most plants make their own food through a process called **photosynthesis** (foh toh SIHN thih sihs). Photosynthesis takes place in a plant's leaves. A material in the leaves traps light energy from the Sun. During photosynthesis, plants use carbon dioxide gas from the air and water in soil to make food in the form of sugar. The original source of energy for most living things is the Sun.

Energy flows from the Sun to plants to prey to predators.

Sun

plant

Predator and Prey

Recall that an animal that hunts other animals for food is called a predator. A fox is one kind of predator, and a rabbit is one of its prey. An animal can be both predator and prey. For example, a fox may be the prey of a bobcat.

The photographs show how energy flows from the Sun to plants and to animals. Recall that plants are producers and animals are consumers. When a consumer, such as a rabbit, eats a plant, it receives some of the plant's energy. When the rabbit becomes the prey of the fox, the fox receives some of the plant's energy.

In a pond ecosystem, tiny plants and plantlike organisms are the producers. They use the Sun's energy to make food. Tiny animals eat the plants. The tiny animals are prey to small fish. The small fish are eaten by larger fish.

In almost every ecosystem, energy flows from the Sun to producers, and then to consumers. Among the consumers, energy flows from prey to predator. When tiny animals in a pond eat the tiny plants, energy flows to the tiny animals. When predators eat the tiny animals, energy flows to the predators.

SEQUENCE **What is the relationship between a predator and its prey?**

prey

predator

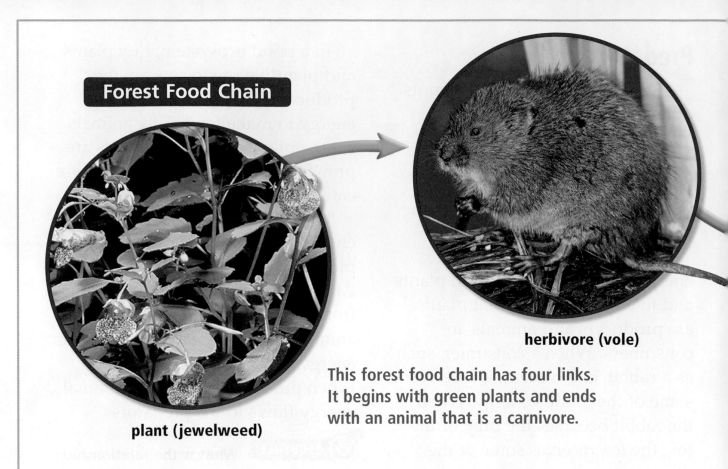

Forest Food Chain

plant (jewelweed)

herbivore (vole)

This forest food chain has four links. It begins with green plants and ends with an animal that is a carnivore.

Food Chains

A **food chain** (chayn) shows the path of food energy in an ecosystem from plants to animals. In the food chain shown, a vole gets energy from eating a plant called jewelweed. A skunk gets energy from eating a vole. An owl gets energy from eating the skunk.

Food chains are different in different ecosystems. But the first link in any food chain is always a producer. In most ecosystems, the producers are green plants. Matter and energy enter the food chain through these plants. This happens when the plants, such as the jewelweed, use the energy in

sunlight to make food through the process of photosynthesis.

The second link in the food chain shown is a vole. A vole is an herbivore (HUR buh vawr). An **herbivore** is an animal that eats only plants. The vole gets energy from the green plants it eats.

The third and fourth links in any food chain are either omnivores (AHM nuh vawrz) or carnivores (KAHR nuh vawrz). An **omnivore** is an animal that eats both plants and animals. A skunk is an omnivore. It eats insects, earthworms, mice, and voles. It also eats berries and nuts. A **carnivore** is an animal that eats only other animals. The great horned owl is a carnivore.

omnivore (skunk)

predator (owl)

In a pond ecosystem, tiny plants and plantlike organisms are the first link in the food chain. The tiny animals that eat these organisms are the second link in the chain. Recall that plant-eating organisms are herbivores. Other links in a pond food chain are the small and large fish that eat the herbivores.

A raccoon is an omnivore that is often a part of a pond ecosystem. A raccoon eats the small fish in the chain. Because it is an omnivore, it also eats plant parts such as berries and acorns.

Seaweed is the first link in some ocean food chains. Small animals called limpets eat the seaweed. Limpets are herbivores and the second link in the chain. Crabs eat limpets. Some crabs are omnivores, but most crabs are carnivores. Seagulls

eat crabs. They are omnivores and the last organisms in this food chain.

Organisms depend on each other for food, but they also compete with each other. Competition for resources can occur at several points in the same food chain. For example, seagulls eat both fish and crabs. But seals and other predators also eat fish and crabs. So seagulls, seals, and other predators compete for the fish and crabs in the ocean.

SEQUENCE **What are the third and fourth links in a food chain?**

Express Lab

Activity Card 8
Put Yourself in a Food Chain

The Energy Pyramid

As shown in the energy pyramid, at each link in a food chain some of the food energy is used. For example, plants do not store all the food that they make. Some of the energy from the food is used to develop flowers and seeds.

Only part of the energy that the plants captured from the Sun is available to jackrabbits that eat the plants. The jackrabbits use some of the energy to look for food, grow, and run from predators. So less energy is available to predators, such as bobcats, that eat jackrabbits.

In a food chain, the further a population of organisms is from producers (plants), the less energy is available to that population. For this reason, the population size of a predator is usually smaller than the population size of its prey. For the same reason, most food chains have only four or five links.

SEQUENCE **What happens to available energy at each link in the food chain?**

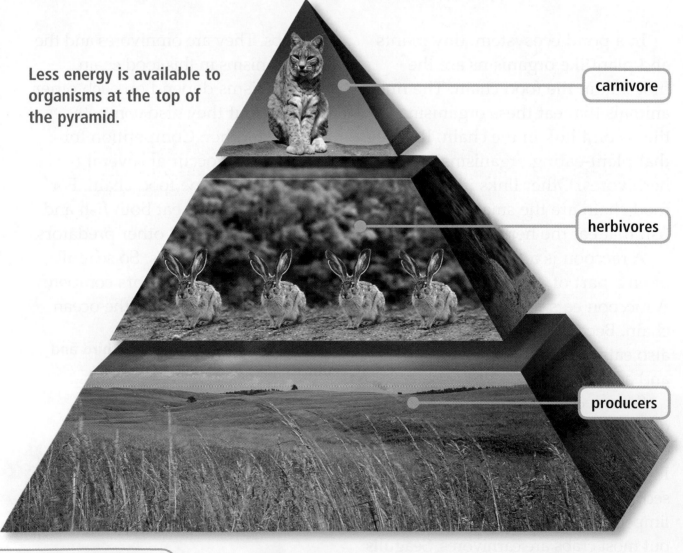

Less energy is available to organisms at the top of the pyramid.

carnivore

herbivores

producers

Visual Summary

Plants can produce their own food using the Sun's energy. Animals that eat the plants get some of that energy.

Many herbivores are prey for carnivores and omnivores. No matter what an animal eats, it is part of a food chain.

At each link in a food chain, some of the food energy is used. Therefore, less energy is available the further a population of organisms is from the producers in the chain.

Reading Review

❶ MAIN IDEA What is the primary source of energy in most ecosystems?

❷ VOCABULARY What does a food chain show?

❸ READING SKILL Show the sequence of energy flow in an ecosystem.

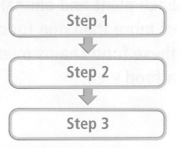

❹ CRITICAL THINKING:
Analyze How can an animal be both predator and prey? Explain.

❺ INQUIRY SKILL: Ask Questions Write a list of questions you have about food chains in a fresh water ecosystem.

 TEST PRACTICE

An herbivore *cannot* be a _____.

A. consumer.

B. prey.

C. plant eater.

D. producer.

 Technology
Visit **www.eduplace.com/cascp** to find out more about food chains.

What Are Food Webs?

Building Background

There are many different plants and animals in an African grassland ecosystem such as the one shown. Each plant and animal may be part of more than one food chain. All these food chains overlap to make a food web.

PREPARE TO INVESTIGATE

Inquiry Skill

Research When you do research, you learn more about a subject by looking in books, searching the Internet, or asking science experts.

Materials

- Food Web Support Master
- reference books
- 4 index cards
- construction paper
- markers or crayons
- scissors

A Tangled Web

Procedure

1. **Research** Work with a partner. Use a reference book. From the Food Web Support Master provided, find a plant-eating animal. In your *Science Notebook*, record that animal and the plants it eats. Then research and record an animal from the list that eats the plant eater. Next, find a new animal that eats that one.

2. On separate index cards, draw and label each living thing from step 1.

3. **Use Models** Place the index cards in order on construction paper to show a food chain. Draw arrows to show how energy flows from one living thing to another.

4. **Experiment** Remove the index cards, and turn over your construction paper. Work with another team. Use cards from both teams to make a food web. A **food web** is two or more overlapping food chains. Draw arrows to show how energy flows.

STEP 2

STEP 3

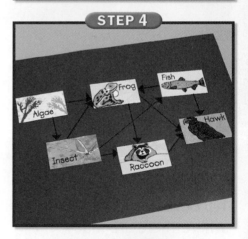

STEP 4

Conclusion

1. **Infer** Does energy flow from plant eaters to animal eaters or from animal eaters to plant eaters? How do you know?

2. **Predict** What might happen if one kind of animal were removed from the web?

Guided Inquiry

Ask Questions What questions do you have about a food web in an ecosystem near your school? **Research** answers for one or two questions by asking an expert.

Food Webs

MAIN IDEA In an ecosystem, overlapping food chains form food webs.

VOCABULARY

food web   p. 96

READING SKILL

Classify

Use the diagram below to list two food chains that overlap.

Group	Group

Chains and Webs

Most ecosystems contain many different kinds of plants and animals. Each plant or animal is part of more than one food chain. When two or more food chains overlap, they form a **food web**. In a food web, at least one plant or animal from each food chain is part of another food chain.

For example, the creosote (KREE uh soht) bush, the grasshopper, the flicker, and the hawk form a food chain. They are also part of a food web. In the food web shown, the creosote bush is food not only for the grasshopper, but also for jackrabbits and kangaroo rats. The creosote bush is part of several food chains.

The hawk is also part of several food chains. The hawk may eat flickers, jackrabbits, and kangaroo rats. The arrows show some of the food chains that form this desert food web.

CLASSIFY What is the difference between a food chain and a food web?

The Mojave Desert is one type of land ecosystem where there are many overlapping food chains. ▶

Creosote bushes give off an odor like tar, but that doesn't stop animals from eating them.

Express Lab

Activity Card 9
Dissect a Food Web

A Desert Food Web

The red-tailed hawk can soar over the desert and spot prey from far away. In the Mojave Desert, it can find small mammals and birds to eat.

The creosote bush grasshopper feeds on only this type of bush. The grasshopper is food for birds in the desert.

A red-shafted flicker snatches insects with its long, barbed tongue.

Kangaroo rats eat the seeds of the creosote bush and burrow under it to avoid the desert Sun.

The jackrabbit moves quickly to escape predators such as the hawk. It may stop where it can hide and eat at the same time.

97

An Ocean Food Web

Seagulls are among many sea birds that dive to feed on fish.

algae

Krill, tiny shrimplike animals, eat algae. Krill are food for fish, sea birds, and marine mammals, such as whales.

Small fish such as Pacific herring are food for sea birds, larger fish, and some marine mammals such as whales.

Some kinds of whales eat krill. Others eat small fish.

salmon

An ocean food web is a huge network of relationships between organisms.

Sharks eat just about any fish they can find, including salmon.

Visual Summary

In every kind of ecosystem, energy enters food webs through plants and plantlike organisms.

Some plants and animals link together in many overlapping food chains to make a food web.

Many organisms, from tiny algae to giant whales, form overlapping food chains to make up an ocean food web.

Reading Review

① MAIN IDEA What is a food web?

② VOCABULARY Describe one food web.

③ READING SKILL: Divide desert organisms into two categories, prey and predator. Are some organisms on both lists? Explain.

Group	Group

④ CRITICAL THINKING: Synthesize What organisms would be affected if there were no algae in the ocean?

⑤ INQUIRY SKILL: Research List five words that you could use to search the Internet for more information on food webs.

✔ TEST PRACTICE

Which of the following animals does not eat creosote bushes?

A. grasshopper

B. red-tailed hawk

C. jackrabbit

D. kangaroo rat

Technology
Visit **www.eduplace.com/cascp** to learn more about food webs.

JOHN MUIR

ADMIRING THE DOUGLAS SQUIRREL

John Muir was a pioneer in the movement to conserve the natural environment. In his first book, published in 1894, *The Mountains of California*, Muir writes about California ecosystems. This passage from the book describes plants eaten by the Douglas squirrel in its forest ecosystem.

No other of the Sierra animals . . . is better fed, not even the deer . . . . His food consists of grass-seeds, berries, hazel-nuts, chinquapins, and the nuts and seeds of all the coniferous trees without exception—Pine, Fir, Spruce, Libocedrus, Juniper, and Sequoia—he is fond of them all, and they all agree with him, green or ripe. No cone is too large for him to manage, none so small as to be beneath his notice. The smaller ones, such as those of the Hemlock, and the Douglas Spruce, and the Two-leaved Pine, he cuts off and eats on a branch of the tree, without allowing them to fall; beginning at the bottom of the cone and cutting away the scales to expose the seeds; not gnawing by guess, like a bear, but turning them round and round in regular order, in compliance with their spiral arrangement. . . .

"When we try to pick out anything by itself, we find it hitched to everything else in the Universe."

Squirrel tracks drawing by Muir

Sharing Ideas

1. **READING CHECK** What does John Muir observe about the Douglas squirrel's food?

2. **WRITE ABOUT IT** Where does the Douglas squirrel fit in a forest food web?

3. **TALK ABOUT IT** Discuss this statement: The Douglas squirrel is an example of something that is "hitched to everything else in the Universe."

What Are Microorganisms?

Building Background

Most microorganisms, like the one shown, produce much of the food and energy that help other living things survive on Earth. Of course, some microorganisms can cause disease. But most do not.

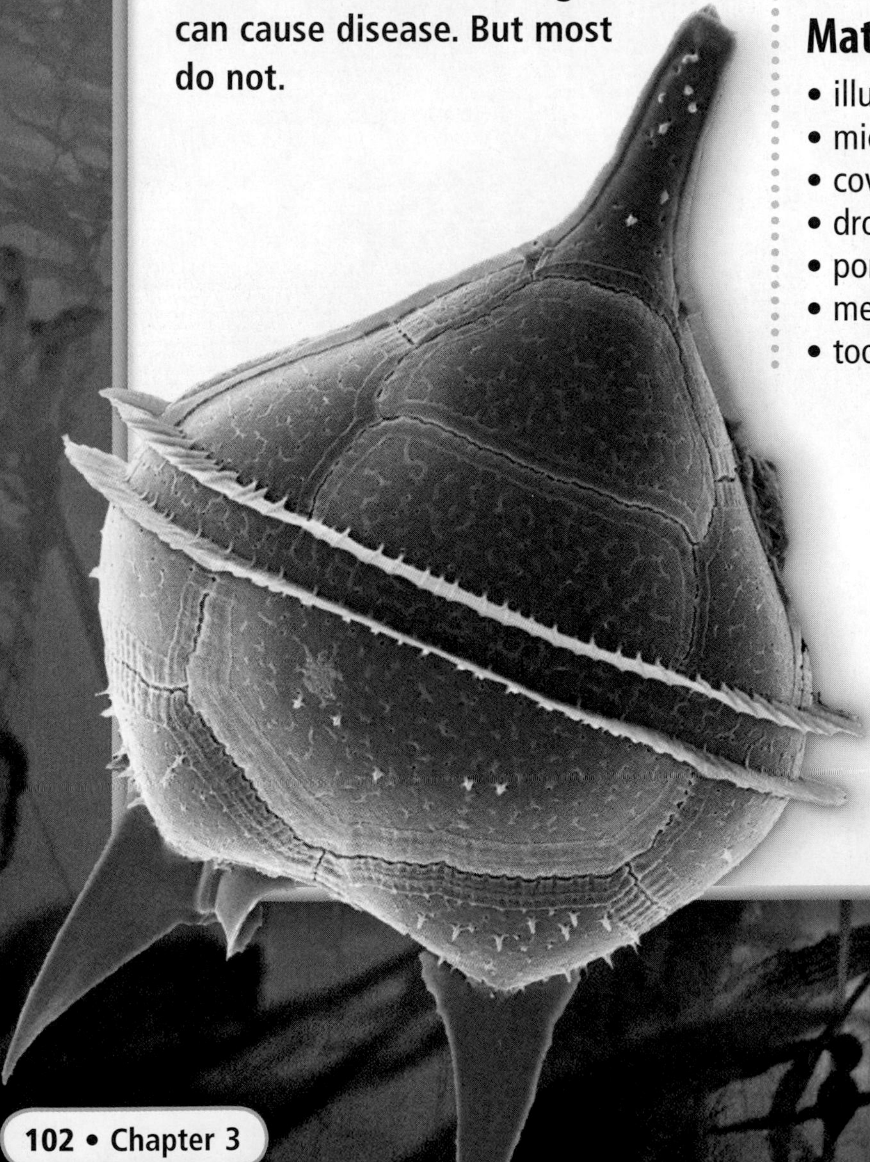

PREPARE TO INVESTIGATE

Inquiry Skill

Record Data When you keep records that are accurate, they can be understood at a later time.

Materials

- illuminated microscope
- microscope slides
- cover slips
- dropper
- pond water
- methyl cellulose
- toothpicks

Observing Microorganisms

Procedure

1 **Collaborate** Work in groups. Use a dropper to place a single drop of pond water on a clean microscope slide. Then add a drop of methyl cellulose and stir gently with a toothpick. Carefully hold a cover slip by its edges with your fingers and place it at an angle over the drop as shown. Lower it slowly to avoid air bubbles as you cover the drop with it.

2 **Observe** Scan the sample of pond water. Look for different kinds of organisms.

3 **Record Data** In your *Science Notebook*, make a drawing of each organism you see. Under each drawing, briefly describe the organism's shape, its method of moving from place to place, and any other details you observe.

Conclusion

1. Describe any organisms that appear animallike and any that appear plantlike. Explain why you would classify them this way.

2. **Compare** Exchange drawings with a student in a different group. Compare the organisms that you each observed. Which organisms were the same? Which were different?

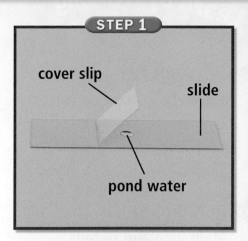

STEP 1

cover slip
slide
pond water

STEP 2

STEP 3

Guided Inquiry

Ask Questions Write a question you might ask to find out how a particular pond microorganism fits into a food web. **Research** the answer to the question in the library or on the Internet.

READING SKILL

Main Idea and Details
Use a diagram like the one shown to organize the main idea and details.

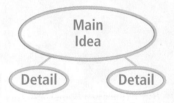

Main Idea

Detail   Detail

A paramecium is a microorganism that propels itself through water by moving tiny hairs. ▼

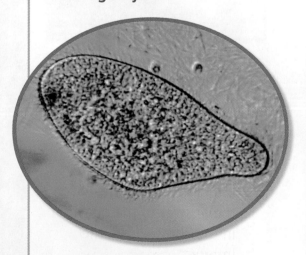

Microorganisms

MAIN IDEA Microorganisms are an important and necessary part of most ecosystems. Many kinds of microorganisms are helpful in making food. Others form the basis of food chains in oceans.

One-Celled Organisms

A **cell** is the basic unit that makes up all living things. Some simple organisms consist of only one cell. This single cell can carry out all of the same life processes as a plant or animal made of many cells. An organism that cannot be seen without the help of a microscope is called a **microorganism** (my kroh AWR guh nihz uhm). Microorganisms include one-celled organisms such as algae, amoebas, yeast, and bacteria.

Bacteria (bak TEER ee uh) are microorganisms found in all living organisms and everywhere on Earth. Because some bacteria cause illnesses, such as strep throat and Lyme disease, bacteria often have a bad reputation. But bacteria and other microorganisms play an important role in the survival of life on Earth.

Some *E. coli* bacteria help your body get nutrients from food. Others can cause disease. ▼

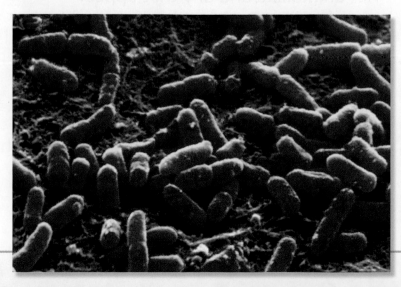

This microorganism helps turn milk into yogurt and cheese. ▶

Microorganisms at Work

Microorganisms are everywhere and doing many different kinds of work. Some foods, such as yogurt, sour cream, and cheese, come from the work of bacteria. Bacteria also help fruit juice become vinegar, cucumbers turn into pickles, and cabbage turn into sauerkraut.

Yeast is another kind of microorganism. It is used to make bread. As yeast eat sugar in the bread dough, they produce bubbles that are trapped in the dough. This causes the dough to expand, or rise. Yeast is also used to make ethanol (EHTH uh nawl). Ethanol is a kind of alcohol fuel that is mixed with gasoline to make it burn cleaner in auto engines.

Without the helpful bacteria that live in your body, you would not be able to digest food and get nutrients that you need. Bacteria also return remains of dead organisms to the environment. They break down dead plants and animals into nutrients that living things can use. In the next chapter you will learn more about this important role of microorganisms.

MAIN IDEA What are two details that support the idea that microorganisms can be helpful?

Express Lab

Activity Card 10
Watch Microorganisms Work

Microorganisms in Water

About three-quarters of Earth is covered by oceans. Plankton are found throughout the waters of the oceans. **Plankton** are microorganisms that live in water and form the beginning of most ocean food chains. There are different kinds of plankton. They form an invisible film over all of Earth's oceans.

Many kinds of plankton are microscopic plants or one-celled algae (AL jee) that use the Sun's energy to make food. They do this by using the same process of photosynthesis that plants on land use. Because they give off oxygen as part of this process, and they are so plentiful, plankton produce most of the oxygen on Earth.

Ocean food webs depend on the ability of these plankton to make food by capturing energy from the Sun. Other kinds of plankton are microscopic animals that feed on the plankton that make food. Larger ocean animals, from small fish to whales, eat plankton.

MAIN IDEA Why are microorganisms important in ocean food chains?

Diatoms are one-celled algae that live in water. Diatoms have two halves that fit together like a box and its lid. This "shell" comes in a variety of amazing shapes.

▲ Plankton produce the food that is the beginning of many ocean food chains.

Visual Summary

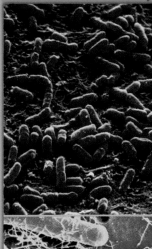

Some kinds of bacteria help you digest food. Other kinds can cause disease.

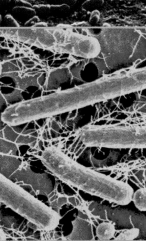

Many microorganisms help in the process of making foods such as yogurt, bread, and pickles.

The ocean is filled with microorganisms. They form the beginning of many ocean food chains and produce much of the world's oxygen.

Reading Review

❶ MAIN IDEA How are microorganisms helpful?

❷ VOCABULARY Use the term *plankton* in a sentence.

❸ READING SKILL Write the main idea of the lesson and two supporting details in the chart.

Main Idea

Detail — Detail

❹ CRITICAL THINKING: Apply How are plankton similar to trees?

❺ INQUIRY SKILL: Record Data Suppose you observe a microorganism and want to describe it to a classmate. Would you draw a picture, write a description, or both? Explain your answer.

 TEST PRACTICE
Bacteria are used in making ____.

A. bread.

B. milk.

C. ethanol.

D. cheese.

 Technology
Visit **www.eduplace.com/cascp** to learn more about beneficial microorganisms.

Dining in the Dark

Extreme pressure, extreme temperatures, no sunlight! What could possibly live near an undersea hydrothermal (hot water) vent? How about 2.4-meter-long tubeworms? Scientists were shocked to discover this new life form living in conditions that would kill most other creatures.

The tubeworm has no eyes, no mouth—and no inside structures! So, how does it eat? It doesn't! Tubeworms get the nutrients they need by absorbing food produced by bacteria that live inside them. The bacteria get their energy from chemicals coming out of the vents. They do not depend on the Sun, because there is no sunlight that deep in the ocean! The discovery that a food chain did not have to start with energy from the Sun was a big surprise to scientists.

Almost all life on Earth depends on solar energy, but the giant tubeworms do just fine dining in the dark!

This hydrothermal vent, called a "black smoker," shoots out water that is more than 400°C—four times as hot as boiling water!

Writing Journal

Imagine you are the scientist who discovered tubeworms. Write in your journal about your discovery and its scientific importance.

MATH Analyze Data

The two circle graphs show what percent of Earth's surface is covered by oceans, desert, forest, and grasslands.

1. How much greater is the percent of grassland than "other" land?

2. Which covers a greater percent of land, forest or grassland? How much greater?

3. What is the total percent of land covered by desert and grassland?

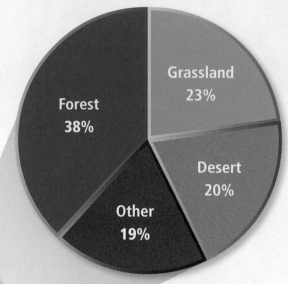

Grassland 23%

Forest 38%

Desert 20%

Other 19%

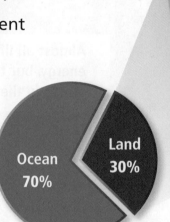

Ocean 70%

Land 30%

WRITING Informative

Choose one plant or animal, such as a tree or an insect, that is part of the ecosystem you live in or one that you have visited. If possible, choose an organism that you have spent some time looking at. Write a description of the plant or animal. In your description include details that you would recognize by using your senses. For example, you would know that a rabbit had soft fur by using your sense of touch.

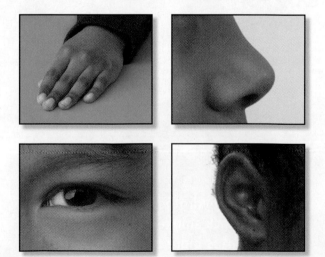

Pet-Store Owner

Squawk! Bark! Meow! If you like to spend your day with animals, you might want to work in a pet store.

A pet-store owner must provide for the needs of many kinds of animals. For example, fish need clean water, birds need perches, and large animals need space to move around. A pet store must provide healthy environments for all the animals it sells.

What It Takes!

• An interest in animals and people

• Skills in running a business

Ecologist

How will building new houses and roads change a nearby forest? Why are there fewer fish in a lake now than in the past? Ecologists look for answers to questions like these.

Ecologists study how living things interact with each other and with their environment. The ecologist's goal is to help people make wise decisions about things that may affect the natural world.

What It Takes!

• An interest in the natural world

• A college degree in life science

Vocabulary

Complete each sentence with a term from the list.

1. Plants make food through the process of _____.

2. Two or more overlapping food chains form a _____.

3. An animal that only eats other animals is a/an _____.

4. A small fish eats algae. A big fish eats the small fish. This describes a/an _____.

5. An organism that can only be seen with a microscope is a/an _____.

6. A bear eats both berries and fish, so it is a/an _____.

7. Microorganisms that float in water are called _____.

8. Pickles are made using helpful _____.

9. An animal that eats only plants is a/an _____.

10. The basic unit that makes up all living things is a/an _____.

bacteria p. 104
carnivore p. 90
cell p. 104
food chain p. 90
food web p. 96
herbivore p. 90
microorganism p. 104
omnivore p. 90
photosynthesis p. 88
plankton p. 106

Test Practice

Write the letter of the best answer choice.

11. Plankton form the _____ of an ocean food chain.

   A. middle
   B. end
   C. beginning
   D. consumers

12. An herbivore might eat _____.

   A. grass.
   B. worms.
   C. omnivores.
   D. insects.

13. A food web may include _____.

   A. carnivores.   **C.** producers.
   B. herbivores.   **D.** all of the above.

14. In a food chain, as an organism gets further from the producer, the amount of energy available _____.

   A. increases.
   B. decreases.
   C. remains the same.
   D. decreases then increases.

15. **Ask Questions** Write a question about a food chain you might find in an ocean ecosystem. What research would you have to do to answer your question?

16. Look back at pages 86 and 87. Describe each part of the instructions for the investigation and tell why each is important.

Map the Concept

Use the concept map to show a food chain. Write each term in the correct place on the map.

hawk   insect   grass   skunk

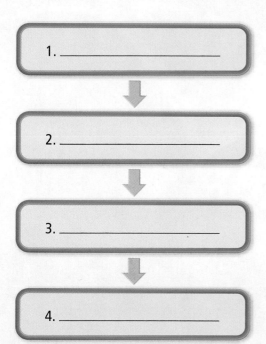

1. _____

2. _____

3. _____

4. _____

Critical Thinking

17. **Analyze** How does an herbivore benefit from the Sun's energy?

18. **Evaluate** Tell whether the following statement is accurate: Herbivores and carnivores are more important to a food web than are omnivores. Give reasons for your answer. Use examples in your explanation.

19. **Synthesize** What would be the likely effect on an ocean food web if one type of fish in the web were to die off?

20. **Apply** Why are there usually only four or five links in a food chain?

Performance Assessment

Parts of a Food Chain
What food chains might exist in a city park? Draw a diagram of a food chain in a city park that includes plants and animals. Compare your diagram with those of other students. Evaluate whether any of the food chains overlap to form a food web.

Writing Journal

Review your answers to the questions on page 83 at the beginning of this chapter. Change your answers, as needed, based on what you have learned.

Chapter 4

Matter in Ecosystems

Mushrooms, forest ecosystem

LESSON 1

When a tree falls, its trunk, leaves, and branches soon begin to rot. Mushrooms, mosses, and molds grow on the rotting log. What happens to the material that made up the tree?

LESSON 2

People change natural ecosystems when they build roads and buildings to meet their needs. How does this affect the other organisms in the ecosystem?

LESSON 3

Habitat destruction, pollution, and the use of natural resources are harmful to ecosystems. What can be done to preserve ecosystems?

Writing Journal

In your Writing Journal, show what you know by writing or drawing answers to each question.

Vocabulary Preview

Vocabulary

Glossary

Vocabulary Skill

Multiple-Meaning Words

litter

The word *litter* means trash that is not disposed of in a way that prevents harm to ecosystems.

Litter also means the multiple offspring produced at one time by an animal, as in *a litter of kittens*.

pollution
The addition of harmful materials to the environment.

compost
Decayed material from the remains of once-living things used to enrich soil.

scavenger
An animal that feeds on the remains of dead animals.

ecotourism

Ecotourism is travel to natural habitats that avoids harming them and helps organisms that live there.

Start with Your Standards

Standard Sets 2., 3. Life Sciences

2.b. *Students know* producers and consumers (herbivores, carnivores, omnivores, and decomposers) are related in food chains and food webs and may compete for resources in an ecosystem.

2.c. *Students know* decomposers, including many fungi, insects, and microorganisms, recycle matter from dead plants and animals.

3.b. *Students know* that in any particular environment, some kinds of plants and animals survive well, some survive less well, and some cannot survive at all.

3.d. *Students know* that most microorganisms do not cause disease and that many are beneficial.

Standard Set 6. Investigation and Experimentation covered in this chapter: 6.a., 6.e., 6.f.

How Is Matter Cycled in an Ecosystem?

Building Background

A vulture's meal may not appeal to you, but vultures and other organisms like them play an important role in ecosystems. Vultures and organisms such as fungi, insects, and microorganisms recycle dead plant and animal material into substances that other organisms can use.

PREPARE TO INVESTIGATE

Inquiry Skill

Use Variables In an experiment, a variable is the condition that is being tested. All conditions in an experiment must be kept the same, except for the variable.

Materials

- marking pen
- 3 resealable plastic bags
- 3 pieces of bread
- dropper
- water
- masking tape
- black construction paper
- hand lens

Growing Mold

Procedure

1 **Collaborate** Work with a partner. Use a marking pen to label three plastic bags *A*, *B*, and *C*. In your *Science Notebook*, make a chart like the one shown.

2 **Experiment** Put a piece of bread into each bag. Use a dropper to put 10 drops of water on the bread in each bag. Seal the bags and tape them closed with masking tape. **Safety:** Do not open any of the bags after sealing. Your teacher will dispose of them.

3 **Observe** Record in your chart the appearance of the bread in each bag.

4 **Use Variables** Place bag *A* in a refrigerator and bag *B* in a dark closet. Use a sheet of black construction paper to cover bag *C*. Place it in a sunny window. Temperature is the variable you are testing.

5 **Record Data** Use a hand lens to observe the bread in each bag every day for about two weeks. In your chart, record any changes. Look for the growth of mold, a type of organism. Draw what you see.

Conclusion

1. **Analyze Data** How was the growth of mold different in the three bags?

2. **Infer** Under which condition did the mold grow best?

STEP 1

Appearance of Bread

Day	Bag A (cold)	Bag B (room temp)	Bag C (warm)
1			
2			
3			
4			
5			

STEP 2

Guided Inquiry

Experiment Plan an experiment to find out how light affects the growth of bread mold. To **use variables** properly, make sure you set up all the bags in the same way except for the variable of light.

READING SKILL

Cause and Effect
Use the diagram below to describe the effects that decomposers have on an ecosystem.

Cause ▶ Effect

Recycling Matter in Ecosystems

MAIN IDEA Organisms such as scavengers and decomposers recycle matter from dead plants and animals. They turn this matter into a form that can be used by other organisms.

Scavengers

Have you ever gone on a scavenger (SKAV-uhn jur) hunt? If so, you know that it involves looking for things in the environment. Some animals spend much of their time "on a scavenger hunt." Unlike predators, they are not hunting for living prey. They are looking for the remains of dead animals to eat. A **scavenger** is an animal that feeds on the remains or wastes of dead animals.

Scavengers are consumers. Like all consumers, they get energy from the food they eat. For a scavenger, the energy comes from eating the remains of once-living things. Often a scavenger eats the remains of prey that was killed by another animal. Examples of scavengers include raccoons, vultures, hyenas, and some crabs.

Carrion beetles lay their eggs in dead animals. The remains of these animals provide food for the developing young. ▶

Scavengers in Food Webs

Predators and scavengers are both carnivores. Predators hunt and kill other animals for food. Scavengers eat what is left by predators. For example, when a wolf kills a moose for food, it does not eat all of the moose. The leftovers provide hearty meals for coyotes, ravens, and other scavengers.

Scavengers take in nutrients that would otherwise be wasted. If a scavenger becomes the prey of another animal, the nutrients are passed along in the food chain. This is one reason why scavengers are an important part of food webs.

Scavengers are a part of every kind of ecosystem. In the ocean, sharks and crabs are scavengers. Although sharks hunt live prey, they also eat organisms that are no longer alive.

▲ Peccaries are both omnivores and scavengers. They will eat almost anything, including meat, fruit, fish, and birds.

CAUSE AND EFFECT Why are scavengers an important part of food webs?

◀ In Africa, Marabou (MAIR uh boo) storks are commonly seen in garbage dumps. They are both carnivores and scavengers.

Express Lab

Activity Card 11
Model Decay

121

Decomposers

You may recall that bacteria are tiny one-celled organisms found in all environments, including in living things. Fungi (FUHN jy) are another group of organisms that include mushrooms and mold. Some types of both bacteria and fungi can cause disease. Mold can cause foods to spoil.

Most fungi and bacteria are helpful, not harmful. They play an important role as decomposers (dee-kuhm POH zurz). A **decomposer** is a living thing that breaks down the remains of dead organisms.

Although many dead organisms are eaten by scavengers, some are not. Instead, their remains **decay** (dih KAY), or break down into simpler materials. Decomposers help this process. All food chains end with decomposers.

A fallen tree, or log, is a good place to find decomposers that break down wood. For example, insects such as ants, termites, and beetles tunnel holes into the log. The holes weaken the wood.

Other decomposers that might be found on a fallen log include worms, fungi, and bacteria. Fungi release chemicals that break down dead plants, as well as the remains of animals.

A Home for Many Living Things

This log provides food and shelter for the decomposers, scavengers, producers, herbivores, and carnivores living on it.

oyster fungus

beetle

ant

salamander

By helping the wood log decay, decomposers help new plants grow. Nutrients that were in the wood are released back into the soil by decomposers. This process of breaking down materials into a different form that can be used again is called **nutrient recycling**.

Recycling of nutrients by decomposers is important to ecosystems. Much of this recycling is done by microorganisms such as bacteria. As you've learned, bacteria help in the decay of dead plants and animals. Nutrients released by bacteria from these remains enrich the soil. Many types of plants in an ecosystem benefit from this enriched soil.

Decomposers also help clean up the environment. They keep it from becoming filled with the remains of dead plants and animals.

Rates of decay vary with conditions. Decay occurs faster under warm, moist conditions than under cold, dry conditions. An animal that dies on a cold mountain might not decay for a long time. In a warm, rainy area, its body would decay rapidly. The reason for this difference is that most decomposers need moisture and warmth to survive. In cold, dry areas there are fewer decomposers, so decay happens more slowly.

CAUSE AND EFFECT What is one way that decomposers are helpful?

mouse

fern

moss

termites

millipede

Composting

You know that decomposers are important to ecosystems because they release nutrients that other organisms need to survive.

Decomposers also free up living space in the environment. When the remains of dead plants and animals decay, the space they took up becomes available to other living things.

Because decomposers are helpful, it makes sense to encourage their growth. People can create an ideal environment for decomposers. They can do this by making a place where natural materials, including garbage and trash, can become compost (KAHM pohst). **Compost** is decayed material from once-living things that is used to enrich soil.

Often, materials that can be useful in making compost are thrown away. When these materials end up in a landfill, they take up space and may not decay much.

Materials that should be put into compost piles or bins include grass clippings, leaves, kitchen scraps, and some papers. These materials are recycled by decomposers such as fungi and bacteria that live in great numbers in compost piles and bins. The resulting decayed material can be mixed with soil. The enriched soil that results can be used to grow plants for food.

CAUSE AND EFFECT How can compost improve soil?

Garbage by Percent

- yard waste 16%
- food 7%
- other 17%
- paper and cardboard 37%
- plastics, metal, glass 23%

Food, yard waste, and paper and cardboard can all be composted. What percent of all garbage is that?

Visual Summary

Scavengers are consumers that get energy from the remains of dead organisms. They play an important role in ecosystems.

Decomposers help decay, or break down, the remains of dead organisms.

People can create an ideal environment for decomposers by making a compost pile or bin.

Reading Review

❶ MAIN IDEA Why does an ecosystem need decomposers?

❷ VOCABULARY Use the term *scavenger* in a sentence.

❸ READING SKILL Use the diagram to show the effect that warmer temperature has on the decaying process.

Cause ➔ Effect

❹ CRITICAL THINKING: Evaluate What would happen if there were no decomposers in a forest?

❺ INQUIRY SKILL: Use Variables How might you check to see what material breaks down fastest in a compost pile?

✔ TEST PRACTICE

Decomposers include _____.

A. fungi.

B. insects.

C. bacteria.

D. all of the above.

Technology
Visit **www.eduplace.com/cascp** to find out more about scavengers and decomposers.

Nothing Wasted!

Hey, what's this beetle pushing around?
Don't laugh, but it's a big ball of animal dung! The beetle has carefully rolled up the dung to make it into a nursery for its baby. The dung is food for the adult beetle and its baby. Dung beetles are among the most important scavengers on Earth. Without them, the dung of millions of plant-eating animals would overwhelm some ecosystems.

These amazing beetles roll up and bury most of the thousands of tons of dung dropped by plant-eaters in the Serengeti of Africa. ▶

The Dung Beetle Cycle

Elephants eat plants and drop dung.

Beetle rolls up ball of dung.

Beetle buries dung ball with egg inside.

New beetle hatches from dung ball.

Buried dung ball fertilizes plants.

Writing Journal

In your writing journal, describe the role of the dung beetle in its ecosystem. If all dung beetles died off, what would likely happen to its ecosystem?

How Do People Affect Ecosystems?

Building Background

Sometimes ecosystems change because people change them. For example, what is now a quiet forest might become a busy city or town. Trees will be cut down and schools and homes will be built. When people change ecosystems, the changes affect the plants and animals that live there. Some living things may survive well, some may survive less well, and some may not survive at all.

PREPARE TO INVESTIGATE

Inquiry Skill

Use Numbers You use numbers when you measure, estimate, record, and interpret data.

Material

• graph paper

Vanishing Ecosystem

Procedure

1 **Compare** The maps show the amount of land in Ecuador that was covered by forest for the years 1938, 1958, 1988, and 2005. Compare the maps. In your *Science Notebook*, describe how the area of forest changed from 1938 to 2005.

2 **Analyze Data** Estimate the area of Ecuador that is covered by forest for each year shown. Do this by counting the number of green squares on each map. Record, in square units, the estimated area of forest for each year.

3 **Use Numbers** Make a line graph of the data you recorded in step 2. Label the horizontal axis *Years*. Label the vertical axis *Number of Square Units*.

4 **Use Numbers** Make a line graph of the following data of the estimated population of Ecuador: 1938, 2 million; 1958, 4 million; 1988, 10 million; 2005, 13 million. Label the horizontal axis *Years*. Label the vertical axis *Population*.

Conclusion

1. **Compare** Compare the graphs you made in steps 3 and 4. How are they alike?

2. **Predict** If the population of Ecuador continues to grow, what do you think might happen to the area of the rainforest?

Ecuador

SOUTH AMERICA

Forest Cover

1938

1958

1988

2005

Guided Inquiry

Ask Questions With a classmate, brainstorm several questions about rainforest conservation. Select one question to **research**.

Human Activities Affect Ecosystems

VOCABULARY

hazardous waste p. 132
litter p. 131
pollutant p. 131
pollution p. 131

READING SKILL

Compare and Contrast
Use the diagram below to compare an ecosystem that does not include humans and one that does.

Compare	Contrast

MAIN IDEA Like other organisms, people change the ecosystems in which they live. Human changes to an ecosystem can affect the ability of other organisms to survive in those ecosystems.

Effects on Land Ecosystems

As people meet their needs in land ecosystems, they change those ecosystems. For example, forests may be cleared to use the land for farming. Forest plants are replaced by crop plants and forest animals are replaced by farm animals.

Towns, cities, roads, and farms are built in natural areas. Often the living things in these places cannot survive once the places are changed for human use. For example, plants cannot grow where parking lots or stores have been built.

Humans clear land for other resources, such as wood or minerals.

Some farmers spray liquid weed killers to prevent weeds from growing in crop fields. Weed killers are pollutants that can kill plants in surrounding areas.

People can use technology to change a forest into a city or a river into a lake. These changes can have both helpful and harmful effects. Dams are built to control flooding, bring water to dry areas to grow crops, and to provide water for people in cities.

Dams can also be harmful. Before a dam is built, river flooding can deposit soil rich in nutrients along the land beside the river. After the dam is built, this flooding no longer occurs. The soil along the river will no longer be enriched. Changes in the flow of the river may also cause decreases in fish populations.

People sometimes add harmful materials to ecosystems. For example, some farms use materials such as weed killers and pesticides. Runoff from these products can seep into the soil and cause pollution (puh LOO shuhn). **Pollution** is the addition of harmful materials to the environment. A material that causes pollution is called a **pollutant**. Pollutants can harm many kinds of organisms.

Human activities produce a lot of waste, such as trash from homes and businesses. **Litter** is trash that is not disposed of in a way that prevents harm to ecosystems. Most litter is trash that is thrown carelessly on the ground or in water. Litter can harm ecosystems. For example, plants cannot grow where litter covers the soil. Young animals sometimes eat trash, causing them to become ill.

COMPARE AND CONTRAST What helpful and harmful effects can river dams have?

Effects on Water Ecosystems

When people do not dispose of waste products properly, pollution can result. Pollution can affect both land and water ecosystems. For example, sea animals can be harmed by some kinds of litter when they get tangled in it.

A **hazardous** (HAZ ur duhs) **waste** is a waste that can pollute the environment even when it occurs in very small amounts. Hazardous wastes are a danger to the health of people and other organisms. Substances such as motor oil, paint, insect sprays, and many cleaning supplies are hazardous wastes.

If containers of used motor oil are not disposed of properly, oil can seep into the ground and pollute it. Over time, this oil may be washed into lakes, streams, and rivers and pollute them as well.

Sometimes large oil spills occur that harm vast ocean habitats and the organisms that live in them. Such large spills usually happen when oil is being transported. For example, underwater oil pipelines can burst or ships carrying oil can overturn. Sea birds, seals, whales, fish, and shellfish may be killed as a result of such accidents.

COMPARE AND CONTRAST What is the difference between litter and hazardous waste?

◄ Some litter can directly harm animals by getting caught on their bodies and injuring them.

Express Lab

Activity Card 12
Model the Effects of Pollution

Cause	Effect
 People clear forests.	Forest plants and animals lose habitat and don't survive.

Cause	Effect
People pollute land ecosystems and dam rivers.	Pollutants harm many kinds of organisms. Dams change river flow, affecting fish populations.

Cause	Effect
 People pollute water ecosystems.	Sea birds, seals, whales, fish, and shellfish may be killed.

 Technology
Visit **www.eduplace.com/cascp** to learn more about how humans change ecosystems.

Reading Review

1 MAIN IDEA What are two ways that humans change land ecosystems?

2 VOCABULARY What is a pollutant?

3 READING SKILL How do humans affect water ecosystems?

Compare	Contrast

4 CRITICAL THINKING:
Evaluate Suppose that stores are built in a meadow. The builder says that the stores will not affect the meadow ecosystem. Evaluate this statement.

5 INQUIRY SKILL: Use Numbers
A study shows that a population of 4,000 coyotes is reduced by 2,900 coyotes after a forest is cleared. How many coyotes are left?

✔ **TEST PRACTICE**
Which of the following is likely to have a positive affect on ecosystems?

A. building a dam

B. littering

C. preventing pollution

D. using pesticides in farming

How Can Ecosystems Be Conserved?

Building Background

The survival of the San Joaquin kit fox species is in danger. The biggest threat to the fox is the loss of its habitat to farms and development. People have the power to destroy ecosystems and drive species to extinction. They also have the power to save ecosystems and encourage the survival of species.

PREPARE TO INVESTIGATE

Inquiry Skill

Hypothesize If you think you know why something that you observe happens, you can make a hypothesis, or an educated guess, about it.

Materials

- 4 clear plastic cups
- 4 labels
- 4 items of trash
- clear plastic wrap
- 4 rubber bands
- disposable gloves
- potting soil
- water
- dropper
- goggles
- newspapers
- marking pen

Recycling Waste

Procedure

1 **Collaborate** Work with a partner. Put one item of trash in the bottom of each of four plastic cups. Use a marking pen to label each cup with the item it contains. Then add soil to each cup so it is about three-fourths full. Moisten the soil with a few drops of water. **Safety:** Wear goggles.

2 **Hypothesize** Cover each cup with plastic wrap held in place with a rubber band. Place the cups in a sunny window for a week. Make an educated guess about what will happen to each trash item by the end of the week. Record your hypothesis in your *Science Notebook*.

3 **Observe** After one week, dump the contents of one cup onto a sheet of newspaper. Look closely at the trash item you put in the cup. Record your observations in your *Science Notebook*. **Safety:** Wear disposable gloves.

4 Repeat step 3 for each of the other cups.

STEP 1

STEP 2

plastic cap

STEP 3

Conclusion

1. **Hypothesize** Based on your data, form a hypothesis about what happens to different items of trash you throw away.

2. **Ask Questions** What else do you want to know about what happens to different kinds of trash? Make a list of such questions about trash.

Guided Inquiry

Experiment Plan and carry out a similar experiment using other items you throw away. **Observe** the condition of each item at the end of one week. Record all your observations.

READING SKILL

Problem and Solution
Use the diagram to record solutions to the problems of pollution and habitat destruction.

Problem	Solution

Conserving Ecosystems

MAIN IDEA Some of the ways ecosystems can be conserved include using biodegradable materials, recycling, and practicing green agriculture.

Biodegradable Materials

A **biodegradable material** is matter that breaks down easily in the environment. Paper, cardboard, and untreated wood are biodegradable materials. Materials that are not biodegradable can exist as trash or hazardous waste for thousands of years. Metals, many chemicals, and most plastics are not biodegradable.

Scientists are finding ways to make biodegradable versions of nonbiodegradable materials. For example, there are new biodegradable plastics, foams, and fabrics.

Day 1

Day 38

Day 58

▲ This new kind of plastic is made of plant materials. It acts like regular plastic when it is in use. But when it is thrown away, microorganisms can break it down into materials that will not pollute the environment.

A landfill is designed to stop pollutants from leaking into the surrounding environment.

Problems with Landfills

Over time a biodegradable newspaper should break down, right? It may not if the newspaper goes to a landfill.

A landfill is an outdoor area, usually a pit, set aside to bury wastes. Today, landfill pits are lined with plastic and sealed. This is done to prevent hazardous waste from leaking out of the landfill and harming ecosystems around it.

Why wouldn't a newspaper break down in a landfill? The garbage in a landfill is packed so tightly that there is little air or water. Many microorganisms that break down materials cannot survive there. So the garbage does not decay. When one scientist dug through a landfill, she found 30-year-old newspapers that could still be read!

Another problem with landfills is that they take up a lot of space. And because no one wants to live near landfills, it's hard to find new places to put them.

Often the best way to make sure that biodegradable trash decomposes safely is to keep it out of a landfill. Recycling, reusing, and composting biodegradable materials can save space in landfills. These practices can also prevent trash from causing pollution.

PROBLEM AND SOLUTION **What is one way to solve the problems with landfills?**

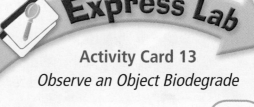

Express Lab

Activity Card 13
Observe an Object Biodegrade

Preserving Rainforests

Some people consider rainforests the most important ecosystems on the planet. Rainforests contain a huge number of different kinds of plants and animals. Rainforests are the source of many resources that people use. For example, chemicals found in rainforest plants are used to make medicines that treat cancer, muscle diseases, and malaria. Other rainforest plants are a source of many kinds of fruits, nuts, and vegetable oils.

Rainforests also play an important role in keeping gases in Earth's air in the right balance. The plants of the rainforest release large amounts of oxygen into the air. All plants and animals, including humans, need oxygen to live.

Rainforest plants remove the waste gas carbon dioxide from air. If too much carbon dioxide builds up in air, it can cause the climate to warm up. This can alter ecosystems and cause natural disasters such as droughts, strong hurricanes, and floods.

Plants of the rainforest help keep gases in Earth's air in balance. ▼

▲ Ecotourists can kayak on Mono Lake, California, without harming its ecosystem.

Rainforests are being cut down for many reasons. The wood from rainforest trees is used to build houses and furniture and to make paper and cardboard. In some places rainforest land is used for cattle grazing and to grow crops.

How can rainforests be conserved? Rainforest products such as nuts, fruits, vegetable oils, and medicines can provide more income than using the land for cattle or farms. Many of these products can be harvested without cutting down trees. There are also ways to obtain lumber without destroying rainforests. For example, some methods of logging are less harmful than others. Rather than cutting down an entire section of forest, loggers can select a few trees to cut down. Over time, the remaining forest will produce new trees.

Ecotourism involves travel to natural habitats that avoids harming and helps preserve these areas and the organisms that live there. Ecotourists pay to visit rainforests and see wildlife.

Ecotourism can provide a good source of income for people who live near the rainforest. This is a benefit that encourages more and more people to help preserve the rainforests of the world.

PROBLEM AND SOLUTION What is one way rainforests can be preserved?

Green Agriculture

You have learned some ways that farming can affect ecosystems. Forests, grasslands, and even desert areas can be used as farmland. Rivers, streams, and lakes are often used to provide water for crops and livestock. Recall that some farmers spray chemicals, such as weed killers and pesticides, on crop fields. These chemicals can pollute nearby land and water.

Farmers also use chemical fertilizers to help crops grow. The chemicals can run off into nearby lakes or streams. They can cause these bodies of water to become overrun with algae or plants. Too many plants can kill fish and other animals in the water.

There are ways of farming that do not harm ecosystems. These methods are called green agriculture. Green agriculture involves practices that help conserve water, improve soil, and do not harm surrounding ecosystems.

A common form of green agriculture is organic farming. Organic farming uses only materials that occur naturally in an ecosystem. Organic farmers do not use chemical pesticides, weed killers, or fertilizers.

Many people prefer to buy food produced by green agriculture, such as these organic vegetables. ▶

Organic farmers often use organisms in place of harmful materials. For example, chemical pesticides are often used to control aphids, an insect pest. But organic farmers might release ladybeetles in their fields. These insects eat aphids and do not pollute the environment. Organic farmers also use natural fertilizers, such as manure.

Crop rotation is another green agriculture practice. It involves growing a different kind of crop on the same field each year. If the same crop is grown on a field year after year, it uses up certain nutrients in the soil. Then, the farmer must add fertilizer to the soil.

When crops are rotated, only small amounts of different nutrients are taken from the soil. With crop rotation, farmers need to use much less fertilizer.

Farmers practicing green agriculture also grow cover crops. These are crops that are usually grown for one year and then plowed into the soil. Cover crops help enrich the soil, conserve moisture, and control erosion. They even provide habitats for wildlife.

PROBLEM AND SOLUTION How can farmers prevent nutrients in soil from being used up?

◀ Organic farms use many methods to avoid using chemical pesticides and fertilizers.

Zero Waste

The goal of zero waste is to recycle or reuse as much natural and manufactured material as possible so that very little or no waste is produced. This keeps waste materials from ending up in landfills and causing pollution.

Reaching the goal of zero waste can also help conserve ecosystems. For example, using cloth bags to carry groceries can greatly reduce the number of paper bags that are made. Fewer trees will need to be cut down to make the paper. Forest ecosystems can be conserved.

Recycling is an important practice in conserving resources. Materials that can be recycled include glass bottles, aluminum cans, magazines, newspapers, and some plastics. Recycling helps conserve resources such as minerals, metals, and oil products. Many of these are in short supply.

Products that can be made from recycled plastic include fabric for clothing, CD cases, playground equipment, and ballpoint pens. Products that can be made from recycled paper products include newspapers, packaging material, greeting cards, and even furniture.

▼ **Paper recycling center, San José, California**

▲ Many paper products, such as this wrapping paper, are made from recycled paper.

Visual Summary

A biodegradable material is one that will be broken down in the environment by microorganisms.

Green agriculture involves farming methods that do not harm ecosystems.

Waste materials do not break down in landfills because microorganisms cannot live there. Zero waste practices can help conserve ecosystems.

Reading Review

❶ MAIN IDEA How do biodegradable materials help conserve ecosystems?

❷ VOCABULARY What is ecotourism?

❸ READING SKILL What are two problems that recycling can help solve?

Problem	Solution

❹ CRITICAL THINKING: Apply How can people who are not farmers support green agriculture?

❺ INQUIRY SKILL: Hypothesize A wet pile of leaves rots more rapidly than a dry pile. Write a hypothesis to explain this.

✔ TEST PRACTICE

Which of the following are *not* biodegradable materials?

A. untreated wood

B. cardboard

C. paper

D. metals

Technology
Visit **www.eduplace.com/cascp** to learn more about beneficial microorganisms.

Environmental Conservation

To protect the natural beauty of the United States, people in the mid-1800s began the conservation movement. They wrote books and articles about their concerns. They feared that wilderness areas would be overrun with farms, train tracks, and other development.

Their hard work began to pay off. In 1872, Yellowstone National Park was created in Wyoming. In 1916, the National Park Service was created. This agency oversees more than 400 national parks, recreation areas, and historic monuments.

In 1973, the Endangered Species Act was signed. It created a list of plants and animals that have federal protection.

Yellowstone National Park The first national park in the world is created.

Sierra Club John Muir forms the Sierra Club to protect wilderness areas.

Everglades National Park Due mainly to Marjory Stoneman Douglas, Everglades National Park is created.

1872   **1892**   **1947**

John Muir

Marjory Stoneman Douglas

"Everybody needs beauty as well as bread, places to play in . . . , Where Nature may heal and cheer and give strength to body and soul alike."
—John Muir

First Earth Day Twenty million people take part in activities and demonstrations on behalf of the environment.

Bald Eagles Once endangered, bald eagles have increased in numbers. They may be removed from the endangered species list.

1970   2004

Sharing Ideas

1. **READING CHECK** What concerned the people who started the conservation movement?

2. **WRITE ABOUT IT** What is the Endangered Species Act, and how did it help the bald eagle?

3. **TALK ABOUT IT** Discuss what you think the world might be like today without the conservation movement.

MATH Analyze Data

A student performed an experiment in which she modeled two methods of waste disposal—composting and landfill. In the compost model, she placed newspapers in a bucket of wet soil that contained microorganisms. In the landfill model, she placed newspapers in a sealed plastic bag. She measured the mass of each model once a week for 8 weeks. Her data is in the chart.

Week	Mass of newspaper in soil (in grams)	Mass of newspaper in bag (in grams)
1	250	250
2	246	250
3	239	250
4	230	248
5	218	248
6	203	245
7	187	245
8	168	245

1. Use the data to create two line graphs to show how the mass of each model changed.

2. Which model had the least mass at the end of 8 weeks? How much less was its mass?

3. Suppose the student extended the experiment for another 8 weeks. Hypothesize how your line graphs would look. Estimate the mass of each model at the end of 8 weeks.

WRITING Informative

Write a report about conserving the environment. Choose a local ecosystem you would like to conserve. Identify issues that you think need to be addressed. Include facts and details to support your ideas. Explain why people should act on your suggestions. Present your report to your class.

Dana Bolles

At NASA's Ames Research Center, scientists study new technology for flight and space travel. The center has runways, fuel tanks, and a huge hangar for storing aircraft.

Dana Bolles makes sure that Ames is a good neighbor in its community. She works as an Environmental Protection Specialist. Her job is to prevent the center from polluting the air, land, and water.

"This job is challenging," says Bolles. "We are located in the San Francisco Bay area, where local regulations often are some of the most stringent in the country."

Bolles also faces the challenge of being a wheelchair rider. However, she does not let this stop her from reaching her goals. She inspires many people.

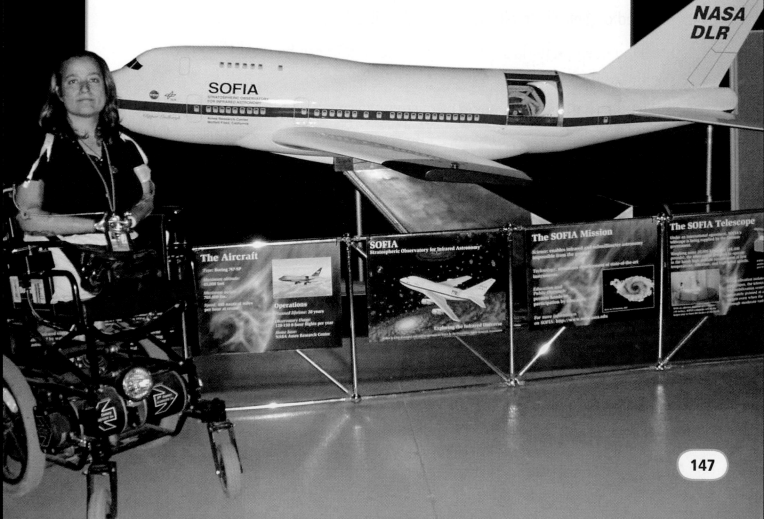

Vocabulary

Complete each sentence with a term from the list.

1. A material that causes pollution is called a/an _____.

2. An animal that feeds on the remains of dead animals is a/an _____.

3. Trash that is thrown on the ground or in water is _____.

4. The process by which the remains of dead organisms break down into simpler materials is called _____.

5. Travel to places where natural habitats have been successfully preserved without harming those places is called _____.

6. An organism that breaks down the remains of dead organisms into simpler materials is a/an _____.

7. A waste that can pollute the environment even when it is present in very small amounts is a/an _____.

8. Decayed organic material used to enrich soil is _____.

9. Breaking down materials into a different form that can be used again is known as _____.

10. A material that is broken down by microorganisms is a/an _____.

biodegradable material p. 136
compost p. 124
decay p. 122
decomposer p. 122
ecotourism p. 139
hazardous waste p. 132
litter p. 131
nutrient recycling p. 123
pollutant p. 131
pollution p. 131
scavenger p. 120

✔ Test Practice

Write the letter of the best answer choice.

11. Scavengers and decomposers get matter and energy from _____.

    A. dead organic material.   C. sunlight.
    B. living organic material.   D. bacteria.

12. Farming practices that help preserve ecosystems are called _____.

    A. zero waste.   C. ecotourism.
    B. green agriculture.   D. pollution.

13. One way to keep material out of landfills is to _____.

    A. recycle.
    B. litter.
    C. rotate crops.
    D. practice green agriculture.

14. Decomposers that are living things that are too small to see are _____.

    A. scavengers.   C. microorganisms.
    B. insects.   D. mushrooms.

15. Use Numbers Suppose the number of pairs of bald eagles in the lower 48 states was 791 in 1974; 1,757 in 1984; 4,449 in 1994; and 7,600 in 2004. Which ten-year-period showed the largest increase in the number of pairs of bald eagles?

16. Suppose a plastic bottle ends up in a landfill. Twenty years later, a scientist researching the landfill digs up the bottle. It is still whole. Could the bottle be made of biodegradable plastic? What evidence supports your answer?

Map the Concept

Use the terms below to fill in the concept map.

nutrient recycling	biodegradable
compost	material
hazardous waste	pollution
	litter

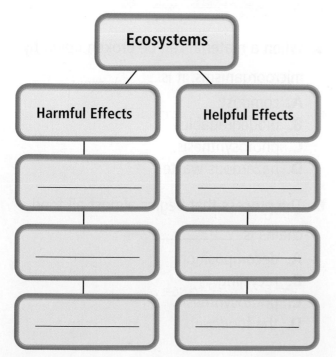

Critical Thinking

17. Analyze How are scavengers and decomposers alike and different?

18. Evaluate Many trees shed their leaves in the fall. In areas with very cold winters, the layer of leaves is still on the forest floor when spring arrives. Based on this observation, what effect do cold temperatures have on microorganisms?

19. Synthesize How might organic farmers use compost?

20. Apply What steps can you take to reduce the amount of garbage that you send to the local landfill?

Performance Assessment

Make a Plan for Garbage

Write a plan for what should happen to the garbage that is thrown away at your school. Think about garbage that is produced in your classroom and the school lunchroom. What items could be recycled? What could be composted? What would have to go to a landfill? Can the composted material be used to help create a school garden?

Writing Journal

Review the answers you wrote in your journal before you read the chapter. Change your answers, as needed, based on what you learned.

Write the letter of the best answer choice.

1. Which of the following is an animal that eats only other animals?
   A. carnivore
   B. producer
   C. herbivore
   D. omnivore

2. Which of the following is an animal that eats only plants?
   A. carnivore
   B. decomposer
   C. herbivore
   D. omnivore

3. The use of plastic bottles to make fabric is an example of _____.
   A. composting.
   B. recycling.
   C. littering.
   D. decay.

4. Which of the following is an example of litter?

   A.

   B.

   C.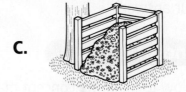

   D.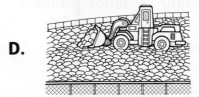

5. When a material can be broken down by microorganisms, it is _____.
   A. compost.
   B. biodegradable.
   C. photosynthesis.
   D. hazardous waste.

6. The process that begins almost all food chains is _____.
   A. decomposition.
   B. recycling.
   C. photosynthesis.
   D. the food web.

7. Which organism is most likely to be the basis of a food chain?

A.

B.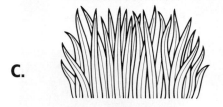

C.

D.

8. A food web is made up of many overlapping _____.
   A. food chains.
   B. microorganisms.
   C. bacteria.
   D. carnivores.

Answer the following in complete sentences.

9. Plankton are tiny organisms that live in the ocean. What might happen to ocean food chains and food webs if plankton became extinct?

10. Write a short paragraph describing an entire food chain. Include the terms *carnivore, photosynthesis, decomposer, compost,* and *herbivore.*

You Can...

Discover More

A coral reef is an ocean ecosystem that forms in clear shallow warm water. Under these ideal conditions, tiny coral animals play a role in building huge reefs that exist for many years.

A single coral animal is called a polyp. When some types of coral die, they leave behind their stony casings. These types of coral animals are natural recyclers. The nonliving material left behind by the dead coral animal becomes home for other coral animals. Through the years new layers build up on top of the old layers. Coral reefs may continue to grow for thousands of years. Only the most recent layers of a coral reef contain living polyps.

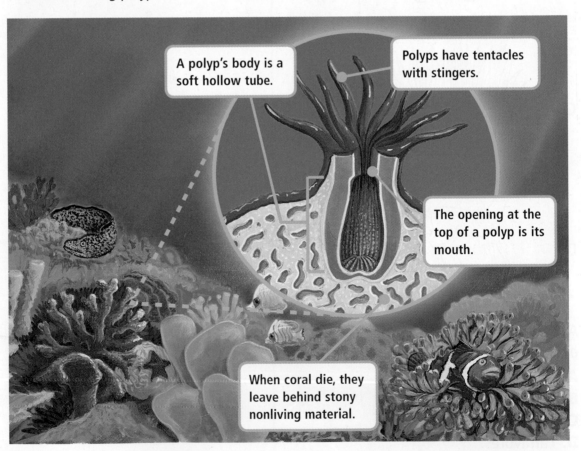

A polyp's body is a soft hollow tube.

Polyps have tentacles with stingers.

The opening at the top of a polyp is its mouth.

When coral die, they leave behind stony nonliving material.

 Simulations Go to **www.eduplace.com/cascp** to explore the colorful organisms that interact in a coral reef ecosystem.

The Solid Earth

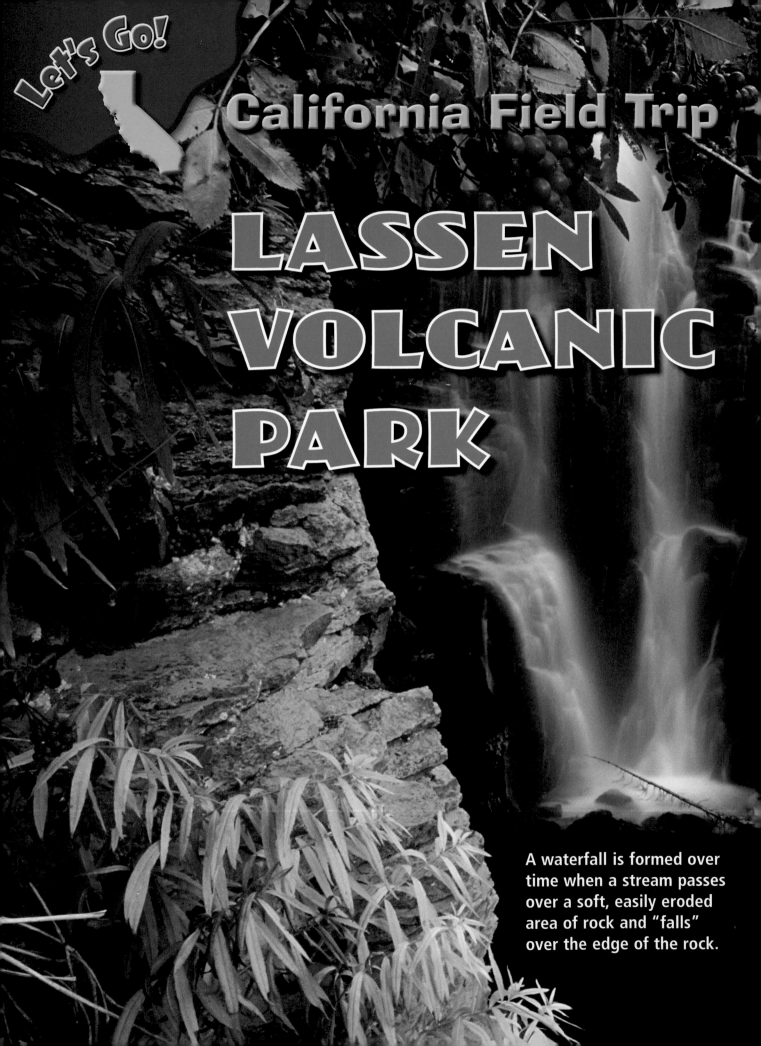

Let's Go!

California Field Trip

LASSEN VOLCANIC PARK

A waterfall is formed over time when a stream passes over a soft, easily eroded area of rock and "falls" over the edge of the rock.

The steam coming out of these vents can reach temperatures as high as 322°F (161°C).

Mount Lassen last erupted during a three-year period, from 1914 to 1917.

The Solid Earth

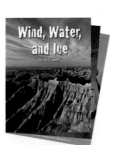
Stalactites forming in caves

The properties of rocks and minerals reflect the processes that formed them. Waves, wind, water, and ice shape and reshape Earth's land surface.

Chapter 5

Rocks and Minerals

Tufa formations, Mono Lake, California

LESSON 1

Look around you. Many things you see are made from minerals. Each type of mineral has its own set of properties. What are the properties of minerals that you use?

LESSON 2

One property of the mineral talc is that it is easily scratched. Besides hardness, what other properties can you use to identify a mineral?

LESSON 3

Igneous rock, sedimentary rock, and metamorphic rock each have different properties. What are some of the properties of each of these types of rock?

LESSON 4

Igneous rock, sedimentary rock, and metamorphic rock are formed in different ways in the rock cycle. How does each type of rock form?

Writing Journal

In your Writing Journal, show what you know by writing or drawing answers to each question.

Vocabulary Preview

Vocabulary

Glossary

Vocabulary Skill

Word Origins

metamorphic rock

The word *metamorphic* comes from two Greek words. The word part *meta* means "to change," and *morphe* means "form." Metamorphic rock is formed when existing rocks are changed by heat, pressure, or chemicals.

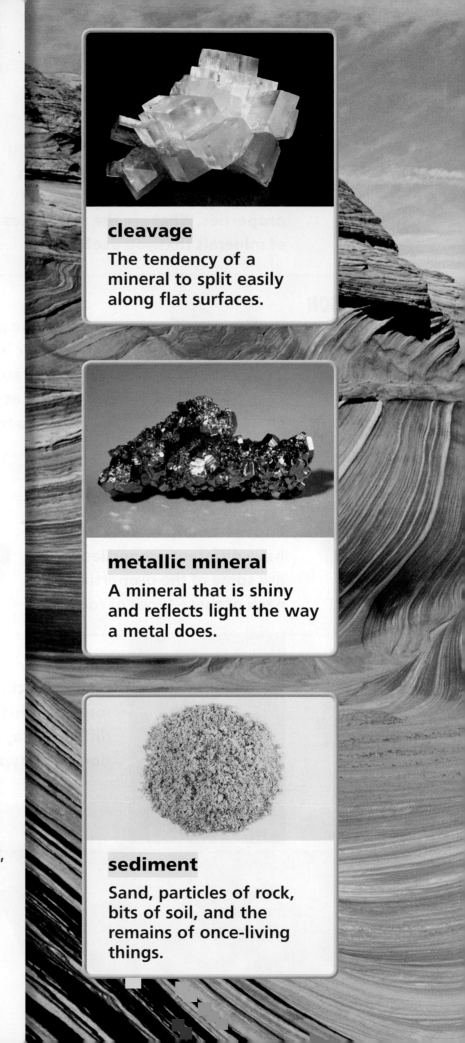

cleavage
The tendency of a mineral to split easily along flat surfaces.

metallic mineral
A mineral that is shiny and reflects light the way a metal does.

sediment
Sand, particles of rock, bits of soil, and the remains of once-living things.

Start with Your Standards

Standard Set 4. Earth Sciences (Rocks and Minerals)

4.a.   *Students know* how to differentiate among igneous, sedimentary, and metamorphic rocks by referring to their properties and methods of formation (the rock cycle).

4.b.   *Students know* how to identify common rock-forming minerals (including quartz, calcite, feldspar, mica, and hornblende) and ore minerals by using a table of diagnostic properties.

Standard Set 6. Investigation and Experimentation covered in this chapter: 6.a., 6.c., 6.f.

sedimentary rock

A type of rock that forms when sediment becomes pressed together and hardens.

What Are the Properties of Minerals?

Building Background

Most rocks are made up of two or more kinds of minerals. This unusual looking rock contains the minerals quartz, mica, and amethyst. Each mineral has its own set of properties. These properties include whether the mineral looks shiny or dull and how hard it is compared to other minerals.

PREPARE TO INVESTIGATE

Inquiry Skill

Observe It is important to know the difference between what you observe using your senses and tools and what you think about those observations.

Materials

- cardboard egg carton
- 10 numbered mineral samples
- white unglazed ceramic tile
- marker
- goggles

Science and Math Toolbox

For step 1, review **Making a Chart to Organize Data** on page H10.

Properties of Minerals

Procedure

STEP 1

Mineral Sample	Luster	Color	Streak	
			Prediction	Result
1				
2				
3				
4				
5				

① In your *Science Notebook*, make a chart like the one shown. Your chart should have 10 numbered rows.

② **Collaborate** Work with your group. Number the pockets of the egg carton from *1* to *10*. Put a mineral labeled with the same number into each pocket. A **mineral** (MIHN ur uhl) is a solid material that has a definite chemical makeup.

③ **Observe** Look at each mineral. Decide if it shines like a metal, like glass, or is dull. **Luster** is the way a mineral shines. In the *Luster* column of your chart, write *metallic*, *glassy*, or *dull* depending on the luster of the mineral.

④ Record the color of each mineral.

⑤ **Predict** Scratch the tile with three of the minerals. The powder left on the tile is the mineral's **streak**. Predict the streak color for the rest of the minerals. Record the results. **Safety:** Wear goggles.

STEP 3

STEP 5

Conclusion

1. **Compare** For each mineral, was the color of the mineral and the color of its streak the same?

2. **Classify** Sort the minerals into two groups—metallic or nonmetallic—based on the property of luster. Glassy or dull minerals have nonmetallic luster.

Guided Inquiry

Experiment Which minerals can be scratched with a fingernail? **Predict** and then test your ideas. Rub the mineral where you scratched it. A scratch will not rub off. Record your results.

Properties of

Properties of Minerals

MAIN IDEA Minerals can be described according to a set of properties including luster, color, streak, hardness, and cleavage.

READING SKILL

Main Idea and Details
Use the diagram to give the main idea and four details about mineral properties.

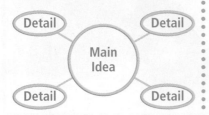

Luster

A **mineral** (MIHN ur uhl) is a nonliving solid material that has a definite chemical makeup. It is found in Earth's outermost layer. Minerals have many uses. It's likely that many types of minerals were used to build your school. Window glass is made from the minerals talc, quartz, limestone, and feldspar. Copper is used in some plumbing pipes. Steel girders made from iron may support the building. The properties of minerals make them useful in a variety of ways.

One property of a mineral is luster. **Luster** is the way a mineral shines, or reflects light. Some minerals, such as pyrite, are shiny like the metals gold and silver. Some minerals, such as gypsum, have a dull luster. The mineral fluorite has a glassy luster.

fluorite

silver

▲ The luster of a mineral is a clue to its identity. The mineral can be shiny like silver or have a glassy luster like fluorite.

Color and Streak

The color of a mineral depends on its chemical makeup. Some minerals can be easily identified by their color. For example, azurite is deep blue. Malachite is green.

While color is easy to observe, it is not the best way to identify a mineral. Impurities in a mineral can affect its color. For example, the mineral beryl is blue when it contains bits of iron. It is pink when it contains bits of manganese, and green when it contains bits of chromium.

The color of a mineral when it is ground to a powder is called its **streak**. Scratching a mineral against a ceramic tile, which grinds it to a powder, is a test of its streak.

For many minerals, the streak is the same color as the mineral. Sometimes the color of the streak is different than the color of the mineral. Therefore, streak can be a good way to identify minerals like these.

MAIN IDEA What property of a mineral is streak?

▲ The streak of the mineral hematite is different than the color of the mineral.

pink beryl

blue beryl

green beryl

azurite

▲ Pure azurite is a deep blue color.

▲ The color of the mineral beryl can vary with impurities in the sample.

Mohs Hardness Scale

Photo	Mineral	Hardness
	talc	1
	gypsum	2
	fingernail	2.5
	calcite	3
	copper penny	3.2
	fluorite	4
	apatite	5
	glass	5.5
	feldspar	6
	steel file	6.5
	quartz	7
	topaz	8
	corundum	9
	diamond	10

Hardness

The **hardness** of a mineral is a measure of how easily that mineral can be scratched. You can test for the property of hardness by using different objects, such as a fingernail, copper penny, steel nail, or piece of glass, to scratch the mineral.

Another way to test hardness is to compare a mineral to the minerals listed in the Mohs scale of hardness. Ten minerals are listed in the scale. They are ordered from softest to hardest. Talc, which is number 1, is the softest. Diamond is number 10 and is the hardest mineral.

Suppose the mineral you are testing can scratch quartz but cannot scratch topaz. Look at the Mohs scale. The hardness of the mineral being tested is between 7 and 8.

Like all matter, minerals are made of tiny particles. The way in which a mineral's particles are arranged determines the hardness of the mineral. Graphite and diamond are both made only of carbon. The arrangement of carbon particles in graphite makes it one of the softest minerals. Diamond, the hardest mineral, has a different arrangement of the carbon particles.

◄ The Mohs scale lists the hardness of ten common minerals. Which mineral's hardness is greater than feldspar but less than topaz?

Mica

Calcite

Ruby

Mica cleaves, or splits, along one plane. Calcite has three cleavage planes. Ruby does not split along cleavage planes.

Cleavage

Another mineral property is cleavage. **Cleavage** is the tendency of a mineral to split easily along flat surfaces. These flat surfaces are called cleavage planes.

Mica has cleavage planes that are all in the same direction. Mica splits into thin sheets. The mineral halite is commonly referred to as rock salt. Halite and calcite split along three cleavage planes. When these minerals split, they form cube-shaped pieces. Other minerals split differently to form other geometric solid figures.

Some gemstones, such as rubies and diamonds, do not split naturally along cleavage planes.

Instead, gem cutters grind these minerals to produce shiny, sparkling surfaces that reflect light. The smooth surfaces are called facets.

The number of facets and the way they are ground give gemstones different looks. A stone may have a few facets or many. One popular gem cut has 57 facets.

MAIN IDEA What are some of the properties of minerals?

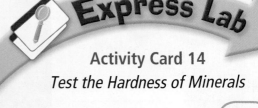

Express Lab

Activity Card 14
Test the Hardness of Minerals

titanium

bauxite

quartz

zincite

talc

Using Mineral Properties

You've learned some ways minerals are used in your school building. Read about some of the ways minerals are useful to this baseball player.

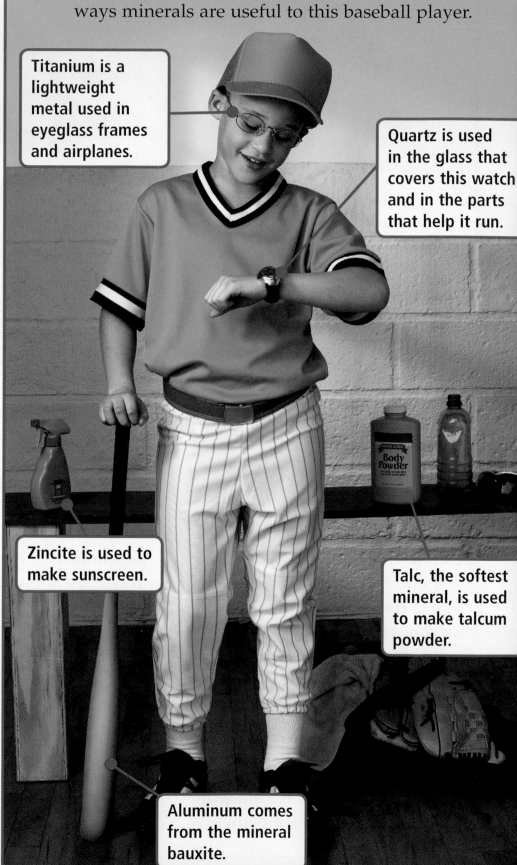

Titanium is a lightweight metal used in eyeglass frames and airplanes.

Quartz is used in the glass that covers this watch and in the parts that help it run.

Zincite is used to make sunscreen.

Talc, the softest mineral, is used to make talcum powder.

Aluminum comes from the mineral bauxite.

Visual Summary

silver

fluorite

One property of a mineral is luster, or the way a mineral reflects light. Some minerals are shiny like metal. Others have a dull or glassy luster.

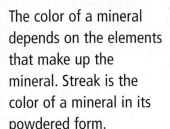

hematite

The color of a mineral depends on the elements that make up the mineral. Streak is the color of a mineral in its powdered form.

talc

A mineral's hardness is a measure of how easily that mineral can be scratched. Talc is the softest mineral.

Reading Review

1 MAIN IDEA What is a mineral?

2 VOCABULARY Use the terms *luster* and *mineral* in a sentence.

3 READING SKILL What are four properties that can be used to describe a mineral?

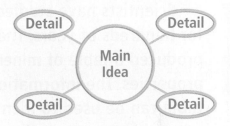

4 CRITICAL THINKING: Apply Using the Mohs hardness scale, what would you conclude about the hardness of a mineral that could scratch calcite but not apatite?

5 INQUIRY SKILL: Observe Look around your classroom. Identify one mineral and explain how it is being used.

✓ **TEST PRACTICE**

The color of a mineral in its powdered form is the _____ of that mineral.

A. hardness

B. cleavage

C. streak

D. luster

Technology
Visit **www.eduplace.com/cascp** to find out more about minerals.

How Are Minerals Identified?

Building Background

Scientists have studied minerals for hundreds of years. They have produced a table of mineral properties. The information in the table can be used to identify any mineral by its properties. You can identify a mineral by performing tests and then comparing the results to the information in the table of mineral properties.

PREPARE TO INVESTIGATE

Inquiry Skill

Classify When you classify, you sort objects, organisms, or events according to their properties.

Materials

- Properties of Minerals table, page 170
- chart from Directed Inquiry, page 159
- egg carton and minerals from Directed Inquiry, page 159
- glass plate
- steel nail
- copper penny
- goggles

Mineral Properties

Procedure

1. **Classify** Use the chart you made for the activity on page 159 to help you classify the minerals into two groups: metallic minerals (shiny like metal) and nonmetallic minerals (dull or glassy). Record your results.

2. **Compare** Make a chart like the one shown. Use a fingernail to test each mineral for hardness. Record *N* in your chart for minerals that can be scratched with a fingernail.

3. Repeat step 2 using a copper penny. Record *C* in your chart for minerals that can be scratched with copper. Repeat using a steel nail. Record *S* for minerals that can be scratched with the steel nail.

4. Finally, see if you can scratch a glass plate with the remaining minerals. Record *G* for minerals that can scratch glass. **Safety:** Wear goggles.

5. Compare the properties you recorded in your charts to those listed in the Properties of Minerals table on page 170. Record the name of each mineral.

Conclusion

1. **Infer** How did the properties you observed help you identify the minerals?

2. **Hypothesize** Why might you be unable to identify some of the minerals you observed?

STEP 2

Mineral Sample	Hardness	Name
1		
2		
3		

STEP 3

STEP 4

Guided Inquiry

Ask Questions What questions do you have about identifying minerals? **Observe** the minerals again and then make a list of questions. Can you use these questions to design other tests to identify minerals? Explain.

VOCABULARY

metallic mineral   p. 169
nonmetallic
    mineral   p. 168

READING SKILL

Classify

Use the chart to help you classify minerals as metallic or nonmetallic.

Group	Group

Identifying Minerals

MAIN IDEA The properties of a mineral can be determined by observing and by carrying out a series of tests. Then, by comparing its properties with those listed in a table of mineral properties, the mineral can be identified.

Nonmetallic Minerals

Look at the Properties of Minerals table on page 170. Notice that it is divided into nonmetallic and metallic minerals. A **nonmetallic mineral** is dull or glassy. You can use the table to identify an unknown mineral by using these tests.

Luster How does the mineral shine? If the sample is dull or glassy, it is listed under *Luster* as *nonmetallic*. You can rule out all metallic minerals listed.

Hardness What scratches the mineral? If it can be scratched by a fingernail, there is an *F* in the *Hardness* column.

Color What color is the mineral? In the *Color* column, find a mineral that has that color.

Cleavage Does the mineral split along a flat surface? If it does, the *Cleavage* column will indicate *yes*.

Other Properties Sometimes a mineral has unusual properties. For example, which mineral in the table peels in thin sheets?

Express Lab

Activity Card 15
Tell If a Mineral Is Metallic

Metallic Minerals

A **metallic mineral** is shiny like a metal. You can use luster to find out whether your mineral is metallic or nonmetallic. Then you can test for hardness. Suppose the mineral you want to identify is a metallic mineral that can scratch glass. What other properties should you look for in metallic minerals?

Color Compare the color of the mineral with the colors listed in the table. What is the color of the metallic mineral you are trying to identify? Is there a mineral in the table that lists that color?

Streak What color is the mineral's streak? Suppose you were able to scratch the mineral on a ceramic tile. Find a mineral on the table that has the same color streak as your mineral.

Other Properties Does the mineral have special properties? Suppose you test the mineral for magnetism and find that it attracts iron objects. Which mineral in the table is magnetic?

CLASSIFY What test is used to classify a mineral as metallic or nonmetallic?

Luster

Hardness

Cleavage

Streak

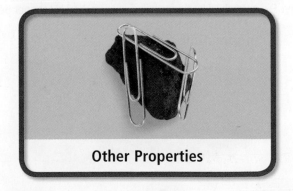

Other Properties

Properties of Minerals

Luster	Hardness	Color	Cleavage	Other	Name
Nonmetallic	C	colorless, white	yes; parallelograms	bubbles when acid is placed on it	Calcite
Nonmetallic	G	colorless, beige, pink	yes	hardness very close to glass	Feldspar
Nonmetallic	F	colorless, white	yes	tastes salty	Halite
Nonmetallic	G	dark green to black	yes; diamond shape	splits easily	Hornblende
Nonmetallic	F	dark brown, black, or silver-white	yes	flakes when peeled	Mica
Nonmetallic	G	colorless, white, rose, smoky, purple, brown	no	looks glassy, chips like glass	Quartz
Nonmetallic	F	white, greenish to gray	yes	usually flaky	Talc

Luster	Hardness	Color	Streak	Other	Name
Metallic	C	gray	gray to black	heavy for its size	Galena
Metallic	F	yellow	golden yellow	used for jewelry	Gold
Metallic	G	steel gray	reddish	may have reddish patches	Hematite
Metallic	G	black	black	magnetic	Magnetite
Metallic	G	brassy yellow	greenish black	looks like gold	Pyrite

Key: F = scratched by fingernail, C = scratched by copper penny; S – scratched by steel nail; G = scratches glass

nonmetalic

metalic

Visual Summary

Scientists have developed ways to identify the minerals by completing a series of tests to determine a mineral's properties. One of these properties is color.

Luster is one property of a mineral. A nonmetallic mineral has a dull or glassy luster.

A metallic mineral has a shiny luster. It reflects light the way a metal does.

Reading Review

1 MAIN IDEA How can you use a table of mineral properties to identify a mineral?

2 VOCABULARY What is the difference between a metallic and a nonmetallic mineral?

3 READING SKILL What does the property of luster allow you to do?

Group	Group

4 CRITICAL THINKING: Draw Conclusions Use the table on page 170 to identify the nonmetallic mineral that has a hardness greater than glass; can be colorless, white, rose, smoky, purple, brown; looks glassy; and chips like glass.

5 INQUIRY SKILL: Classify Into what two groups are minerals classified in the Properties of Minerals table?

✔ **TEST PRACTICE**
What property do you use to determine if a mineral is nonmetallic or metallic?

A. luster   **C.** hardness

B. cleavage   **D.** color

Technology
Visit **www.eduplace.com/cascp** to find out more about identifying minerals.

MINERAL LIGHT SHOW

Intense! Are those vivid colors of mineral samples real? They are, but they can be seen only under special conditions. First you need the right kind of mineral. Then you need to be in a dark place. Finally, you need to have a special kind of light, called ultraviolet. Ultraviolet light, also known as black light, or UV, makes certain minerals glow, or fluoresce (flu REHS), in brilliant colors.

Only some minerals fluoresce under ultraviolet light. For this reason, the property of fluorescence can sometimes help identify a mineral. For example, fluoride and calcite sometimes fluoresce due to impurities they contain. The mineral sheelite is always fluorescent.

Wow! Lettuce, honey, and even peanut butter sandwiches glow under UV light!

These plain-looking rocks contain fluorescent minerals. Ultraviolet light causes them to give off brilliant colors that can help identify their minerals.

Writing Journal

In your writing journal, create an advertisement for a new product that uses fluorescent minerals. Tell how the product can be used.

173

How Do Rocks Differ?

Building Background

Rocks vary in appearance depending on the minerals that they contain. The properties of rocks also depend on how the rocks formed. Like minerals, it is possible to identify different kinds of rocks by their properties. Some kinds of rock have properties that make them useful as building materials. This famous statue of Abraham Lincoln is carved from marble.

PREPARE TO INVESTIGATE

Inquiry Skill

Infer When you infer, you interpret your observations.

Materials

- rock specimen set
- marker
- paper labels
- hand lens

Science and Math Toolbox

For step 3, review **Using a Hand Lens** on page H2.

Looking at Rocks

Procedure

STEP 1

	Colors	Texture	Grain
A			
B			
C			
D			
E			
F			

1. In your *Science Notebook*, make a chart like the one shown.

2. **Collaborate** Work with a partner. Choose six rocks from the rock specimen kit. Using paper labels and a marker, label each rock *A, B, C, D, E,* or *F.*

3. **Observe** Closely observe each rock for different colored pieces or layers. Record your observations of color in your chart. Run your fingers over each rock to feel its texture. Record the texture as *rough* or *smooth* in your chart.

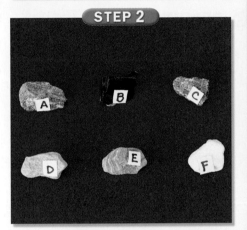

STEP 2

4. **Experiment** Use a hand lens to observe the grain in each sample. Rub each rock with your fingers to see if any bits of rock break off. Record each rock's grain size in the chart as *no grain*, *large grain*, or *small grain*.

5. **Classify** Work with another team. Combine your rock collections and group similar rocks. Record the properties you used to classify each group.

STEP 4

Conclusion

1. **Classify** Discuss with your classmates other ways you may classify the rocks.

2. **Infer** Based on what you have observed, how do you think these rocks formed? For example, which might have formed by melting? by pressure?

Guided Inquiry

Experiment Suppose you wanted to further **classify** your rocks by other properties. Make a plan to test for two properties. Then, with your teacher's permission, carry out your plan on each rock specimen. Record your results.

Identifying Rocks

VOCABULARY

igneous rock	p. 178
metamorphic rock	p. 180
rock	p. 176
sediment	p. 179
sedimentary rock	p. 179

MAIN IDEA Three basic kinds of rock—igneous, sedimentary, and metamorphic—make up Earth's crust. Each kind of rock forms in a different way and has different characteristics.

Earth's Layers

If you could take a section out of Earth, you would see that Earth is made up of layers. The outer layer is the crust. The ocean floor and the large areas of land called continents (KAHN tuh nuhnts) are part of the crust. The continents are North America, South America, Europe, Asia, Africa, Australia, and Antarctica.

The crust is the thinnest layer of Earth and is made up of rock. **Rock** is a solid material made up of one or more minerals.

READING SKILL

Compare and Contrast
Use the chart to compare and contrast the properties of the three types of rock.

Group	Group	Group

Earth is made up of different layers. ▶

Express Lab

Activity Card 16
Model the Earth

The next layer of Earth is the mantle (MAN tuhl). The mantle is a thick layer of rock between the crust and the core. The lower part of the mantle is solid. In the upper part of the mantle, the rock is soft enough to move like modeling clay.

The innermost layer of Earth is the core (kawr). The core is a dense ball with a liquid outer part and a solid inner part. The solid inner part is the hottest part of Earth.

COMPARE **Identify one way in which each of Earth's layers differ.**

Earth's Layers

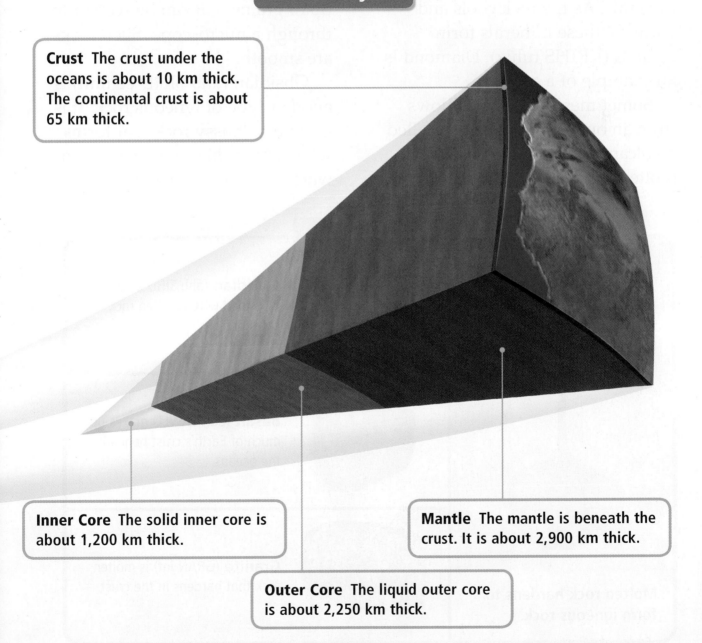

Crust The crust under the oceans is about 10 km thick. The continental crust is about 65 km thick.

Inner Core The solid inner core is about 1,200 km thick.

Mantle The mantle is beneath the crust. It is about 2,900 km thick.

Outer Core The liquid outer core is about 2,250 km thick.

Igneous Rock

Three basic kinds of rock make up Earth's crust. Each kind forms in a different way and has different characteristics.

Igneous (IHG nee uhs) **rock** is rock that forms when melted, or molten, rock from deep below Earth's surface cools and hardens. The molten rock contains different minerals. As the rock cools and hardens, these minerals form crystals (KRIHS tuhlz). Diamond is an example of a crystal.

Sometimes molten rock flows from an opening in the crust called a volcano (vahl KAY noh). This molten rock cools quickly. The crystals that form are very small, or there may be none. Large crystals form when molten rock cools more slowly below Earth's surface.

Igneous rocks can be classified by grain size. Some igneous rocks, such as granite (GRAN iht), have a visible grain. Others, such as basalt (buh SAWLT), are made up of grains that can be seen only through a microscope. Such rocks are smooth.

Obsidian (ahb SIHD ee uhn) is another type of igneous rock. It is a smooth, glassy rock that forms when lava comes in contact with water and cools quickly.

Igneous Rock

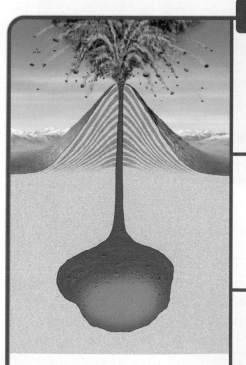

Molten rock hardens to form igneous rock.

Obsidian (ahb SIHD ee uhn) is formed when molten rock cools quickly.

Basalt (buh SAWLT) makes up much of Earth's crust beneath the oceans.

Granite (GRAN iht) is molten rock that hardens in the crust.

Conglomerate (kuhn GLAHM-ur iht) is formed from sediments of different sizes.

Limestone sometimes forms when the remains of ocean animals become cemented together.

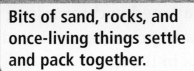

Bits of sand, rocks, and once-living things settle and pack together.

Shale is formed from thin layers of clay. Shale is smooth and breaks easily into layers.

Sedimentary Rock

Sedimentary (sehd uh MEHN tuh ree) **rock** is rock that forms when sand, particles of rock, bits of soil, and remains of once-living things are pressed together and harden. These materials are called **sediment** (SEHD uh muhnt). Rock is broken into sediment by natural forces in a process called weathering. Sediment is carried by wind, moving water, and moving ice. Over time, layers of sediment are deposited on top of another.

As the layers build up, their weight produces more and more pressure on the bottom layers. Over millions of years, the bottom layers become rock. Dissolved minerals fill in any cracks and cement, or glue, all of the particles together. Sedimentary rock usually forms in low places.

Limestone is one type of sedimentary rock. Some limestone forms when the remains of ocean animals become cemented together. Limestone formed in this way may contain fossil shells. Limestone is used in making concrete, glass, and building stones.

Shale is another type of sedimentary rock. It is a fine-grained rock formed from tiny clay particles. The particles become compacted by pressure. Shale is is the most common sedimentary rock. Finely ground shale is used as a filler in some plastics, paint, and roadbed material.

COMPARE Contrast the conditions under which large crystals and small crystals form in igneous rock.

Metamorphic Rock

Metamorphic (meht uh MAWR fihk) **rock** is new rock that forms when existing rocks are changed by heat, pressure, or chemicals beneath Earth's surface. Both igneous rock and sedimentary rock can be changed into metamorphic rock. Existing metamorphic rocks can also be changed into new metamorphic rock.

How do sedimentary and igneous rocks change into metamorphic rock? Beneath Earth's surface, these rocks are under great pressure. The pressure causes heat to build up, which causes the rocks to change.

If you look closely at samples of metamorphic rock, you'll notice that some of the grains in the rock are flattened. This is due to the great pressure that formed the rock.

Gneiss (nys) is one type of metamorphic rock. Gneiss can form when granite, an igneous rock, is changed by great heat and pressure.

Compare the grains of granite and gneiss in the photos. You can see the grains in granite are rounded. The grains in the gneiss sample are flattened and form long bands. Heat and pressure produced these patterns in the gneiss.

Slate is another type of metamorphic rock. Shale is a soft sedimentary rock. When shale is buried, and heat and pressure build up, slate is formed.

One metamorphic rock, schist, can be formed from another metamorphic rock, slate. Schist can also be formed from the igneous rock basalt.

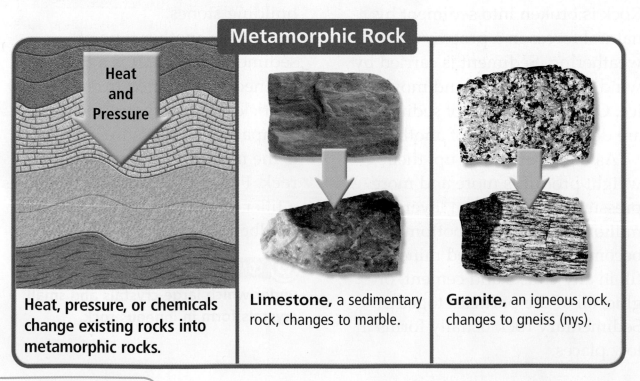

Metamorphic Rock

Heat, pressure, or chemicals change existing rocks into metamorphic rocks.

Limestone, a sedimentary rock, changes to marble.

Granite, an igneous rock, changes to gneiss (nys).

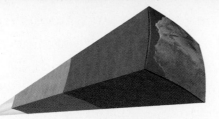

Lesson Wrap-Up

Visual Summary

Three basic kinds of rock—igneous, sedimentary, and metamorphic—make up Earth's crust. Each kind of rock forms in a different way and has different characteristics.

granite   **basalt**   **obsidian**

Igneous rock is rock that forms when melted, or molten, rock from Earth's mantle cools and hardens.

shale   **limestone**   **conglomerate**

Sedimentary rock is rock that forms when sand, particles of rock, bits of soil, and remains of once-living things harden.

marble   **gneiss**

Metamorphic rock is new rock that forms when existing rocks are changed by heat, pressure, or chemicals beneath Earth's surface.

 Technology
Visit **www.eduplace.com/cascp** to find out more about identifying rocks.

Reading Review

1 MAIN IDEA What are the three basic types of rock that make up Earth's crust?

2 VOCABULARY Use the terms *sediment* and *sedimentary rock* in a sentence.

3 READING SKILL: Compare the ways in which sedimentary rock and metamorphic rock form.

Group	Group

4 CRITICAL THINKING:
Hypothesize What would happen if heat and pressure were added to sediments?

5 INQUIRY SKILL: Infer Suppose you find a rock that contains fossil shells. Which of the three types of rocks is it likely to be? Explain your answer.

 TEST PRACTICE
Which of the following is a type of glassy igneous rock with sharp edges that forms when lava cools quickly above Earth's surface?

A. granite   **C.** gypsum

B. scheelite   **D.** obsidian

HEAT From EARTH

Geothermal energy is heat from within Earth. It can be used to warm buildings and generate electricity. The term *geothermal* is from two Greek roots. *Geo* means "earth" and *therm* means "heat." Thus, *geothermal* means "earth-heat."

You know that igneous rock is rock that forms when molten rock from Earth's mantle cools and hardens. If you could travel about 3,048 m (10,000 ft) below ground, you would find the temperature of the rock is hot enough to boil water. Scientists and engineers have found a way to use superheated water and steam from deep within Earth to generate electricity.

The first geothermal power plants in the United States were built in northern California at the Geysers dry steam field. The Geysers is still the largest geothermal field in the world.

Geothermal energy is a clean power source. It can be renewed as long as water can be pumped back into the ground. One drawback is that it is available only where large amounts of underground water are in contact with heated rock.

Dry Steam Power Plant

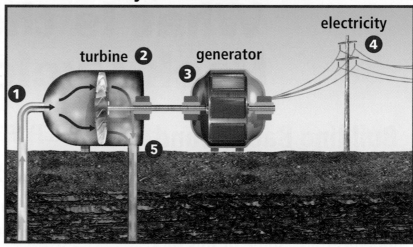

1. Steam is pumped from deep within Earth.
2. The steam turns a turbine.
3. The turbine powers a generator.
4. The generator produces electricity.
5. The condensed steam (water) is pumped back into the ground to be reheated.

Sharing Ideas

1. **READING CHECK** What is geothermal energy?

2. **WRITE ABOUT IT** What must be done to keep geothermal energy from being used up?

3. **TALK ABOUT IT** Discuss with your classmates how increased use of geothermal energy could have a positive effect on the environment.

What Is the Rock Cycle?

Building Background

Earth's rock is always changing. For example, melted rock from an erupting volcano cools to form igneous rock. Some of this rock will break down into sediment. Some of the sediment will become sedimentary rock. Heat and pressure turn this rock into metamorphic rock. The continuous changes that rocks undergo is called the rock cycle.

PREPARE TO INVESTIGATE

Inquiry Skill

Collaborate When you collaborate, you work with others to carry out investigations and share data and ideas.

Materials

- Rock Cycle diagram (Activity Support Master)
- rock specimen set from Directed Inquiry, p. 175
- sand
- hand lens

Rock Cycle Model

Procedure

1. **Observe** Carefully examine each rock in your rock set. Use a hand lens to make close observations. In your *Science Notebook*, record a list of the properties for each rock.

2. **Collaborate** Share your list with your group. Add properties to your list that other students identify.

3. **Classify** Use what you know about each rock type to classify each of the rocks in your set. Make groups of sedimentary, igneous, and metamorphic rocks. Label each group.

4. **Use Models** Study the Rock Cycle diagram. The rock cycle is the continuous series of changes that rocks undergo. Then use rocks from your rock set and sand to make a model of the rock cycle. Place the rocks and sand on the rock cycle diagram in the correct places.

5. **Record Data** Your teacher will provide you with a key to the rocks in your set. Use the key to label your rock cycle diagram with the names of the rock samples you used.

Conclusion

1. **Communicate** How does your model represent the rock cycle?

2. **Classify** Classify basalt, shale, and slate by how they are formed.

STEP 1

STEP 3

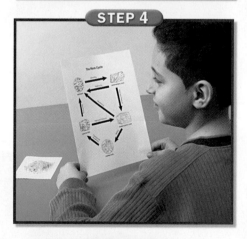
STEP 4

Guided Inquiry

Experiment Collect rock specimens near your school and home. Carry out steps 1 and 2 using these rocks. Have another student **classify** each rock.

How Rocks Form

VOCABULARY

rock cycle   p. 186

READING SKILL

Sequence
Use the diagram to show how metamorphic rock changes to igneous rock and igneous rock changes to sedimentary rock.

Step 1

↓

Step 2

↓

Step 3

MAIN IDEA Any type of rock—metamorphic, igneous, or sedimentary—can change into any other type of rock. The continuous series of changes that rocks undergo is called the rock cycle.

Heat and Pressure

Any type of rock can change into any other type of rock. For example, metamorphic rock can become sedimentary rock. Scientists call the continuous series of changes that rocks undergo the **rock cycle**. The rock cycle shows the processes that change rock.

When heat and pressure are great enough, metamorphic rocks become molten, or melted. When this melted rock cools and hardens, it forms igneous rock. When igneous rock, in turn, is subject to heat and pressure, igneous rock becomes metamorphic rock. Find these changes in the rock cycle diagram on page 187.

The metamorphic rock marble is used in building. It is removed from the ground in places called quarries. ▼

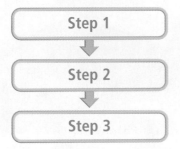

limestone

marble

▲ Great heat and pressure change limestone into marble.

Sedimentary rock forms near Earth's surface. Over time, sedimentary rock may become buried deep beneath Earth's surface. There, great heat and pressure act on the rock. With enough heat and pressure, the sedimentary rock changes into metamorphic rock. Find this change in the diagram.

SEQUENCE Describe the changes that metamorphic rocks undergo to become igneous rocks.

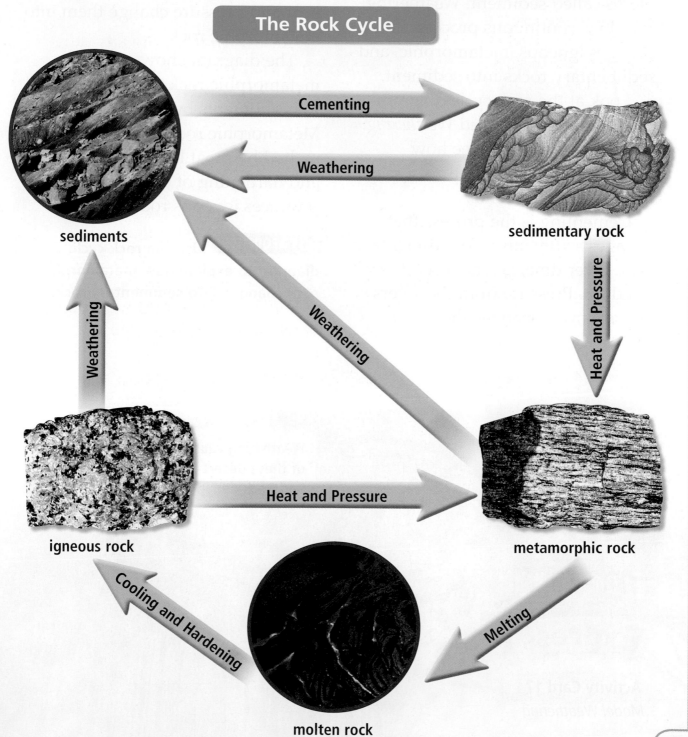

The Rock Cycle

Cementing

Weathering

sediments

sedimentary rock

Heat and Pressure

Weathering

Weathering

Heat and Pressure

igneous rock

metamorphic rock

Cooling and Hardening

Melting

molten rock

Weathering and Cementing

One way rocks can change is through the process of weathering. Weathering is the breaking down of rocks. Weathering occurs when wind, moving water, chemicals, and ice break rocks into smaller pieces called sediment. Weathering is a slow, continuous process. It changes igneous, metamorphic, and sedimentary rocks into sediment.

Look at the rock cycle diagram. Find the arrows labeled *Weathering*. Follow the arrows to see how weathering changes all three types of rock into sediments.

Cementing is the process that changes sediments into sedimentary rock. Over time, layers of sediment build up. Pressure from the layers above slowly changes the lower layers of sediments into rock. Dissolved minerals fill in any cracks in the rock, cementing, or gluing, the particles of sediment together.

Look for the arrows labeled *Heat and Pressure* that point from the sedimentary rock and the igneous rock. Follow the arrows to see how heat and pressure change them into metamorphic rock.

The diagram shows that metamorphic rock may be broken into sediments by weathering. Metamorphic rock can also be melted by great heat. Cooling and hardening of this melted rock produces igneous rock.

SEQUENCE Use the rock cycle diagram to explain how metamorphic rock changes into sedimentary rock.

Weathering caused the features of these desert cliffs in California's Red Rock Canyon State Park.

Express Lab

Activity Card 17
Model Weathering

Lesson Wrap-Up

Visual Summary

When heat and pressure are great enough, they can change igneous, sedimentary, and metamorphic rock into new metamorphic rock.

Dissolved minerals fills in cracks in the rock, cementing the sediments together. Weathering breaks sedimentary rock, as well as metamorphic and igneous rock, into sediments.

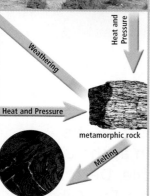

The rock cycle is the name scientists give to the continuous series of changes that rocks undergo.

Technology
Visit **www.eduplace.com/cascp** to find out more about the rock cycle.

Reading Review

1 MAIN IDEA Give two examples to support the statement: Any type of rock—metamorphic, igneous, or sedimentary—can change into any other type of rock.

2 VOCABULARY What is the rock cycle?

3 READING SKILL Describe in order the processes that change igneous rock into sedimentary rock, and sedimentary rock into metamorphic rock.

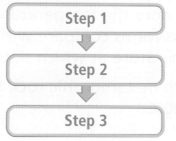

Step 1

Step 2

Step 3

4 CRITICAL THINKING:
Compare What is similar about the way in which metamorphic and igneous rock change into sedimentary rock?

5 INQUIRY SKILL: Use Models Draw and label a rock cycle diagram.

TEST PRACTICE

The process by which dissolved minerals fill in cracks between sediments is called _____.

A. weathering.　　**C.** cooling.

B. cementing.　　**D.** heating.

Math Data Analysis

Different types of metamorphic rock form under different conditions of temperature and depth within Earth. The diagram shows the temperatures at which some metamorphic rocks form. Use it to answer the questions. Provide all answers in both degrees Celsius and Fahrenheit.

1. What is the difference in temperature at which quartzite and slate form?

2. How does the temperature at which gneiss forms compare with the temperature at which slate forms?

3. Which metamorphic rock forms at 600°C?

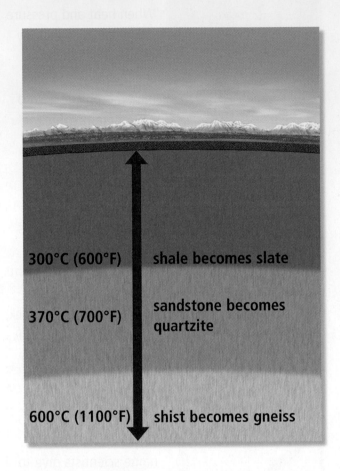

300°C (600°F)   shale becomes slate

370°C (700°F)   sandstone becomes quartzite

600°C (1100°F)   shist becomes gneiss

Writing Descriptive

Many sculptures and statues, such as the famous statue of Abraham Lincoln at the Lincoln Memorial, were carved from marble. Decorative parts of buildings, among them the Taj Mahal in India, are also made of marble.

Select a statue or building in your area that is made of or decorated with marble, granite, or other type of rock. Provide a detailed description of the statue or building. Also describe the properties of the stone. Explain which properties make it a good choice for the particular use.

Lori Dengler

Dr. Lori Dengler has dug up and collected rocks and sand from all over California and other places. By studying these materials, she can discuss earthquakes that struck hundreds of years ago!

Dr. Dengler is a geologist at Humboldt State University in northern California. She also is the director of an earthquake education center. The center works with teachers to prepare schools for earthquakes.

In California, an earthquake could occur at any time. Dr. Dengler's message is that changes on Earth affect everyone. Being prepared and knowing what to do can save lives.

Vocabulary

Complete each sentence with a term from the list.

1. The way a mineral shines is called its _____.

2. A solid material made up of one or more minerals is _____.

3. The tendency of a mineral to split easily along flat surfaces is _____.

4. Rock that forms when existing rock is changed by heat, pressure, or chemicals beneath Earth's surface is _____.

5. A measure of how easily a mineral can be scratched is its _____.

6. A nonliving solid material that has a definite chemical makeup and is found in Earth's outermost layer is called a/an _____.

7. A mineral that is shiny like a metal is called a/an _____.

8. Rock that forms when sand, particles of rock, bits of soil, and remains of once-living things are cemented is called _____.

9. Rock that forms when melted, or molten, rock from deep below Earth's surface cools and hardens is called _____.

10. A mineral that is dull or glassy is called a/an _____.

cleavage p. 163
hardness p. 162
igneous rock p. 178
luster p. 160
metallic mineral p. 169
metamorphic rock p. 180
mineral p. 160
nonmetallic mineral p. 168
rock p. 176
rock cycle p. 186
sediment p. 179
sedimentary rock p. 179
streak p. 161

✔ Test Practice

Write the letter of the best answer choice.

11. The color of a mineral when it is ground to a powder is its _____.

    A. hardness.   **C.** streak.
    B. black.   **D.** cleavage.

12. Sand, bits of rock, and the remains of once-living things are called _____.

    A. sediment.   **C.** nonmetallic mineral.
    B. core.   **D.** metallic mineral.

13. The continuous series of changes that rocks undergo is called the _____.

    A. mantle.   **C.** crust.
    B. hardness scale.   **D.** rock cycle.

14. What is not a property that can be used to identify a mineral?

    A. luster.   **C.** hardness.
    B. streak.   **D.** talc.

Inquiry Skills

15. Classify There are minerals with metallic luster and minerals that are glassy or dull. What other properties can help you identify minerals?

16. A scientist observes that a rock sample has grains that are flat and form long bands. What inference can the scientist make about what type of rock the sample is?

Map the Concept

Fill in the concept map to classify the following different types of rocks.

limestone	obsidian	gneiss
schist	granite	shale

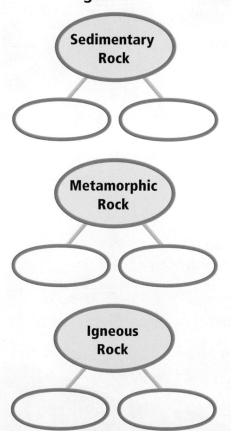

Critical Thinking

17. Apply Use the Properties of Minerals table on page 170 to answer the following question. What mineral is nonmetallic, can be scratched by a fingernail, breaks in cubes, is colorless, and tastes salty?

18. Synthesize You have two igneous rock samples. Sample A has large crystals and Sample B has very small crystals. What could you conclude about how quickly each sample cooled as it formed?

19. Analyze In the rock cycle, what must occur for igneous rock to become sedimentary rock?

20. Evaluate A friend has a set of mineral samples and wants to identify them. What would you suggest he or she do?

Performance Assessment

Your teacher will give you two mineral samples, **A** and **B**. Use the Properties of Minerals table on page 170 to identify each sample. Make a two-column chart with the headings *Observations* and *Inferences*. Record any observations you make and inferences you can draw from them. Keep a record of each test you perform and the results. What is the name of each mineral sample?

Writing Journal

Review your answers to the questions on page 155. Change your answers as necessary, based on what you have learned.

Chapter 6

Rapid Changes on Earth

Volcanoes can rapidly change Earth's surface.

LESSON 1

It happens in an instant. People over a large area feel the ground begin to shake. It's an earthquake. Earthquakes are one way that Earth changes rapidly. How do earthquakes change Earth?

LESSON 2

A volcano remains quiet for many years. Then suddenly it erupts, raining melted rock and hot ash on Earth. What are some ways an erupting volcano changes the surface of Earth?

LESSON 3

There is a deep rumble. Suddenly rocks and soil come tumbling down a steep slope. How do landslides change Earth's surface?

Writing Journal

In your Writing Journal, show what you know by writing or drawing answers to each question.

Vocabulary Preview

Vocabulary

Glossary

Vocabulary Skill

Compound Word

earthquake

The word *earthquake* is a compound word made up of two words. You can figure out the meaning of *earthquake* by thinking about the meaning of the two words that make it up. An *earthquake* is a sudden movement of part of Earth's crust.

landslide

The sudden movement of loose rock and soil down a steep slope.

lava

Molten rock that reaches Earth's surface when a volcano erupts.

volcano

An opening in Earth's crust through which hot ash, gases, and molten rock escape from deep within Earth.

fault

A crack in Earth's crust.

Start with Your Standards

Standard Set 5. Earth Sciences
(Waves, Wind, Water, and Ice)

5.a.   *Students know* some changes in the
earth are due to slow processes, such
as erosion, and some changes are due
to rapid processes, such as landslides,
volcanic eruptions, and earthquakes.

**Standard Set 6. Investigation and
Experimentation** covered in this chapter:
6.d., 6.f.

What Are Earthquakes?

Building Background

Some changes to Earth's surface take place slowly over thousands or millions of years. Some changes happen suddenly. An earthquake can occur with no warning. When an earthquake does occur, it can change Earth's surface in just a few minutes.

PREPARE TO INVESTIGATE

Inquiry Skill

Use Models You can use a model of an object, process, or idea to better understand or describe how it works.

Materials

- cardboard sheet
- scissors
- newspaper
- aluminum pan
- damp sand
- tray
- 4 paper cups
- goggles

Earthquake Model

Procedure

1. **Collaborate** Work with a partner. Half fill a pan with damp sand. Pack it down.

STEP 2

2. Cut a cardboard sheet in half lengthwise to form two strips. Place the cardboard strips side by side on the sand and extending up the edge of the pan. Fill the pan with sand. Pack down the sand.

3. **Use Models** Place a tray on the pan. With your partner, turn the pan and tray upside down onto a newspaper. Slowly remove the pan. Place four cups upside down on the sand formation.

STEP 3

4. **Predict** The cardboard strips represent parts of Earth's crust. Predict what will happen when you tug back and forth on the strips. Record your prediction in your *Science Notebook*.

5. **Observe** Gently move one cardboard strip back and forth. Observe and record what happens to the sand and the cups.

STEP 4

6. Repeat steps 1–5 several more times to see if your results vary.

Conclusion

1. **Infer** What does pulling the strips represent? What do the sand and the paper cups represent?

2. **Infer** How do you think earthquakes affect Earth's surface?

Guided Inquiry

Experiment Repeat this activity using wet sand instead of damp sand. What differences do you notice? Do the cups take a longer or shorter time to fall over? **Hypothesize** about the reason for the difference.

READING SKILL

Main Idea
Use the chart below to list two details that support the main idea that earthquakes cause rapid changes to Earth's surface.

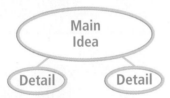

Earthquakes

MAIN IDEA Earth's surface is constantly changing. Earthquakes cause rapid changes to Earth's surface.

Faults

Suppose that you are standing in a level field. A friend is standing not far from you. Suddenly, the ground beneath you thrusts upward. You look for your friend and see that she is now standing on ground lower than where you are. An earthquake (URTH kwayk) has just occurred. An **earthquake** is a sudden movement of part of Earth's crust.

Along the San Andreas Fault, pressure builds between huge sections of Earth's crust. Earthquakes are frequent along this fault line.

fault

Earthquakes occur when sections of the crust come together, move apart, or slide past each other. These movements of the crust usually take place along a **fault** (fawlt), or crack, in Earth's crust.

The San Andreas Fault is a crack or break in Earth's crust that extends from northern California south to Cajon Pass near San Bernardino. This fault system is over 1,200 km (800 mi) long and in some places as deep as 16 km (10 mi).

Some of the strongest earthquakes in the United States have occurred along the San Andreas Fault. In 1857 there was movement along this fault from the cities of Parkfield to Wrightwood, California. The ground shifted as much as 9 m (30 ft) along the line of the earthquake. The earthquake was felt as far away as Las Vegas, Nevada. In 1906 an earthquake and the fire that resulted from it destroyed the city of San Francisco.

Slow movement occurs all the time along some parts of the San Andreas Fault and along other faults. Such slow movement along a fault is called **creep**.

Since 1979, scientists have measured the amount of creep movement in Hollister, California. In one place, the creep has been about 12 mm ($\frac{1}{2}$ in.) a year. In another, the movement has been about 6 mm ($\frac{1}{4}$ in.) a year.

MAIN IDEA **Describe two kinds of movement that occur along faults.**

Large Faults in California

——	fault
≡≡≡	part of fault in which creep occurs

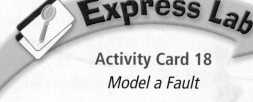

Express Lab

Activity Card 18
Model a Fault

Causes of Earthquakes

Earth's crust is always changing. Forces deep inside Earth put pressure on the rock layers above. This pressure may build up for hundreds or thousands of years. During this time, sections of Earth's crust may move continuously and slowly. The movement is so slow that it's not noticeable.

Sometimes the pressure on the rock layers becomes too great. When this happens, one or both sections on either side of a fault may move suddenly. This sudden movement is an earthquake.

An earthquake that occurs in the ocean floor can sometimes cause a **tsunami** (tsoo NAH mee), a very large ocean wave. Whether or not a tsunami will form after an earthquake depends on the motion of the earthquake and its strength. Tsunamis can cause great damage on land.

The study of earthquakes is called **seismology** (syz MAHL uh jee). Seismologists measure an earthquake's energy. The amount of energy, or magnitude, of an earthquake is measured using the Richter scale. For example, an earthquake that measures less than 3.5 on the Richter scale may not be felt. An earthquake that measures 7.5 is a major earthquake.

What people feel on Earth's surface depends on how far they are from the earthquake's focus (FO kus). The **focus** is the point underground where an earthquake starts.

Earthquake Waves

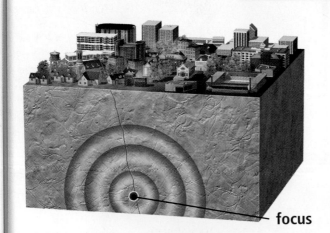

① The intensity of an earthquake is felt most strongly at the epicenter, which is directly above the focus.

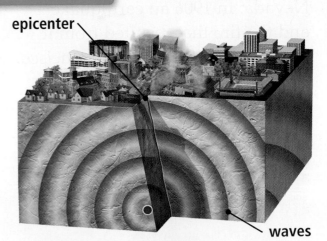

② The farther the waves are from the focus, the less strongly the earthquake is felt.

Energy moves in waves away from the focus point. Most focus points are less than 72 km (45 mi) below Earth's surface.

The point on the surface that is directly above the focus is an earthquake's epicenter (EHP ih sehn tur). The **epicenter** is where an earthquake is felt most strongly, or has the greatest intensity. Seismologists measure the effects of an earthquake on an intensity scale.

Violent earthquakes can move rock on Earth's surface and produce new landforms. Over time, mountains can be pushed up and valleys can be formed. New faults may be formed as well.

MAIN IDEA What effect can a violent earthquake have on Earth's surface?

In 1995 an earthquake in Kobe, Japan, measured 7.2 on the Richter scale.

1906 San Francisco Earthquake

Santa Rosa

N

Point Reyes

San Francisco

San Mateo

Stanford University

SAN ANDREAS FAULT

Chittendon

Moss Landing

Earthquake Intensity

I
II–III
IV
V
VI
VII
VIII
IX
X+

0   20   40 Miles
0   20   40 Kilometers

Earthquake Intensity Scale

Value	Intensity	Description
I–III	Very Light	Not felt by most people.
IV–V	Light	Sleepers awaken. Doors swing open. Small objects move.
VI–VII	Moderate to Strong	Felt by everyone. Trees are shaken. Some caving in along sand or gravel banks happens.
VIII–IX	Very Strong to Violent	Chimneys fall. Tree branches break. Cracks are in ground.
X	Very Violent	Serious damage. Water is thrown from rivers and lakes. Sand and mud shifts on beaches.

X-bracing, shown here on the Alcoa Building in San Francisco, helps buildings resist earthquake damage.

Earthquake-Safe Design

Depending on their magnitude or intensity, earthquakes can be very dangerous. Very violent earthquakes in and near cities can topple buildings and kill many people.

Buildings can be designed so they are less likely to collapse during an earthquake. Materials such as brick and stone tend to crack and break when the ground beneath them shakes.

To withstand earthquakes, materials need to bend, or be flexible. Wood and steel are flexible. Buildings made with these materials will move and sway, but usually will not crack and fall. Using steel frames to reinforce homes and other buildings provides support during an earthquake.

Earthquake Safety

Here are some guidelines for staying safe during and after an earthquake.

Know how to telephone the police and fire departments.

In case of a gas leak, do not turn lights on or off. Do not use candles or matches.

Know which radio station to tune to.

If you are indoors, stay indoors. Take cover near an inside wall and under a sturdy desk or table. Stay there until the shaking stops.

If you are outdoors, find an open area away from buildings and power lines. Crouch down and cover your head.

If you are in a car, stay there with your seatbelt fastened.

When the shaking stops, take these steps.

Listen to the radio for the latest emergency information.

Use the telephone only to report life-threatening emergencies.

MAIN IDEA Considering the effect that an earthquake can have on buildings, how can you stay safe during and after an earthquake?

Visual Summary

Earthquakes occur when sections of Earth's crust come together, move apart, or slide past each other. These movements usually take place along a fault, or crack, in Earth's crust.

Violent earthquakes can change Earth's surface. Over time, mountains can be pushed up and valleys can be formed. New faults may be formed as well.

Buildings made of wood or steel withstand earthquakes better than buildings make of brick or stone. X-bracing helps buildings resist earthquake damage.

Reading Review

❶ MAIN IDEA How can an earthquake affect Earth's surface?

❷ VOCABULARY How is the focus of an earthquake different from the epicenter?

❸ READING SKILL: Write a paragraph that describes creep.

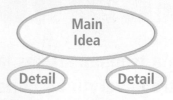

❹ CRITICAL THINKING: Apply Suppose you interview an engineer about how buildings withstand earthquakes. What questions would you ask to learn as much as possible about what building materials to use?

❺ INQUIRY SKILL: Use Models Make a drawing that shows Earth's surface and the focus and epicenter of an earthquake.

 TEST PRACTICE

A tsunami is a very large ocean wave that is caused by a/an _____.

A. landslide.

B. volcano.

C. underwater earthquake.

D. seismograph.

 Technology
Visit **www.eduplace.com/cascp** to find out more about earthquakes.

205

Tsunami Early Warning

When a tsunami strikes land, it can destroy everything in its path. The Tsunami Warning System helps alert Pacific Ocean communities to tsunamis.

There is no warning system in the Indian Ocean. In December 2004, a very destructive tsunami struck there. It destroyed property. Many lives were lost.

Dr. Lee-Lueng Fu is a senior research scientist at the Jet Propulsion Laboratory, California Institute of Technology. He is also part of an international team studying the world's oceans.

Satellite images made by his team captured information about the Indian Ocean tsunami, but not in time to warn anyone. This information may help save lives in the future. Dr. Lee-Lueng Fu commented, "These observations are unique and of tremendous value for testing and improving tsunami computer models and developing future tsunami early warning systems."

Pacific Ocean Tsunami Early Warning System

1. A gauge on the ocean floor detects a passing tsunami.
2. Data is sent from the gauge to a surface buoy.
3. Data is relayed from the buoy to a satellite.
4. The satellite transmits data to ground stations. People at ground stations warn communities that may be affected by the tsunami.

Sharing Ideas

1. **READING CHECK** In a tsunami warning system, how is a tsunami detected and how is this information relayed to people in danger?

2. **WRITE ABOUT IT** What five items would you pack in advance in a Tsunami Prep Kit? Write a list and give a reason for each item you select.

3. **TALK ABOUT IT** Discuss with your classmates the importance of having tsunami warning systems in all areas where tsunamis are a threat.

What Are Volcanoes?

Building Background

Some changes to Earth's surface happen very quickly. Volcanic eruptions can rapidly change the shape of mountains and other land forms. In a short time, material from a large eruption can cover the land and everything on it for many kilometers.

PREPARE TO INVESTIGATE

Inquiry Skill

Observe It is important to know the difference between what you observe using your senses and tools and what you think about those observations.

Materials

- small plastic cup
- newspaper
- modeling clay
- grass, leaves, and twigs
- red and yellow food coloring
- liquid dishwashing soap
- dropper
- baking soda
- vinegar
- metric measuring cup
- plastic spoon
- goggles

Erupting Volcano

Procedure

STEP 1

1 Collaborate Work in a small group to build a volcano. Place a plastic cup on newspaper on a flat surface. Use modeling clay to build a volcano around the cup. Leave an opening in the volcano, directly over the opening in the cup. **Safety:** Wear goggles during this activity.

2 Place grass, leaves, and twigs around the sides of the volcano. Stand up some of the twigs to look like trees.

STEP 3

3 Carefully put 2 spoonfuls of baking soda in the cup. Add 6 drops each of red and yellow food coloring. Use a dropper to add 6 drops of dishwashing soap. Stir the mixture.

4 Observe Pour 125 mL of vinegar into a metric measuring cup. Slowly add the vinegar to the mixture so your volcano "erupts." Record your observations in your *Science Notebook*.

STEP 4

Conclusion

1. **Observe** What happened to the grass, leaves, and twigs on the sides of the model volcano during the eruption?

2. **Hypothesize** How do you think a real lava flow would affect the land near a real volcano?

Guided Inquiry

Ask Questions What questions would you ask to learn why a volcano erupts? Decide which questions might be answered by doing **research** in the library, on websites, or by asking an expert.

VOCABULARY

lava	p. 210
magma	p. 210
volcano	p. 210

READING SKILL

Cause and Effect
Use a chart to show the causes and effects of volcanoes.

Cause → Effect

Volcanoes

MAIN IDEA A volcano erupts when pressure pushes molten rock up through cracks in Earth's crust and onto the surface. Volcanoes change Earth's surface.

How Volcanoes Erupt

A **volcano** (vahl KAY noh) is an opening in Earth's crust through which hot ash, gases, and molten rock escape from deep within Earth. The molten rock beneath Earth's surface is called **magma** (MAG muh). Molten rock that reaches Earth's surface is called **lava** (LAH vuh).

Recall that deep within Earth's mantle, temperatures are very high. It is so hot in some places that rocks become magma. As magma rises to the surface, some of it slowly hardens and becomes igneous rock. Pressure beneath the surface causes some magma to push its way through faults and flow onto Earth's surface as lava.

Volcanoes can erupt in different ways. Some volcanoes release thick, slow-moving lava from their openings. Other volcanoes spew hot lava, ash, and gases into the air. Any erupting volcano can quickly change Earth's surface.

CAUSE AND EFFECT What causes magma to push its way through faults and flow onto Earth's surface?

Express Lab

Activity Card 19
Compare Volcanic Eruptions

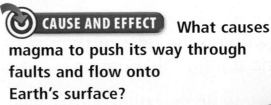

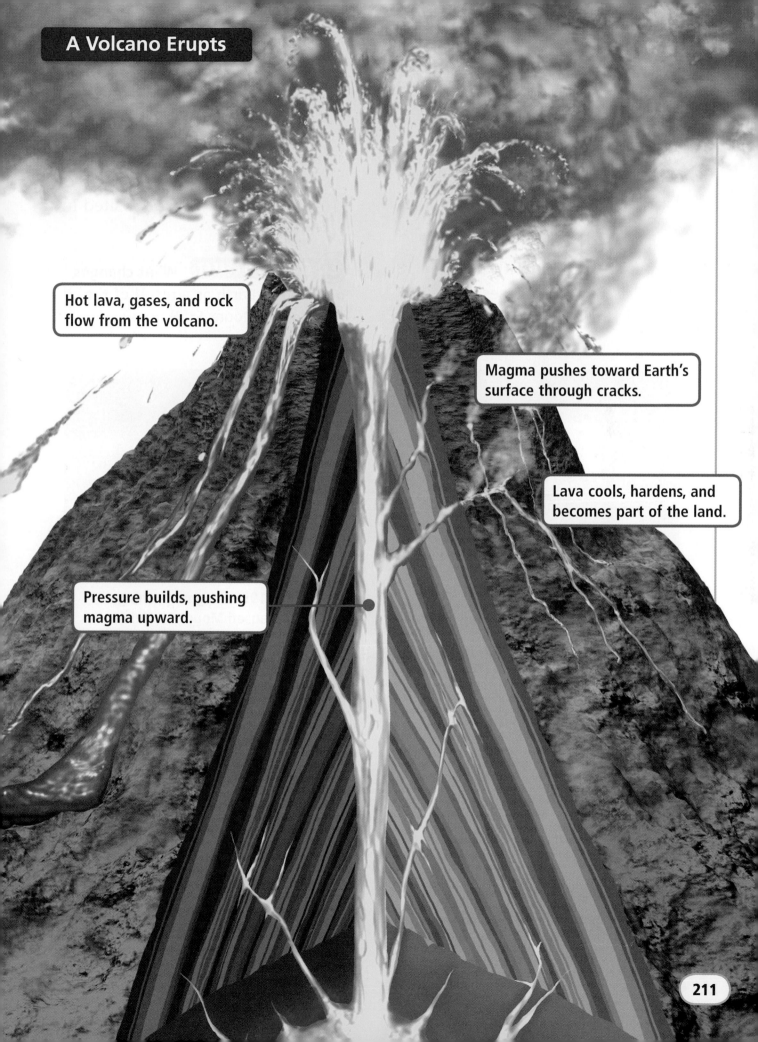

A Volcano Erupts

Hot lava, gases, and rock flow from the volcano.

Magma pushes toward Earth's surface through cracks.

Lava cools, hardens, and becomes part of the land.

Pressure builds, pushing magma upward.

Mount St. Helens

Mount St. Helens, in the state of Washington, is a volcano that has existed for 40,000 years. There were periods when the volcano was active, and periods when it was quiet.

Mount St. Helens erupted suddenly and violently on May 18, 1980. Ash and hot gases blew into the air. Rocks, soil, mud, and water crashed down the mountainside. More than 380 sq km (145 sq mi) of forest were destroyed. The entire north side of the mountain blew away, leaving a huge crater over 3 km (2 mi) long and almost 2 km (1 mi) wide. Ash was deposited in 11 states.

CAUSE AND EFFECT What changes occurred to Earth as a result of the eruption of Mount St. Helens?

Mount St. Helens has existed for about 40,000 years. Eruptions of gases, ash, and lava formed it.

In March 1980, magma pushing upward caused Mount St. Helens to begin to erupt.

The major eruption in May lasted for nine hours. Rock, mud, and water crashed down the mountain.

When the eruption was over, the surrounding landscape was completely changed.

Visual Summary

A volcano is an opening in Earth's crust from which ash, gas, and lava flow. Any volcanic eruption can change Earth's surface.

Sometimes volcanoes release lava slowly. At other times they can erupt suddenly and violently. Volcanoes can affect Earth's surface for hundreds of miles around.

When Mount St. Helens erupted, ash and hot gases blew into the air. Rocks, soil, mud, and water came down the mountain. The north side of the mountain was blown away.

Reading Review

1 **MAIN IDEA** How does a volcano change Earth's surface?

2 **VOCABULARY** How does magma differ from lava?

3 **READING SKILL** What causes rock in Earth's mantle to become magma?

Cause ➡ Effect

4 **CRITICAL THINKING:** **Apply** Suppose you interview someone who witnessed a volcanic eruption. What questions would you ask the witness?

5 **INQUIRY SKILL: Observe** Look again at the photos of Mount St. Helens on p. 212. What do you think happened to the trees after the volcano erupted?

 TEST PRACTICE

What was NOT a result of the 1980 Mount St. Helens eruption?

A. Ash blew into the air.

B. The landscape was changed.

C. Rock, mud, and water crashed down the mountain.

D. Slow-moving lava built up the mountain.

 Technology
Visit **www.eduplace.com/cascp** to find out more about volcanoes.

Extreme Science

Cool Lava!

Do not touch! Volcanoes are known for spouting red-hot lava. But did you know there is actually a volcano in eastern Africa that is famous for its *cool* lava?

The volcano is called Ol Doinyo Lengai, and it has the coolest lava on Earth. Like all volcanoes, an eruption of Ol Doinyo Lengai causes rapid changes to Earth's surface. But, because of its unusual mineral content, the lava from this volcano comes up looking like dark mud. Fountains of it can solidify in mid-air and then even shatter like glass.

Don't be fooled by Ol Doinyo's cool look. Its goopy dark lava is still around 538°C (1,000°F). That's twice as hot as the highest setting on a kitchen oven.

Red-hot lava from the Kilauea volcano in Hawaii pours into the ocean. Since 1983, lava flows have added 2 square kilometers of new land to the Island of Hawaii.

Writing Journal

If you were a scientist studying volcanoes, which lava would you like to study? The cool lava of Ol Doinyo Lengai, or the hot lava of Mauna Loa? Explain your reasons in your writing journal.

215

What Are Landslides?

Building Background

Some changes on Earth happen very slowly, and some happen quite rapidly. Landslides can begin and end in a matter of minutes. Landslides quickly change the surface of Earth. When mud and rocks slide, they carry trees and other living things with them.

PREPARE TO INVESTIGATE

Inquiry Skill

Analyze Data When you analyze data, you look for patterns to help you predict, infer, and draw conclusions.

Materials

- wax paper
- sand
- pebbles
- diatomaceous earth
- milk carton with one end and one side cut away
- metric measuring cup
- goggles

Landslide Model

Procedure

STEP 1

1 **Make a Model** Work in a group. Use a milk carton that has one side and one end cut away to model a hill and a landslide. Set it up on a tray with a sheet of waxed paper on it. Add 1-cm layers of sand, pebbles, and diatomaceous earth to the bottom of the carton. Prop up the end of the carton with two books. **Safety:** Wear goggles.

STEP 2

2 **Experiment** Slowly pour water on the material at the top of the "hill" until you cause a "landslide."

3 When the landslide occurs, measure the volume of material that fell in the slide by pouring the material into a measuring cup. Record the amount as trial 1.

STEP 3

4 **Analyze Data** Clean out the carton and measuring cup. Repeat steps 1–3 two more times, changing the number of books to three and then four. Compare the volume of the material in the cup for each trial.

5 **Collaborate** To get more data, compare results with other groups.

Conclusion

1. **Infer** What effect does the steepness of a hill have on a landslide?

2. **Analyze Data** In step 5, what might account for any differences in data?

Guided Inquiry

Experiment Make another model of a landslide. Use materials such as clay, larger rocks, and small pieces of sod. Repeat the experiment three times and average your results. **Infer** reasons for any differences.

READING SKILL

Compare and Contrast
Use the chart to compare and contrast different ways landslides can occur.

Compare	Contrast

Landslides

MAIN IDEA Landslides cause rapid changes to Earth's surface. There are many causes of landslides including heavy rains, melting snow, earthquakes, and volcanic eruptions.

Causes and Effects

When Mount St. Helens erupted in 1980, it caused a massive landslide. A **landslide** is the sudden movement of loose rock and soil down a steep slope. Mudslides and rockslides are also types of landslides.

Earthquakes and volcanic eruptions often trigger landslides. Soil and rock that have been loosened by the shaking land will slide downhill. The steeper the slope, the faster the materials will move downhill.

How might people be affected by a mudslide? ▶

Express Lab

Activity Card 20
Explore Plants and Landslides

▲ A 2005 landslide destroyed these homes in Laguna Beach, California.

One type of landslide is caused by heavy rain, or the sudden melting of snow. These conditions often result in mudslides in hilly areas.

Wildfires can lead to landslides. If fire destroys all the plants on a mountain, the slopes are left bare. Without trees and bushes to hold soil in place, the sudden movement of rocks and soil down the slope is more likely. Landslides are more likely to occur on steep slopes.

Landslides can be very destructive in places where people have built houses on hillsides and near the edges of cliffs. Every year landslides cause millions of dollars in damage to property. Tilted telephone poles, cracked house foundations, and curved tree trunks are some signs that an area may be subject to landslides.

The problems caused by landslides can be reduced. Local governments can limit where people are allowed to build houses or businesses. Supporting walls can be built to change the direction of landslides away from developed areas. Before buying or building a home on sloped land, people can consult with an expert to learn if the site is likely to have landslides.

COMPARE AND CONTRAST Compare and contrast two causes of landslides.

Types of Landslides

There are many steep slopes in mountain regions, including those in California. Landslides commonly occur along these steep slopes. When the soil is damp or wet, a large, heavy mass of soil can slide down the slope. This type of landslide can carry away trees, boulders, cars, and even houses.

Rockslides occur when loosened rocks suddenly fall from cliffs. Many rockslides occur on the steep cliffs in Yosemite Valley. They also occur in other areas of California where there are steep rocky slopes.

COMPARE AND CONTRAST What are two ways that landslides and rockslides are alike?

Landslide

In this type of landslide, a thick, heavy mass of rock material flows down a hillside.

Original position

Moving mass

Rockslide

In a rockslide, large sections of rock break along cracks and topple over each other as they fall down the hill.

Visual Summary

Landslides are sudden movements of loose rock and soil down a steep slope. They cause rapid changes to Earth's surface. Mudslides and rockslides are types of landslides.

Landslides can be very destructive in places where people have built houses on hillsides and near the edges of cliffs.

There are different types of landslides, including mudslides and rockslides.

Technology
Visit **www.eduplace.com/cascp** to find out more about landslides.

Reading Review

❶ MAIN IDEA What are landslides and how do they affect Earth's surface?

❷ VOCABULARY Write a sentence about a landslide.

❸ READING SKILL How are rockslides and mudslides alike and different?

Compare	Contrast

❹ CRITICAL THINKING: Predict Would loose rock be more likely to become a landslide on a steep slope or a gradual slope?

❺ INQUIRY SKILL: Analyze Data In *Town A*, rainfall on a steep slope is about 39 cm in one week. A steep slope in *Town B* receives an average of 3.5 cm of rain each day for two weeks. Which town is more likely to have a landslide?

✔ TEST PRACTICE
Which of the following is NOT a cause of landslides?

A. earthquake

B. tsunami

C. erupting volcano

D. heavy rain

Math Geometry

You have learned that landslides occur on steep slopes. The drawing shows the net, or pattern, for making a three-dimensional model of a steep-sided mountain.

Copy the net on a sheet of construction paper. Then use scissors and transparent tape to make the model. Fold along the dotted lines and tape the edges of the model together.

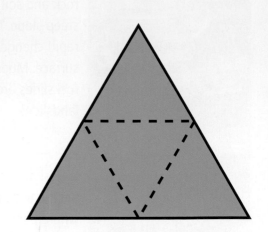

1. What geometric shape is the model mountain?

2. How many faces, edges, and vertices does your three-dimensional shape have?

3. How can you change the net to make a model mountain with even steeper sides? Describe the changes.

Writing Informative

Research a description of a volcanic eruption from the point of view of two or more eyewitnesses. Use accounts from newspapers, books, and the Internet. Then write a summary that identifies the time and place of the eruption and gives detailed information from the eyewitness accounts.

As you write your summary, think about the answers to these questions. Were there any details that were common to most eyewitness reports? What terms did most eyewitnesses use to describe the event? Was there information that only one person reported?

Seismologist

Seismologists are scientists who study earthquakes. They analyze data from a seismograph, a device that measures vibrations in Earth. Seismologists also map and monitor changes along fault lines. A seismologist's data help predict future earthquakes. The data also help governments make decisions about safety codes for buildings and emergency planning.

What It Takes!

- A degree in geology, geophysics, or earth science
- Math and computer skills

Emergency Medical Technician

Can you think clearly during a crisis? If so, you could learn to be an emergency medical technician (EMT). Typically, EMTs give first aid to the very sick or injured.

EMTs work especially hard during a disaster, such as a serious earthquake. Their work saves many lives. In areas where earthquakes are common, EMTs often have practice drills for such events.

What It Takes!

- Continuing education and a license
- Skills in dealing with people, especially the very sick and injured

Vocabulary

Complete each sentence with a term from the list.

1. A sudden movement of part of Earth's crust is a/an _____.

2. The point where an earthquake starts is called the _____.

3. Molten rock that reaches Earth's surface when a volcano erupts is _____.

4. A crack in Earth's crust is called a/an _____.

5. Molten rock that is beneath Earth's surface is _____.

6. Sudden movement of loose rock down a slope is called a/an _____.

7. The slow, continuous movement along a fault line is _____.

8. The study of earthquakes is called _____.

9. An opening in Earth's crust through which hot ash, gases, and molten rock escape from deep within Earth is a/an _____.

10. The point on Earth's surface directly above the focus where an earthquake is felt most strongly is the _____.

creep p. 201
earthquake p. 200
epicenter p. 203
fault p. 201
focus p. 202
landslide p. 218
lava p. 210
magma p. 210
seismology p. 202
tsunami p. 202
volcano p. 210

✓ Test Practice

Write the letter of the best answer choice.

11. Which does NOT cause a rapid change to Earth's surface?

    A. volcano erupting   **C.** tsunami
    B. earthquake   **D.** fault

12. In which place is a landslide most likely to occur?

    A. dry, flat desert
    B. rainy, bare slope
    C. rainy, mountain forest
    D. sunny, grassy field

13. Which natural event can lead to a landslide?

    A. weathering   **C.** tornadoes
    B. wildfires   **D.** rock cycle

14. A very large ocean wave that is caused by an underwater earthquake is a/an _____.

    A. landslide.   **C.** tsunami.
    B. volcano.   **D.** rockslide.

Inquiry Skills

15. **Analyze Data** Suppose there are two earthquakes in different regions. One earthquake has a magnitude of 8.0. Another has a magnitude of 4.0. What would each event be like? What kind of damage would you expect to find from each? What may have happened to the surrounding land and buildings closest to the epicenter?

16. Suppose scientists are trying to draw conclusions about how warning floats work in detecting tsunamis. Why would the scientists want to conduct multiple trials?

Critical Thinking

17. **Apply** If you wanted to construct an earthquake safety kit for your family, what would you include?

18. **Synthesize** Suppose you have to construct a new kind of house that could be built to withstand an earthquake. What kind of materials would you use?

19. **Analyze** How might studying the causes of volcanoes help people?

20. **Evaluate** Make an argument about why it might be a bad idea to build homes and buildings on steep slopes or near the edges of cliffs.

Map the Concept

Select one rapid change to Earth's surface that you have learned about. Fill in the Cause and Effect table to show the cause or causes of that rapid change. Then describe the effects of the rapid change.

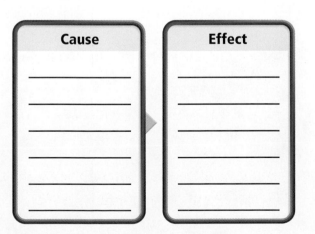

Cause	Effect

Performance Assessment

Design a pamphlet that teaches people about the dangers of earthquakes or tsunamis. Identify ways to be prepared for such an event. Include safety guidelines to follow during and after the event. Keep your paragraphs short and include drawings.

Writing Journal

Review your answers to the questions on page 195 at the beginning of this chapter. Change your answers, as needed, based on what you have learned.

Chapter 7

Slow Changes on Earth

Rock formations, Joshua Tree
National Park, California

LESSON 1

The sand on beaches was once rock or shells. What processes change rock into the sand?

LESSON 2

Moving water can change Earth's surface. How do rivers and ocean waves change the shape of land?

LESSON 3

Glaciers and wind are two forces that cause weathering. How do ice and wind change Earth's surface?

Writing Journal

In your Writing Journal, show what you know by writing or drawing answers to each question.

227

Vocabulary Preview

Vocabulary

Glossary

Vocabulary Skill

Compound Word

headland

The word *headland* is a compound word. A head is the top or uppermost part of something. A headland is a point of land, usually high, that extends out into the water.

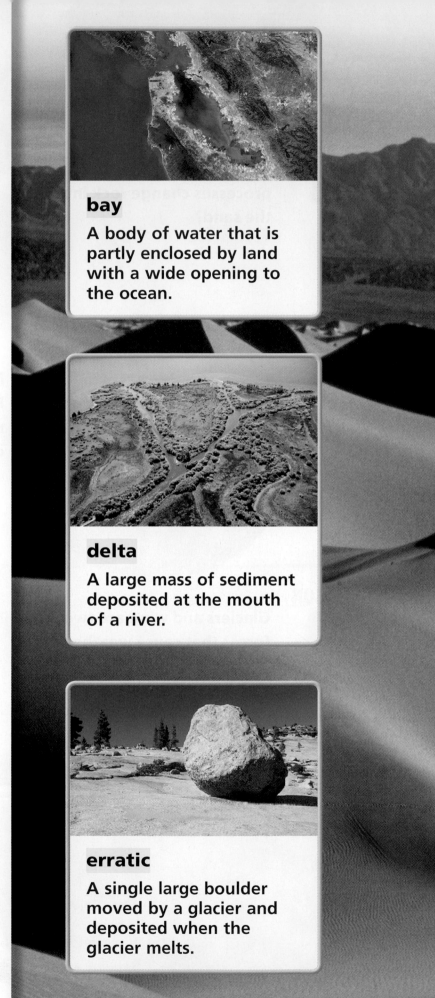

bay
A body of water that is partly enclosed by land with a wide opening to the ocean.

delta
A large mass of sediment deposited at the mouth of a river.

erratic
A single large boulder moved by a glacier and deposited when the glacier melts.

Start with Your Standards

Standard Set 5. Earth Sciences (Waves, Wind, Water, and Ice)

5.a. *Students know* some changes in the earth are due to slow processes, such as erosion, and some changes are due to rapid processes, such as landslides, volcanic eruptions, and earthquakes.

5.b. *Students know* natural processes, including freezing and thawing and the growth of roots, cause rocks to break down into smaller pieces.

5.c. *Students know* moving water erodes land forms, reshaping the land by taking it away from some places and depositing it as pebbles, sand, silt, and mud in other places (weathering, transport, and deposition).

Standard Set 6. Investigation and Experimentation covered in this chapter: 6.a., 6.b., 6.c.

sand dune

A hill or pile of sand formed by the wind.

What Are Weathering and Erosion?

Building Background

The land has many different shapes. Weathering slowly wears away rock into smaller pieces. Erosion moves these rock materials—pebbles, sand, and soil—from one place to another. Over time, these and other processes change the surface of Earth.

PREPARE TO INVESTIGATE

Inquiry Skill

Measure In some science investigations, you can estimate a measurement of weight, length, or volume.

Materials

- small plastic soft drink bottle with cap
- water
- 250-mL graduated cylinder
- funnel

Science and Math Toolbox

For steps 1 and 5, review **Measuring Volume** on page H7.

Freezing Effects

Procedure

STEP 1

1. **Measure** Work with a partner. Completely fill a soft drink bottle with water. Pour the water into a graduated cylinder to find out how much water it takes to fill the bottle. In your *Science Notebook*, record this amount of water in mL. This is the volume of the liquid that the bottle can hold.

2. Refill the bottle with water. Then firmly tighten the cap on it.

STEP 2

3. Put the bottle into a freezer and allow it to remain overnight.

4. **Observe** Take the bottle out of the freezer. Observe any effects that the ice had on the bottle.

5. **Measure** Estimate the difference in volume between the water-filled bottle and the ice-filled bottle.

STEP 5

Conclusion

1. **Infer** What caused the changes you observed in the bottle?

2. **Infer** How do the effects that you observed relate to things that happen in nature?

Guided Inquiry

Ask Questions What questions would you ask about how sediment and water interact in nature? Choose one question to **research** in the library, on websites, or by asking an expert.

Weathering and Erosion

VOCABULARY

erosion   p. 234
glacier   p. 234
weathering   p. 232

READING SKILL

Sequence
Use the chart like the one below to show the processes of weathering and erosion.

> Step 1
> ↓
> Step 2
> ↓
> Step 3

MAIN IDEA Earth's surface is slowly built up and worn down. The processes of weathering and erosion change Earth's surface.

Weathering

Have you ever picked up a smooth stone from the beach? If so, you have observed an example of weathering (WETH ur ihng). **Weathering** is the slow wearing away of rock into smaller pieces. Ice, plant roots, moving water, and chemicals are causes of weathering.

Weathering caused this huge boulder in Yosemite to break off from the top of the hill. ▼

boulder   ice

boulder

▲ Acid rain has damaged this stone figure on a building in Paris, France.

◄ The roots of plants can break apart large rocks.

Most rocks have tiny cracks in them. In cold climates, rainwater that enters the cracks can freeze and expand. The expanding ice makes the cracks bigger. Over time, periods of freezing and melting cause rocks to break.

A similar thing happens when plant roots grow into cracks in a rock. The growing roots widen the cracks, and the rock breaks.

Streams flow over rocks, moving them. Over and over rocks bump against other rocks. As the rocks wear down, sharp edges become smooth and the rocks get smaller.

Outer layers of rock can peel off when a forest fire or the Sun heats up the outside of a rock. When cool rainwater falls on heated rocks, it can also cause them to break.

Chemicals can weather rocks. Gases in the air react with iron in some rocks to form rust, which crumbles. Other gases in air react with rainwater to form acid rain. Acid rain weakens rock, causing it to break apart.

SEQUENCE Describe the sequence of events that might smooth down a sharp-edged rock that falls into a stream.

Express Lab

Activity Card 21
Model Weathering and Erosion

This balanced rock formation is the result of weathering and erosion.

Erosion

After a heavy rainstorm, have you ever noticed soil and pebbles being carried by running water? If so, you have seen an example of erosion (ih ROH zhuhn). **Erosion** is the movement of rock material from one place to another. The materials that result from weathering are carried away by erosion.

Water is the main cause of erosion. Suppose a drop of water splashes onto soil. The water loosens and picks up tiny particles. When the water moves downhill, it carries the tiny particles with it. As the water flows over the soil, it picks up more particles.

Weathering and erosion of rock take place over thousands and even millions of years. The water of a fast-moving river breaks down rock. Over many years, the running water carries enough weathered material away to form a deep canyon. The Grand Canyon in Arizona was formed this way.

A **glacier** (GLAY shur) is a large mass of slow-moving ice. A glacier moves so slowly that its movement is difficult to see. As it moves, a glacier causes both weathering and erosion of the rocks over which it moves. A glacier can dig out huge areas of rock and soil to form deep valleys and canyons.

Wind is another cause of weathering and erosion. Some areas have few plants to hold soil in place. In these areas, the wind carries away dry sand and soil.

SEQUENCE How do weathering and erosion form a deep canyon?

This U-shaped valley was shaped by moving water in the form of a glacier.

Visual Summary

Plant roots cause weathering by breaking rock into smaller pieces. Plant roots grow into cracks in a rock. The growing roots widen the cracks.

Gases in air react with rainwater to form acid rain. Acid rain weakens rock, causing it to break.

This balanced rock formation is the result of weathering and erosion. The materials that result from weathering are carried away by erosion.

Reading Review

❶ MAIN IDEA What is the slow process of wearing away rock into smaller pieces?

❷ VOCABULARY Use *erosion* in a sentence about acid rain.

❸ READING SKILL: Describe the steps involved when water and ice weather rocks.

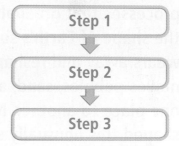

Step 1

Step 2

Step 3

❹ CRITICAL THINKING: Apply Thousands of years ago, enormous sheets of moving ice covered much of New England. Explain why large boulders litter the landscape.

❺ INQUIRY SKILL: Observe In what types of places could you observe weathering?

✔ TEST PRACTICE
The process that moves sediment from one place to another is _____.

A. weathering.

B. acid rain.

C. mountain building.

D. erosion.

Technology
Visit **www.eduplace.com/cascp** to find out more about erosion and weathering.

How Does Water Shape the Land?

Building Background

Moving water is one of the processes that gradually changes the shape of Earth's surface. Water wears away and reshapes rock. It moves pebbles, sand, and soil from one place to another. Moving water shaped this unusually shaped island.

PREPARE TO INVESTIGATE

Inquiry Skill

Predict When you predict, you state what you think will happen based on observations of causes and effects.

Materials

- hand lens
- sediment (sand, bits of rock, soil)
- plastic soft-drink bottle with cap
- metric ruler
- water
- clock or watch
- goggles

Science and Math Toolbox

For step 2, review **Using a Tape Measure or Ruler** on page H6.

Effects of Water on Sediment

Procedure

STEP 1

1. **Collaborate** Work with a partner. Use a hand lens to observe a mixture of sediment. In your *Science Notebook* record what you observe. **Safety:** Wear goggles.

2. **Measure** Make a chart like the one shown. Use a funnel to put about 2 cm of the sediment into a plastic soft drink bottle. Fill the bottle about two-thirds with water. Put the cap back on the bottle and tighten it firmly.

STEP 2

	Sediment with water
Start	
After 2 hours	
After 4 hours	
Prediction	

3. **Observe** Swirl around the material in the bottle for about 30 seconds. Then set the bottle down and do not move it again. Record what you observe.

STEP 3

4. **Predict** Observe the contents of the bottle every 2 hours for the rest of the day. Record what you observe each time. At the end of the day, write a prediction about how the sediment will look in 24 hours.

Conclusion

1. **Compare** How are the observations you made before swirling the bottle similar to the ones you made after swirling it? How are they different?

2. **Infer** How do the effects you have observed relate to things that happen in nature?

Guided Inquiry

Experiment Make a model to show what happens when water runs downhill over sediment. Measure the material that is moved. Repeat this three times. Average your results. **Infer** reasons for any differences.

VOCABULARY

bay	p. 239
delta	p. 240
deposition	p. 238
headland	p. 239
river system	p. 240

READING SKILL

Cause and Effect
Use the chart below to explain what causes beaches to become narrower.

Cause → Effect

How Does Water Shape the Land?

MAIN IDEA Moving water changes Earth's surface through weathering, erosion, and deposition.

The Changing Coastline

You know that erosion moves bits of sand, soil, and rock. But what happens to these materials?

Recall that bits of sand, soil, and rock are called sediment. The dropping of sediment moved by water, wind, and ice is called **deposition** (dehp uh ZIHSH uhn). Wind, glaciers, and moving water are the main causes of weathering, erosion, and deposition. Along the seacoasts, ocean waves easily pick up and carry sand away. Waves also drop the sand, sometimes in new places.

Ocean waves can separate parts of a headland to form tiny islands called sea stacks. ▼

California's Coastline

Eroded rock from land and eroded shells from the ocean form the beaches along California's coastline. Ocean waves and currents move sand along the shore.

Some beaches change with the seasons. Strong winter winds produce strong waves that remove more sand from the shore than they deposit. This erodes the beach, making it narrower. In summer, gentler waves deposit more sand on the beaches than they remove. This widens the beach.

Headlands and bays are other features of the California coastline. A **headland** is a point of land, usually high, that extends out into the water. A headland is surrounded by water on three sides. A **bay** is a body of water that is partly enclosed by land and has a wide opening. The opening, called the mouth, connects the bay to the ocean.

▲ Strong winter waves carry beach sand away and deposit it offshore.

▲ Gentle summer waves deposit sand on the beach.

Express Lab

Activity Card 22
Model a River

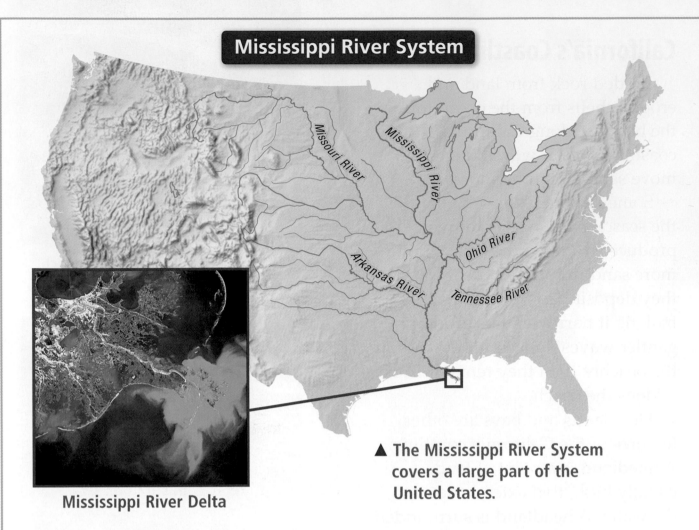

Mississippi River System

Missouri River

Mississippi River

Arkansas River

Ohio River

Tennessee River

Mississippi River Delta

▲ The Mississippi River System covers a large part of the United States.

River Systems

Rainfall on a hill or mountainside begins to trickle down the slope. Several trickles may join to form a small stream. Streams join to form a river. Small rivers can then join larger rivers. The largest river and all the waterways that drain into it are called a **river system**.

Rivers that make up the Mississippi River System begin in the Rocky Mountains in the west and the Appalachian Mountains to the east. These rivers flow into the Mississippi River. The Mississippi River flows into the Gulf of Mexico.

Deposition helps create a variety of land surface features. Some of these features occur as part of river systems. As rivers flow downhill, the fast-moving water picks up sediment. At the mouth of a river, the river empties into a lake or ocean. Here the land tends to flatten out. This flattening tends to slow the river. As the river slows, the sediment drops out of the water.

At the mouth of the Mississippi River sediments have formed a large delta that extends far into the Gulf of Mexico. A **delta** is a large mass of sediment deposited at the mouth of a river.

Another feature that river deposition can create is an alluvial fan. An alluvial fan is a fan-shaped land mass that forms after a river rushes down a steep slope and slows over a flat plain. Death Valley National Park in California is famous for its alluvial fan deposits.

As a river flows over flat land, the river tends to wind in curves called meanders (mee AND urz). The river water erodes the outside of each curve and deposits sediment on the inside.

Sometimes more water flows down a river than the normal river channel can hold. The water overflows the river's banks, or floods. Sometimes swift-flooding

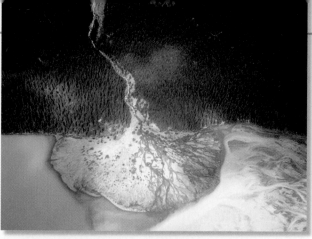

▲ This alluvial fan is at the mouth of a glacial stream in Canada.

rivers can pick up and deposit boulders in new places. The land where a river tends to flood is called a floodplain. Rivers deposit sand, silt, and clay in floodplains.

CAUSE AND EFFECT What happens when a river or stream slows down?

As a river flows over flat land, it tends to wind in curves called meanders. ▼

People Shape the Land

People can also shape the land. For example, when people build dams on rivers, they create large reservoirs and change the natural flow of the water in rivers. They also keep sediments from flowing down river.

The Shasta Dam is part of California's Central Valley flood control system. The dam controls flood water of the Sacramento River. It also supplies irrigation water to farmers in California's Central Valley. These irrigation waters have helped make agriculture in California's Central Valley very important. In fact, Central Valley grows a quarter of all the food Americans eat.

The reservoir formed by Shasta Dam is Shasta Lake. It provides recreational opportunities such as boating, fishing, and swimming.

CAUSE AND EFFECT What effect does the Shasta Dam have on the people of California?

The Shasta Dam provides irrigation water for California's Central Valley. ▼

Shasta Lake

Visual Summary

Moving water in the form of ocean waves deposits sand on beaches. Ocean waves can also cause beach erosion.

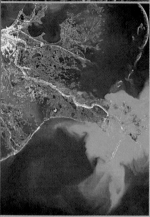

Deposition in river systems creates landforms such as deltas and alluvial fans.

One way people change Earth's surface is by building dams.

Reading Review

❶ MAIN IDEA How is Earth's surface changed through deposition?

❷ VOCABULARY Use the term *headland* in a sentence about the coastline.

❸ READING SKILL: What causes an alluvial fan to form?

Cause → Effect

❹ CRITICAL THINKING: Analyze How might dams change the effects of deposition?

❺ INQUIRY SKILL: Predict What would happen if sediment builds up in a lake created by a dam?

 TEST PRACTICE

A body of water that is partly enclosed by land but has a wide opening to the ocean is called a/an ____.

A. alluvial fan.

B. bay.

C. headland.

D. sediment.

 Technology
Visit **www.eduplace.com/cascp** to find out more about how water shapes the land.

The Powell Expedition

John Wesley Powell wants to learn more about how water changes Earth's surface. He leads an expedition down the Green and the Colorado rivers and through the unexplored Grand Canyon. Over 98 days and 1,600 km, Powell rides rapids, climbs cliffs, and endures rainstorms—not bad for a man who lost an arm in the Civil War!

Characters

Professor John Wesley Powell:
geology professor and Civil War veteran

George Bradley:
expedition member and adventurer

Jack Sumner:
expedition member, hunter, trader

Narrator 1

Narrator 2

Setting:
The Grand Canyon; August 1869

Narrator 1: It's early August, 1869. Powell and his men don't know it yet but they are nearing the end of their journey.

Narrator 2: Some of his men are a bit worse for wear, as we'll see.

Professor Powell: Okay, everybody. Time to get going. We've got a lot of climbing to do before dark. I want to get high enough to see the river from above. It'll help me map our route for tomorrow.

Jack: How high do you think the canyon is here?

Professor Powell: Maybe 4,000 feet.

George: It's just one rock layer after another. [*Sighs*] It never ends!

Jack: Grumbling already, George?

George: Okay, okay. I guess I'd rather be climbing than rowing.

Professor Powell: I've got a theory that those layers you're grumbling about describe millions of years of Earth's history.

George: Millions of years? What are you talking about?

Professor Powell: Earth is millions—if not billions—of years old. The oldest rock is at the bottom of the canyon. The youngest rock is at the top.

George: It's all just a rock. Rock is rock.

Professor Powell: Oh, but the river has carved this canyon to expose different kinds of rock. From here I see shale and sandstone. Farther up, it's limestone.

POWELL points his index finger a little higher each time he mentions a layer of rock.

George: You mean the river used to be way up here?

Professor Powell: Yes, I think so.

George: I can see a difference in the color in the rocks. [*George squints.*] Does that mean something?

Professor Powell: Different layers of rock contain different amounts and kinds of minerals. Iron is a mineral that makes rocks red.

Jack: Hey, Professor! I don't know what kind of rock this is but it's got the outline of a shell in it.

Professor Powell: What a find! That fossil helps prove another of my theories.

George: Another theory? You sure have a lot of theories! What is it this time?

Professor Powell: Well, that shell outline looks just like shells we find in the ocean. Perhaps this area used to be under the ocean. This is a great discovery! I'm going to draw a map of this area so I can find it on my next expedition.

George: Next expedition? You're planning to come back here? Count me out!

◄ A fossil from the Grand Canyon

▲ The Colorado River carved the layers of rock in the Grand Canyon over millions of years.

Jack: We'll be lucky if we survive this expedition!

Professor Powell: We'll make it. I have no doubt we'll finish.

Narrator 1: And he did finish. On August 29, the Powell Expedition completed its journey through the Grand Canyon.

Rock Layers of the Grand Canyon

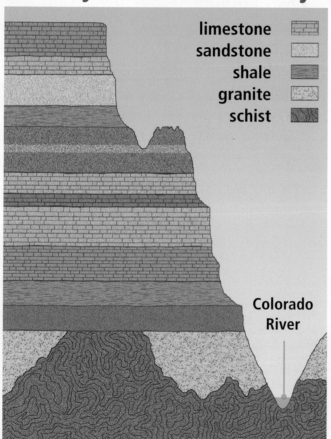

limestone
sandstone
shale
granite
schist

Colorado River

Rock layers wear away in different ways. Some rock wears away more quickly. Some layers have formed slopes and some have formed cliffs.

Narrator 2: After the trip, Powell became a national hero overnight. He conducted a second expedition in 1871.

Narrator 1: Later on, Powell was made the director of the United States Geological Survey. In that job he oversaw mapping and development of the West.

Narrator 2: He also became an expert on Native American culture as director of the Bureau of Ethnology at the Smithsonian Institute.

Narrator 1: And George, as far as we know, never signed up for another expedition again!

Sharing Ideas

1. **READING CHECK** What does John Wesley Powell think that the layers of rock tell about Earth?

2. **WRITE ABOUT IT** Describe how Powell might have felt as he was riding on the Colorado River and looking up at the canyon walls.

3. **TALK ABOUT IT** Powell considered himself a scientist in search of knowledge, rather than an explorer. Discuss how this might have affected the decisions he made during the expedition.

How Do Ice and Wind Shape the Land?

Building Background

Glaciers are rivers of ice. Wind and flowing water in the form of glaciers change and reshape Earth's surface. They remove sediment and other materials from one place and deposit them in other places.

PREPARE TO INVESTIGATE

Inquiry Skill

Infer When you infer, you interpret your observations.

Materials

- bar of soap
- paper cup
- pebbles
- sand
- water
- goggles
- clock or watch

A Model Glacier

Procedure

1 **Collaborate** Work with a partner to make a model of a glacier. A glacier is a large mass of slow-moving ice. Put about 2 cm of sand and small pebbles into a paper cup. Add water until the cup is three-fourths full. Place the cup in a freezer until the water is frozen. **Safety:** Wear goggles.

2 Remove the cup from the freezer. Tear away the bottom part of the paper cup from the ice block. Leave the top of the cup to use as a holder.

3 **Observe** Place your ice block with the sand side down on a bar of soap that is held in place by your partner. Grasp the cup and press down as you rub the ice block over the soap. Observe the effects of your model glacier on the soap.

4 **Record Data** Record your observations in your *Science Notebook*.

STEP 1

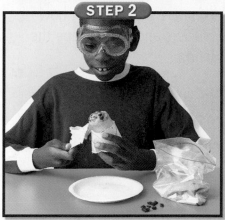
STEP 2

STEP 3

Conclusion

1. **Use Models** What happened to the soap when you rubbed the ice block over it? How might your ice block be like a glacier? How is it different?

2. **Infer** Think about what you observed. What can you infer about the effects that a glacier would have on Earth's surface?

Guided Inquiry

Experiment Design a model to show how wind shapes the land. Write a list of materials you will need and how the experiment will work. **Predict** the results of your experiment.

Ice and Wind Shape the Land

MAIN IDEA Glaciers, which are moving rivers of ice, and wind slowly wear down and build up the land.

READING SKILL

Compare and Contrast
Use the chart below to compare and contrast how glaciers and wind shape the land.

Compare	Contrast

Glaciers

A glacier (GLAY shur) is a large mass of slow-moving ice that flows down a slope. Glaciers formed long ago in cold regions of Earth. Snow piled up year after year. Over time, the weight of the snow added pressure below, and the snow turned to ice.

The weight of the ice in a glacier causes it to move slowly over the land. As it moves, a glacier is a great force of erosion. Huge amounts of soil and rock are pushed ahead of the glaciers. As glaciers melt, they leave behind a changed landscape.

A glacier is a massive river of ice that moves slowly over the land. It pushes rocks and soil ahead of it. ▼

▲ A moving glacier scooped the land. Rain filled in the scooped-out area to form June Lake, in California.

What Glaciers Leave Behind

Glaciers leave signs of their past presence on Earth's surface. They shape the land through erosion and deposition. As they move across the land, they carry away tons of material. When glaciers stop moving and begin to melt, they deposit boulders, rocks, and soil.

The long ridge formed by boulders, rocks, and soil carried and deposited by a glacier is called a **moraine**. A single large boulder moved by a glacier and deposited when the glacier melts is called an **erratic**. A bowl-shaped hollow left by a glacier is called a cirque (surk).

As a glacier moves, rocks embedded in the ice scratch across rocks lying under the ice. Large grooves left in the underlying rock can show the direction the glacier moved.

COMPARE AND CONTRAST Compare how glaciers shape the land through erosion with how they change the land through deposition.

Express Lab

Activity Card 23
Show Wind Erosion

Erratic This large boulder dropped by a glacier is called an erratic.

Cirque This bowl-shaped hollow is called a cirque.

Moraine This rock-strewn ridge is a moraine.

Grooves Rocks embedded in glaciers make grooves in the rocks.

Evidence of Glaciers

Yosemite Valley in California was formed in a variety of ways, including glaciers. Glaciers left erratics, cirques, and moraines in the valley. And glaciers formed nearly all the lakes in Yosemite Valley.

Glaciers have helped shape mountains and carve valleys. They have also left depressions that became lakes. In high mountains, glaciers have carved out bowl-shaped hollows called cirques. Glaciers have created some of the most beautiful landscapes in the world.

Wind Carves the Land

Although it is not as strong as water, wind can change the shape of the land. Have you ever been at the beach on a windy day? Then you probably know that wind can carry sediment.

Wind easily picks up and carries beach and desert sand. The stronger the wind, the more sand the wind can carry away. Wind is even more likely to cause erosion during a dry period. Dry sand is lighter and easier for the wind to carry.

Lack of rain may kill most of the plants in an area. This makes the soil in the area more subject to wind erosion. Windbreaks such as fences, grass, shrubs, and trees can prevent or reduce wind erosion.

Sediments that the wind carries also weather Earth's surface. When windblown grains of sand and sediment are pushed along the ground, they act as sandblasters, which chip, cut, and polish.

Wind-carried sediments can help shape rock formations and their surfaces. These wind-shaped formations include buttes and sandstone towers.

COMPARE AND CONTRAST How are a moraine and erratic alike and different?

▲ Devils Tower in Wyoming was sculpted by the wind.

This rock formation at the Grand Canyon was shaped by wind erosion. ▶

Wind Builds Up the Land

Wind picks up sediment from one place and deposits it in another place. The place where the sediment is deposited is then built up.

Sand dunes form along seacoasts, in dry sandy plains, and in deserts. A **sand dune** is a hill or pile of sand that was formed by the wind.

Sand dunes vary in size. Small beach dunes may be 1 m to 2 m (3 to 7 ft) high. In the Sand Dunes National Park in Colorado, the sand

Dorothea Lange, a famous California photographer, took this and other photographs of the Dust Bowl. ▼

dunes cover an area that is over 80 sq. km (30 sq. mi.). Some of these dunes are as high as 230 m (754 ft).

Where winds are strong and steady, dunes may move as much as 30 m (100 ft) in a year. Dunes can bury towns, cities, and forests.

There are a number of dunes along the coast of California. The largest are the Monterey Bay dunes. California's coastal dunes formed over thousands of years.

In the 1930s, the southern plains of the United States were called the Dust Bowl. Poor farming practices and years of no rain had destroyed the ground cover. Without these plants, the soil was not held in place. Wind-blown soil covered everything.

COMPARE AND CONTRAST **Compare coastal and desert sand dunes.**

What causes sand dunes to form? ▼

Visual Summary

Causes	Effects

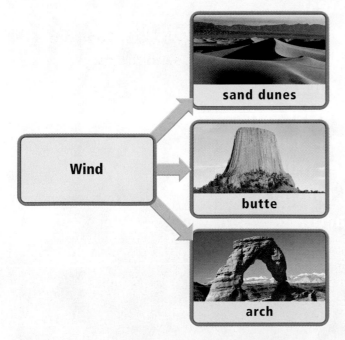

Glaciers → valley

Glaciers → lake

Glaciers → erratic

Wind → sand dunes

Wind → butte

Wind → arch

Reading Review

1 MAIN IDEA How do ice and wind shape the land?

2 VOCABULARY How is a moraine different from an erratic?

3 READING SKILL How do sediments moved by wind compare with materials moved by glaciers?

Compare	Contrast

4 CRITICAL THINKING: Apply Suppose you interview a city planner who is concerned that the city is being threatened by a sand dune. What questions would you ask in order to learn as much as possible about the sand dune?

5 INQUIRY SKILL: Infer How might a moving sand dune be harmful to animals?

✔ **TEST PRACTICE**
Where do sand dunes form?

A. on mountain tops

B. in rivers

C. in deserts

D. on glaciers

Technology
Visit **www.eduplace.com/cascp** to find out more about how ice and wind shape the land.

Galloping Glacier

What would you call this river of ice flowing down the valley? Awesome? Enormous? Whatever you call it, call it a glacier. Most glaciers move just a few inches or feet a year. But this one gallops! Meet Hubbard Glacier, one of the fastest moving glaciers in the world. It moves 10 to 100 times faster than most glaciers do.

As a glacier moves, its thick, heavy ice grinds and carves the land. A large glacier can pick up and transport billions of tons of rock and soil and deposit it dozens of miles from its origin. Whether they gallop or crawl, glaciers are a powerful force of erosion on Earth.

Typical glaciers move a few inches to a few feet a year. The Hubbard Glacier can move 30 meters, or 100 feet, in a single day!

10 20 30 40 50 40 30 20 10

Writing Journal

In your writing journal, predict some of the ways the Hubbard Glacier will change the land that is beneath it.

257

Math Data Analysis

You know that if the wind is steady, a sand dune can move. In fact, sand dunes can move from 6 meters to 30 meters a year. This line graph shows the yearly movement of one sand dune over an eight-year period.

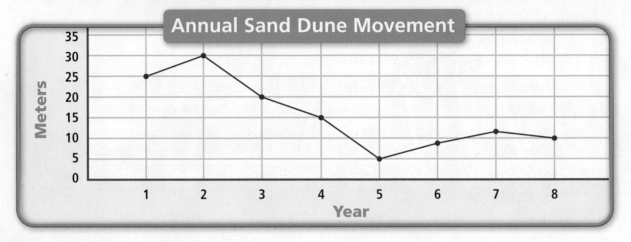

Annual Sand Dune Movement

Meters / Year

1. In which year did the sand dune move the most? How much did it move?
2. In which year did the sand dune move the least? How much did it move?
3. How much did the sand dune move in 8 years?

Writing Informative

Research a description of weathering and erosion caused by a California river. Find out how the river has changed the land.

Write a paragraph to summarize how this river, through weathering and erosion, has changed Earth's surface. Include a main idea and important details that support your main idea.

Dimitri Deheyn

For hundreds of years, sediment from Venice, Italy, has washed into the sea. Some of the sediment is toxic, meaning it can harm living things.

How is sediment changing the waters around Venice? Dr. Dimitri Deheyn is leading a team that is studying these questions. He works for the Scripps Oceanography Institute of San Diego.

Deheyn and his team are digging up layers of sediment from the sea floor. They also are studying the levels of pollution in the water, and how the pollution is affecting living things. Their goal is to recommend a plan for protecting Venice and its ocean environment.

Vocabulary

Complete each sentence with a term from the list.

1. A body of water that is partly enclosed by land and has a wide opening to the ocean is a/an _____.

2. A hill of sand that was formed by the wind is a/an _____.

3. Movement of rock material from one place to another is _____.

4. A point of land, usually high, that extends out into the water is a/an _____.

5. A large mass of slow-moving ice is called a/an _____.

6. The wearing away of rock into smaller bits is called _____.

7. The largest river and all the waterways that drain into it is called a/an _____.

8. A large mass of sediment deposited at the mouth of a river is called a/an _____.

9. A long ridge formed by boulders, rocks, and soil carried and deposited by a glacier is called a/an _____.

10. A single large boulder moved by a glacier and deposited when the glacier melts is a/an _____.

bay p. 239
delta p. 240
deposition p. 238
erosion p. 234
erratic p. 251
glacier p. 234
headland p. 239
moraine p. 251
river system p. 240
sand dune p. 254
weathering p. 232

Test Practice

Write the letter of the best answer choice.

11. What is the dropping of sediment moved by water, wind, and ice?

    A. deposition   **C.** moraine
    B. weathering   **D.** erratic

12. What area of California was partly formed by glaciers?

    A. Central Valley   **C.** Yosemite Valley
    B. Monterey Bay dunes   **D.** Death Valley

13. What causes more erosion than any other form of weathering?

    A. chemicals   **C.** wind
    B. plants   **D.** water

14. Which of the following cause slow changes to Earth's surface?

    A. volcanoes   **C.** earthquakes
    B. rivers   **D.** tsunamis

15. **Communicate** How do tree roots cause weathering?

16. What would you predict may happen to the coastline if a glacier melted next to it? Explain.

Map the Concept

Complete the concept maps using the following terms.

river system   sand dune
moraine   wind
glacier   delta

Cause   Effect

Critical Thinking

17. **Analyze** What might be some of the long-term effects of building many dams along a river system?

18. **Synthesize** What might you expect in some of the ice of a glacier?

19. **Analyze** What is the relationship between erosion, weathering, and deposition and the formation of sand dunes?

20. **Evaluate** Authorities are planning to build a road near the Monterey Bay sand dunes. Scientists know that sand dunes can move as much as 30 m a year. Do you think authorities should go ahead with their plans? Why or why not?

Performance Assessment

Make a poster that shows the effects of glaciers. Draw and label examples of different effects. Include a paragraph that explains what happens before, during, and after a glacier forms and melts.

Writing Journal

Review your answers to the Lesson Preview questions on page 227. Based on what you have learned, change your answers as necessary.

Write the letter of the best answer choice.

1. Which layer of Earth is involved in the weathering of rock to form sediment?

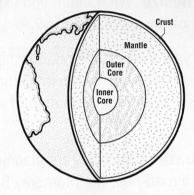

   A. crust
   B. mantle
   C. inner core
   D. outer core

2. What property would you NOT use when trying to identify a mineral?
   A. hardness
   B. color
   C. streak
   D. grain

3. Deep canyons can be formed over thousands of years by _____.
   A. deposition.
   B. erosion.
   C. sedimentation.
   D. volcanoes.

4. Metamorphic rock forms when any rock is subject to _____.
   A. cooling.
   B. cementing.
   C. weathering.
   D. heat and pressure.

5. Which shows ash, gas, and lava flowing from an opening in Earth's crust?

   A.

   B.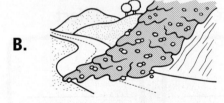

   C.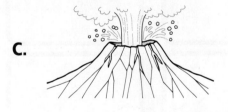

   D.

6. A mudslide is least likely to occur _____.
   A. on a steep hillside.
   B. during hot, dry weather.
   C. early in the spring.
   D. after a volcanic eruption.

7. Which does NOT cause a rapid change to Earth's surface?

A.

B.

C.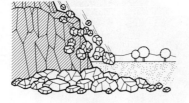

D.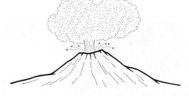

8. Ocean waves change beaches through

_____.

  A. erosion and deposition.
  B. chemical weathering.
  C. volcanic eruptions.
  D. movement of Earth's crust.

Answer the following in complete sentences.

9. How are the processes of weathering, erosion, and deposition related?

10. Describe the rock cycle and the forces that change rocks in each stage of the cycle.

You Can...

Discover More

Why do rocks have different colors? Rocks are made of one or more minerals. The color of a mineral depends on its chemical makeup. Azurite is a deep blue mineral. Malachite is a green mineral.

Some minerals contain impurities that give different samples different colors. For example, the mineral beryl is blue when it contains bits of iron. It is pink when it contains bits of manganese, and green when it contains bits of chromium. Because rocks are made up of different minerals, rocks can have different colors.

black obsidian

red sandstone

green malachite

pink marble

 Go to **www.eduplace.com/cascp** to learn more about the colors of rocks.

Electricity
and
Magnetism

California Connection

Visit www.eduplace.com/cascp to find out how electricity and magnetism help California meet its energy needs.

San Francisco

The electrical lighting on the Golden Gate Bridge was designed to make the bridge appear as if it was floating on air.

Coit Tower is used for displaying pictures, paintings, and exhibits of San Francisco's past.

Lombard Street has eight sharp turns, making it the most crooked street in the United States.

Electricity and Magnetism

Lightning is a large electric discharge.

California **Big Idea!**

Electricity and magnetism are related effects that have many useful applications in everyday life.

Chapter 8

Electricity

Electric lights of San Diego

Lesson Preview

LESSON 1

Clothes stick together when you pull them out of the dryer. A comb makes your hair stand up. What causes these things to happen?

LESSON 2

You flip a switch, and a light comes on. Turn off the switch, and the light goes off. How does electric current travel?

LESSON 3

Look around your classroom. Picture the rooms in your home. How is electricity used in these places?

Writing Journal

In your Writing Journal, show what you know by writing or drawing answers to each question.

Vocabulary Preview

Vocabulary

Glossary

Vocabulary Skill

Related Words

electric charges

electric circuit

electric current

You can use the relationships between similar terms to help you understand new terms. For example, an *electric circuit* carries an *electric current*. An electric current is made up of moving *electric charges*. If you know what an electric charge is, it can help you figure out what an electric circuit is.

series circuit

A circuit in which electric current passes along a single pathway.

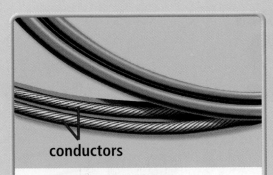

conductors

conductor

A material through which negatively charged particles move easily.

parallel circuit

A circuit in which electric current passes along more than one pathway.

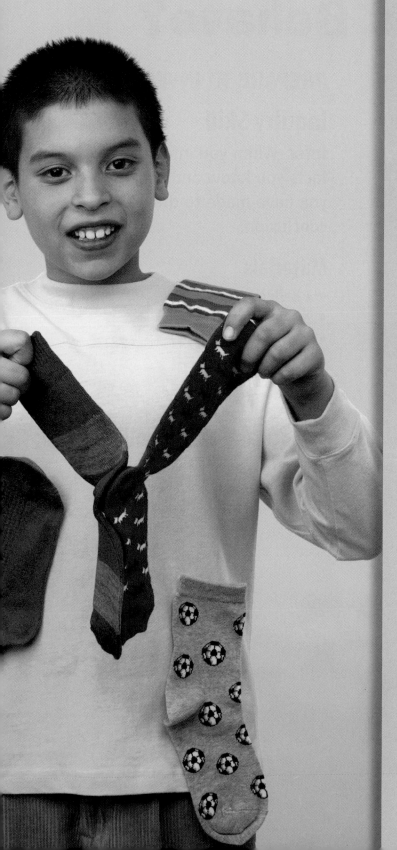

static electricity
An electric charge that builds up on a material.

Start with Your Standards

Standard Set 1. Physical Sciences

1.a. *Students know* how to design and build simple series and parallel circuits by using components such as wires, batteries, and bulbs.

1.e. *Students know* electrically charged objects attract or repel each other.

1.g. *Students know* electrical energy can be converted to heat, light, and motion.

Standard Set 6. Investigation and Experimentation covered in this chapter: 6.a., 6.c., 6.f.

How Do Charges Behave?

Building Background

What's making this girl's hair stand on end? There are many electric charges in her hair. Electric charges can attract or repel each other. The charges in the strands of hair are pushing each other away. Other objects can also have electric charges.

PREPARE TO INVESTIGATE

Inquiry Skill

Infer When you infer, you use facts you know and observations you have made to draw a conclusion.

Materials

- 2 balloons
- 2 pieces of string
- metric ruler
- wool
- plastic wrap

Science and Math Toolbox

For step 1, review **Making a Chart to Organize Data** on page H10.

Build a Charge

Procedure

1. **Collaborate** Work with a partner. Blow up two balloons. Knot the neck of each balloon and tie with a string. In your *Science Notebook*, make a chart like the one shown.

2. **Observe** Hold one string. Have your partner hold the other string so the two balloons hang about 10 cm apart. Observe and record any movement they make.

3. **Record Data** Rub each balloon with a wool cloth. Again hold the balloons so that they hang about 10 cm apart. Observe and record any movements they make.

4. **Record Data** Let the balloons touch. Then let them hang next to each other. Record your observations.

5. **Experiment** Repeat steps 3 and 4, but this time rub one balloon with plastic wrap and one with the wool cloth.

Conclusion

1. **Infer** Rubbing a balloon with wool or plastic wrap gives the balloon an electric charge. Based on your data, infer whether there is more than one kind of electric charge. How do your observations support your inference?

2. **Infer** Based on your data, did the charges attract, repel, or not interact at all? What can you conclude about like charges?

STEP 1

Balloon Setup	Results
No treatment	
Each balloon rubbed with wool	
Balloons touch, then hang side by side.	
One balloon rubbed with wool, the other with plastic wrap	

STEP 2

STEP 3

Guided Inquiry

Experiment Rub one balloon with wool. Rub another balloon with other materials. **Infer** which materials produce the same kind of charge that wool produces.

VOCABULARY

electric charges   p. 272
static electricity   p. 274

READING SKILL

Main Idea and Details
As you read, use charts like the one shown below to record the main idea and details from each section of the lesson.

How Charges Behave

MAIN IDEA All objects are made up of tiny particles. Some of those tiny particles carry positive or negative electric charges. An object can be neutral or have a total negative or positive charge.

Electric Charges

Does your hair ever stand on end after you comb it? All objects, including hair and combs, are made up of tiny particles called atoms. Atoms are made up of even tinier particles. Many of these very tiny particles carry units of electricity called **electric charges**. These charges can make your hair stand on end.

There are two kinds of electric charges, positive and negative. Charges that are the same are called like charges. Charges that are different are called unlike charges. Most objects are electrically neutral. Objects that are electrically neutral have an equal number of positive and negative charges.

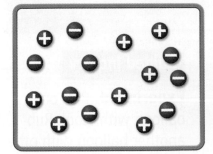

Electrically Neutral
An object that has the same number of positive and negative charges

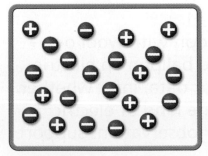

Negatively Charged
An object that has more negative than positive charges

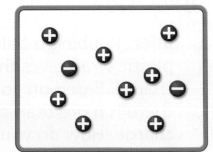

Positively Charged
An object that has more positive than negative charges

How Charges Behave

Electric charges can affect each other, even without touching. For instance, like charges repel, or push away from, each other. Unlike charges attract, or pull toward, each other. Objects with the same charge will push away from each other. Objects with opposite charges will pull toward each other.

Negative charges can move more easily from one material to another than can positive charges. Remember that negative charges are attracted to positive charges. So, negative charges are able to move from one material or object to a material or object that has an overall positive charge.

On their own, negative charges in one electrically neutral object do not usually move toward another object that is electrically neutral. However, negative charges can be made to move. Rubbing can move negative charges from one neutral object to another. For example, when you rub a balloon with a piece of wool cloth, it causes negative charges to move from the cloth to the balloon.

MAIN IDEA What are the two types of electric charges?

Rubbing a balloon with a wool cloth causes negative charges to move from the cloth to the balloon. ▶

Like Charges Repel
When brought close together, objects with like charges repel each other.

Unlike Charges Attract
When brought close together, objects with unlike charges attract each other.

Express Lab

Activity Card 24
See the Effect of Static Electricity

Buildup and Discharge

Sometimes a charge builds up on an object or a material. This built-up electric charge is called **static electricity** (STAT ihk ih lehk-TRIHS ih tee).

When your hair stands on end and moves toward a plastic comb, that is static electricity. Combing your hair rubs the teeth of the comb against strands of your hair. As a result, negatively charged particles move from your hair onto the comb. This gives the comb an overall negative charge.

Once your hair loses negatively charged particles, it has an overall positive charge. Because the hair and the comb have opposite charges, they attract each other. At the same time, each strand of hair has a positive charge. The strands repel each other. They move apart and seem to stand up.

You sometimes get a shock when you touch a metal doorknob. The shock is due to electric discharge. A negative charge has built up on the boy in the picture. When the boy touches the doorknob, the charge quickly jumps from him to the doorknob. This release of the built-up negative charge is called an electric discharge, or spark.

 **MAIN IDEA** What is static electricity?

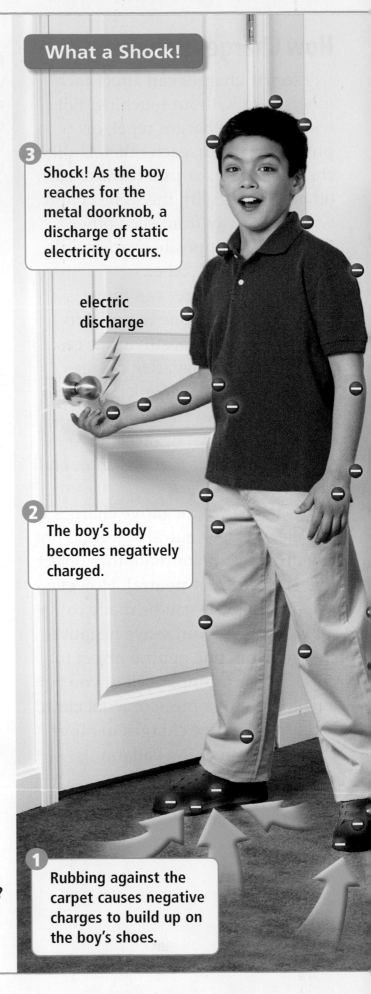

What a Shock!

3 Shock! As the boy reaches for the metal doorknob, a discharge of static electricity occurs.

electric discharge

2 The boy's body becomes negatively charged.

1 Rubbing against the carpet causes negative charges to build up on the boy's shoes.

Visual Summary

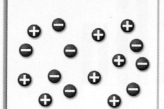

Atoms are made up of tiny particles, many of which carry electric charges.

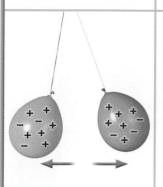

Objects with like charges repel each other. Objects with unlike charges attract each other.

Static electricity can discharge when a negatively charged object comes near another object.

Technology
Visit **www.eduplace.com/cascp** to find out more about electric charges.

Reading Review

1 MAIN IDEA When does an object have an overall positive charge?

2 VOCABULARY Write a short paragraph using the terms *static electricity* and *electric charge*.

3 READING SKILL What two details support the main idea that atoms are made of particles, many of which carry electric charges?

4 CRITICAL THINKING: Apply Suppose you pull a shirt from the dryer, and it has a sock stuck to it. Explain why this happens.

5 INQUIRY SKILL: Infer Object *A* has a positive electric charge. Object *A* and Object *B* attract each other. What can you infer about the overall electric charge of Object *B*?

TEST PRACTICE
A built-up electric charge is _____.

A. electrically neutral.

B. static electricity.

C. positively charged.

D. electric discharge.

Benjamin Franklin
Flies a Kite!

What is lightning? The setting is a cluttered laboratory on a gloomy, rainy day in Philadelphia. It's June 1752. Forty-six-year-old Benjamin Franklin is hard at work on a new theory. He believes that lightning is electrical and that electricity can be collected. And he's come up with a very creative way to test his idea.

Characters

Benjamin Franklin:
scientist, printer, writer

Deborah Reed Rogers:
Benjamin Franklin's wife

William:
Benjamin Franklin's
21-year-old son

Narrator 1

Narrator 2

Benjamin: Well done is better than well said, I always say. [*He ties a string to a homemade kite.*] This experiment may be a little bit—er—unusual, but I can't worry about what others think!

Enter DEBORAH

Deborah: What are you mumbling about, Benjamin?

Benjamin: Isn't it a lovely day to fly a kite, my dear?

Deborah: Are you teasing, Benjamin? It's about to rain!

Benjamin: That's what makes it a perfectly marvelous day!

Deborah: I know everyone thinks you're a genius, what with all those science experiments and the brilliant articles and so forth. But sometimes, Benjamin, I do wonder about you. . . . Well, I'll leave you to your ever-interesting thoughts. I'm off to the market before the rain starts.

Benjamin: Good-bye, my dear.

Exit DEBORAH

Enter WILLIAM, in a rush, wearing his rain jacket.

William: Father, what on Earth are you doing with that kite?

Benjamin: I'm going to fly it. Would you like to come along?

William: But—it's starting to rain!

Benjamin: Exactly! I'm going to use the kite and the rain clouds to prove that lightning is electrical and that electricity can be collected.

William: What? Electrical, you say? But Father . . .

Benjamin: I'll explain when we get to the field. We can stand in that old shed and stay out of the rain.

BENJAMIN, with WILLIAM following, leaves the laboratory and walks quickly toward a nearby field. They arrive at the shed.

Benjamin: William, help me tie this ribbon and this key to the end of the kite string.

William: What for? And what's this pointed wire at the top of the kite?

Benjamin: The wire at the top of the kite will gather electricity from a passing cloud. The wet string will act as a conductor and guide the electricity down to the metal key, which will collect the charge of electricity.

William: I'm baffled. Conductor? Charge?

Benjamin: My new electrical terms! Catchy, eh? Everything will make sense to you soon enough.

William: But Father, aren't you worried the electricity will hurt you? Remember that time you were knocked unconscious?

Benjamin: I do remember, William. That's why I'm going to make sure I stay as dry as possible. Here goes! Fly kite, fly!

How Lightning Forms

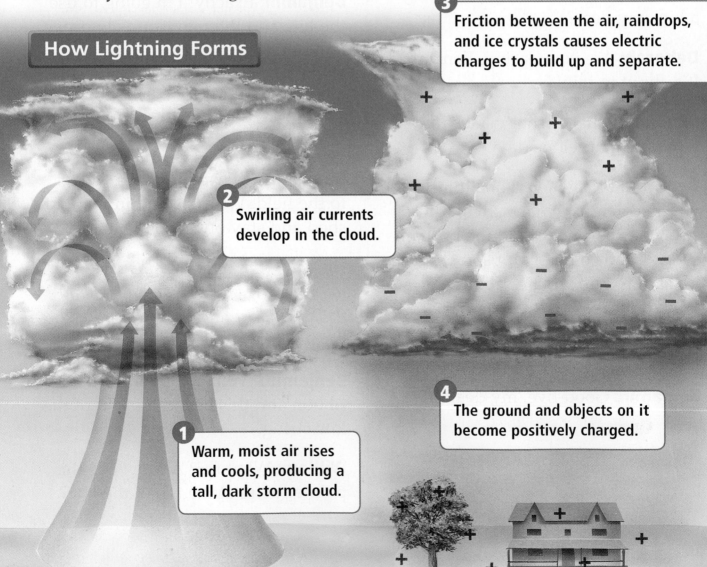

3 Friction between the air, raindrops, and ice crystals causes electric charges to build up and separate.

2 Swirling air currents develop in the cloud.

4 The ground and objects on it become positively charged.

1 Warm, moist air rises and cools, producing a tall, dark storm cloud.

Two hours later, WILLIAM is dozing on the ground while BENJAMIN holds his kite string and scans the sky.

William [*waking up*]: You've been holding that kite string for ages. Nothing's happening! Let's go home.

Benjamin: Wait! See how those loose threads of silk kite string are standing up and away from each other? Watch what happens when I touch the key with my knuckle.

5 The difference in charge between the cloud and the ground continues to grow.

6 Finally lightning, a powerful discharge, occurs.

Narrator 1: When the silk threads on the kite string stood away from each other, they showed that objects with like charges repel each other. The threads became charged and repel each other.

William: A spark! I saw a spark!

Benjamin: What you saw, my son, was electric fire!

Narrator 1: That day, Benjamin Franklin proved that lightning was indeed electric.

Narrator 2: He did it in a way that lots of people considered, well, unsafe. Scientists always need to find new ways to test their ideas.

Narrator 1: In other words, scientists need to come up with new approaches and even new language! Franklin invented new electrical words such as *charge* and *conductor*.

Sharing Ideas

1. **READING CHECK** What idea was Ben Franklin trying to test with his kite experiment?

2. **WRITE ABOUT IT** What clues led Franklin to believe his experiment was successful?

3. **TALK ABOUT IT** Discuss why Franklin's experiment should never be repeated.

What Is Electric Current?

Building Background

You flip a switch and the lights come on. You press a button and your computer screen comes to life. All of these activities use electric current and electric circuits. By understanding how different kinds of electric circuits work, people can safely produce and use electricity.

PREPARE TO INVESTIGATE

Inquiry Skill

Record Data When you keep records that are accurate, they can be understood at a later time.

Materials

- 1.3-volt battery
- battery holder
- electrical tape
- 2 flashlight bulbs
- 4 insulated wires (20-cm lengths, stripped on ends)

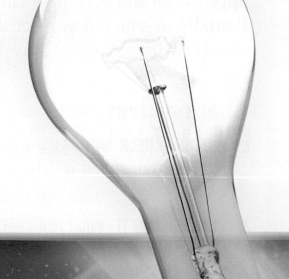

Build Circuits

Procedure

1 **Collaborate** Work with a partner. Read the rules in steps 2, 3, and 4. Then build each circuit and see if it lights the bulb or bulbs.

2 **Experiment** Simple Circuit: Current flows from one side of a battery, through a wire, through a light bulb, and through a second wire to the other side of the battery.

3 **Experiment** Series Circuit: Current flows from a battery, through a wire, through a light bulb, through a second wire, through a second light bulb, and through a third wire to the other side of the battery.

4 **Experiment** Parallel Circuit: Current flows from one side of a battery, through a wire to a light bulb, to a second wire, to another light bulb, to a third wire back to the first light bulb, to a fourth wire, to the other side of the battery.

5 **Record Data** In your *Science Notebook*, draw the circuits you made for steps 2, 3, and 4.

STEP 2

STEP 3

STEP 4

Conclusion

1. **Predict** What do you predict happens to the other bulb when one bulb in a series circuit burns out?

2. **Predict** What do you predict happens to the other bulb when one bulb in a parallel circuit burns out?

Guided Inquiry

Experiment Build a series circuit for three bulbs, then build a parallel circuit for three bulbs. **Compare** how brightly the bulbs glow in each circuit.

Electric Current

READING SKILL

Compare and Contrast
Use the chart below to compare and contrast different types of circuits.

Compare	Contrast

MAIN IDEA An electric circuit is a pathway that electric charges follow. Electric circuits can be used to change electrical energy into other forms of energy.

How Charges Move

You wake up to a beeping alarm clock and flip on a light switch. Later you toast a piece of bread. You started your day by converting, or changing, the energy of moving charged particles to sound, light, and heat.

You have learned about static electricity. The charges that make up static electricity either stay in place or jump in a sudden discharge. This energy is not very useful.

For the energy of moving charged particles to be useful, it must be controlled. Suppose charged particles continuously flow through a material, instead of building up on it. The energy of these particles is controlled and used. This continuous flow of electric charges is called an **electric current**.

How a Toaster Works

1 When the toaster is turned on, electric charges flow from the outlet, through one copper wire, to heating coils in the toaster.

Conductors and Insulators

Electric current easily passes through metals such as copper, aluminum, gold, and silver. These metals are good conductors. A **conductor** (kuhn DUHK tuhr) is a material through which negatively charged particles flow easily.

Electric charges also flow easily through tap water. Tap water contains particles that make it a good conductor. Because the cells of all living things contain water, living things are conductors, too.

A material that electric charges do not flow through easily is called an **insulator** (IHN suh lay tuhr).

Some examples of insulators are plastic, rubber, glass, air, wood, and pure water.

Conductors and insulators are used to control and direct the flow of electric charges. An appliance power cord is usually made of metal wires surrounded by a rubber or plastic covering. Each metal wire is a conductor that carries electric current between the electrical outlet and the appliance. The outer covering is an insulator. It prevents the current from escaping.

COMPARE AND CONTRAST How is electric current different from static electricity?

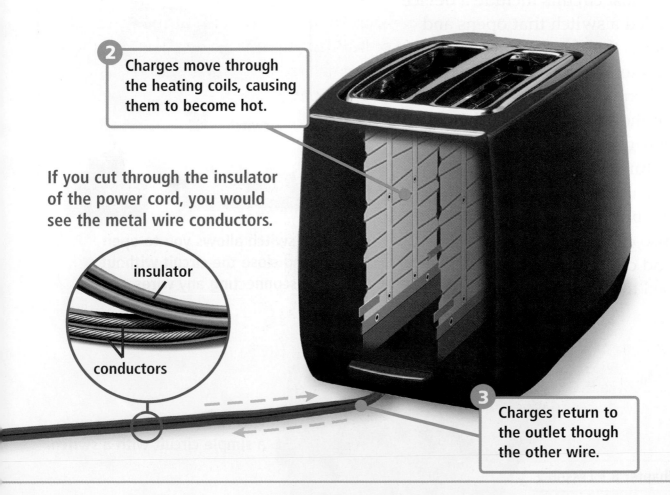

2 Charges move through the heating coils, causing them to become hot.

If you cut through the insulator of the power cord, you would see the metal wire conductors.

insulator

conductors

3 Charges return to the outlet though the other wire.

Circuits and Switches

The pathway that electric current follows is called an **electric circuit** (SUR kiht). A circuit is a closed, or complete, path that does not have any gaps or openings.

You can use wire, a power source, and a light bulb to make a simple electric circuit. You create a closed circuit by connecting these items without gaps. When charges flow through the closed circuit, the light bulb will light.

If there is a gap in the circuit, you have an open or incomplete circuit. When a circuit is open, electric charges cannot flow and the bulb will not light.

Most circuits include a device called a switch that opens and closes the circuit. A switch allows you to turn a light bulb on and off. When you flip the switch to turn on the bulb, you close the circuit. When you flip the switch to turn off the bulb, you open the circuit. Pushing the button of a doorbell also closes a circuit and causes the bell to ring.

Simple Circuit

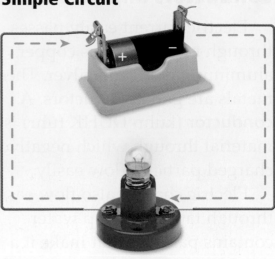

When the parts of the circuit are connected with no gaps, the bulb will light.

Simple Circuit with a Switch

switch

A switch allows you to open and close the circuit without disconnecting any wires.

This flashlight is an example of a simple circuit with a switch.

Series Circuit

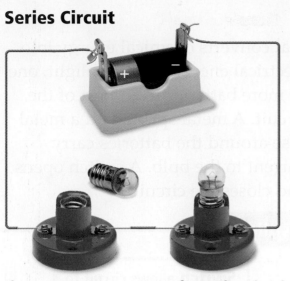

If you remove one part from the circuit, you create a gap. Current no longer moves through any of the parts.

Parallel Circuit

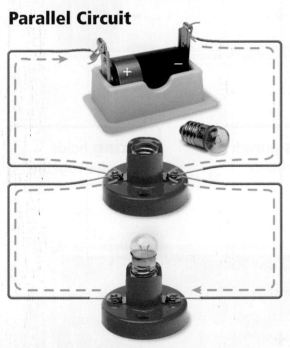

If you remove one part from the circuit, current can still move through the other parts.

Two Types of Circuits

Every working circuit has at least three parts:

- a power source, such as a battery,
- a conductor, usually wire,
- an object that uses electric current, such as a light bulb.

When a circuit has just these three parts, there is only one pathway for the current to follow. However, a circuit can have more parts. It can have a switch, more than one battery, and more than one object using the current.

There are two ways to arrange the pathways of a circuit with many parts. These ways are a series circuit and a parallel circuit.

In a **series circuit**, the parts are connected so that electric current passes through each part, one after another, along a single pathway. In a **parallel circuit**, the parts are connected so that current passes along more than one pathway.

COMPARE AND CONTRAST What is the difference between a series circuit and a parallel circuit?

Express Lab

Activity Card 25
Light a Bulb

Circuits Without Wires

Circuits can use any conductor to carry a current. Current will flow as long as the conductors are connected to the source of electricity in a continuous loop.

One source of electrical energy is a battery. A **battery** is a device that converts chemical energy into electrical energy. In a flashlight, one or more batteries form part of the circuit. A metal spring and a metal case around the batteries carry current to the bulb. A switch opens and closes the circuit.

Circuit in a Flashlight

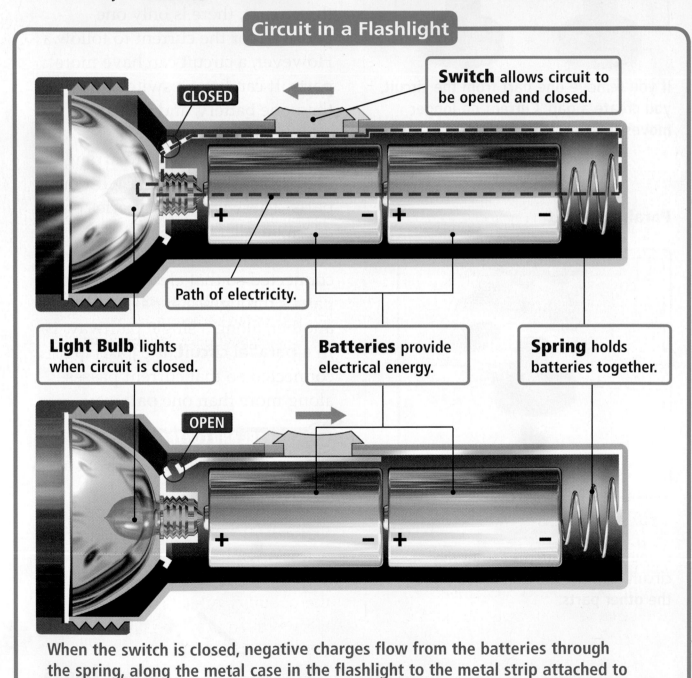

CLOSED

Switch allows circuit to be opened and closed.

Path of electricity.

Light Bulb lights when circuit is closed.

Batteries provide electrical energy.

Spring holds batteries together.

OPEN

When the switch is closed, negative charges flow from the batteries through the spring, along the metal case in the flashlight to the metal strip attached to the switch, to the bulb holder, through the light bulb, and back to the batteries.

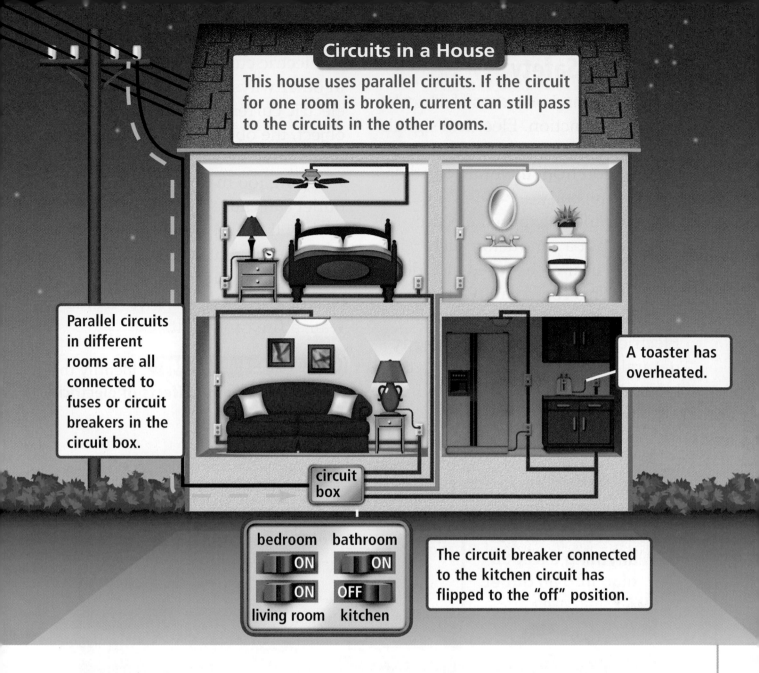

Circuits in a House

This house uses parallel circuits. If the circuit for one room is broken, current can still pass to the circuits in the other rooms.

Parallel circuits in different rooms are all connected to fuses or circuit breakers in the circuit box.

A toaster has overheated.

circuit box

bedroom	bathroom
ON	ON
ON	OFF
living room	kitchen

The circuit breaker connected to the kitchen circuit has flipped to the "off" position.

Circuits in the Home

The electric wiring in a house is connected in parallel circuits. Different circuits control current in different parts of a house. Each circuit is connected to a central circuit box. The box connects all the circuits to an outside source of electric current.

If too much current passes through a circuit, the wires can overheat. Home circuits have a safety device, such as a fuse or a circuit breaker. A fuse contains a metal strip. The strip melts when it overheats, opening the circuit.

A circuit breaker is a switch that opens, or breaks, a circuit when the circuit overheats. This stops the electric current from flowing to that circuit in the home.

 **COMPARE AND CONTRAST** How are a fuse and a circuit alike?

Electrical Safety

The human body uses electrical energy to function. Electrical signals keep the heart beating. They carry information from the brain to other parts of the body.

Never touch exposed electric wires or put a conductor, such as metal, near an exposed electric current. This could cause electric current to pass through your body. Electric current can upset the body's natural electricity. It can also cause burns and injuries.

Electric current can be dangerous in other ways. When too much electric current flows through an object, the object can heat up. It may become hot enough to catch fire. Plugging too many things into one outlet can cause too much current to flow through the outlet. The heat from the current can damage the insulation covering the wires. When electric current heats wires inside a wall, a fire can result.

COMPARE AND CONTRAST **Identify the helpful and harmful effects of electricity.**

Electrical Safety

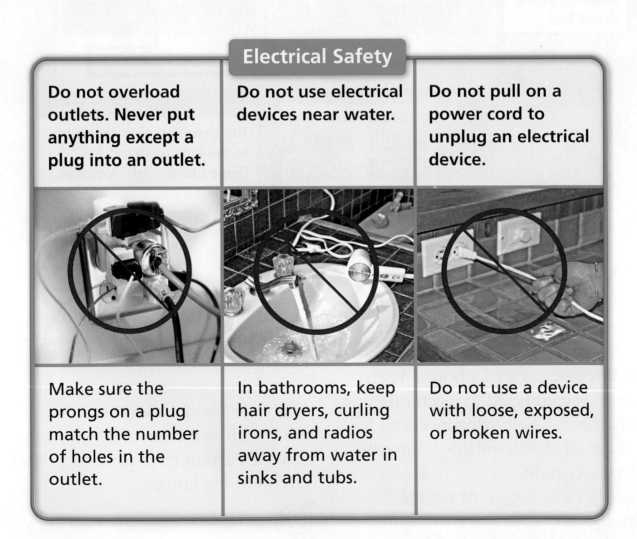

Do not overload outlets. Never put anything except a plug into an outlet.	Do not use electrical devices near water.	Do not pull on a power cord to unplug an electrical device.
Make sure the prongs on a plug match the number of holes in the outlet.	In bathrooms, keep hair dryers, curling irons, and radios away from water in sinks and tubs.	Do not use a device with loose, exposed, or broken wires.

Visual Summary

The flow of electric charges is called electric current. Electric current can be converted to heat, light, and other forms of energy.

A loop that an electric current can follow is called an electric circuit. Electric circuits can be series circuits or parallel circuits.

Electric current can be dangerous. Always follow electric safety rules.

Reading Review

❶ MAIN IDEA How does a switch affect a circuit?

❷ VOCABULARY What is a conductor?

❸ READING SKILL Why is the wiring in a house connected in parallel circuits, not series circuits?

Compare	Contrast

❹ CRITICAL THINKING:
Analyze You flip a switch on a simple circuit to "on." The bulb on the circuit does not light. Is the circuit complete? Explain.

❺ INQUIRY SKILL: Record Data You need to gather data about five devices that convert electrical energy into heat. What data could you collect? How would you organize the data so it would be useful to others?

✓ TEST PRACTICE

The motor that turns a ceiling fan converts electrical energy to _____.

A. motion.

B. heat.

C. light.

D. current.

Technology
Visit **www.eduplace.com/cascp** to learn more about electric current.

289

How Is Electricity Used?

Building Background

After school, you go to your room and turn on the light. You practice on your keyboard. Then you use a computer while you listen to the radio. Electrical energy has allowed you to do all these things. The electrical energy has been converted to different forms, such as light and sound.

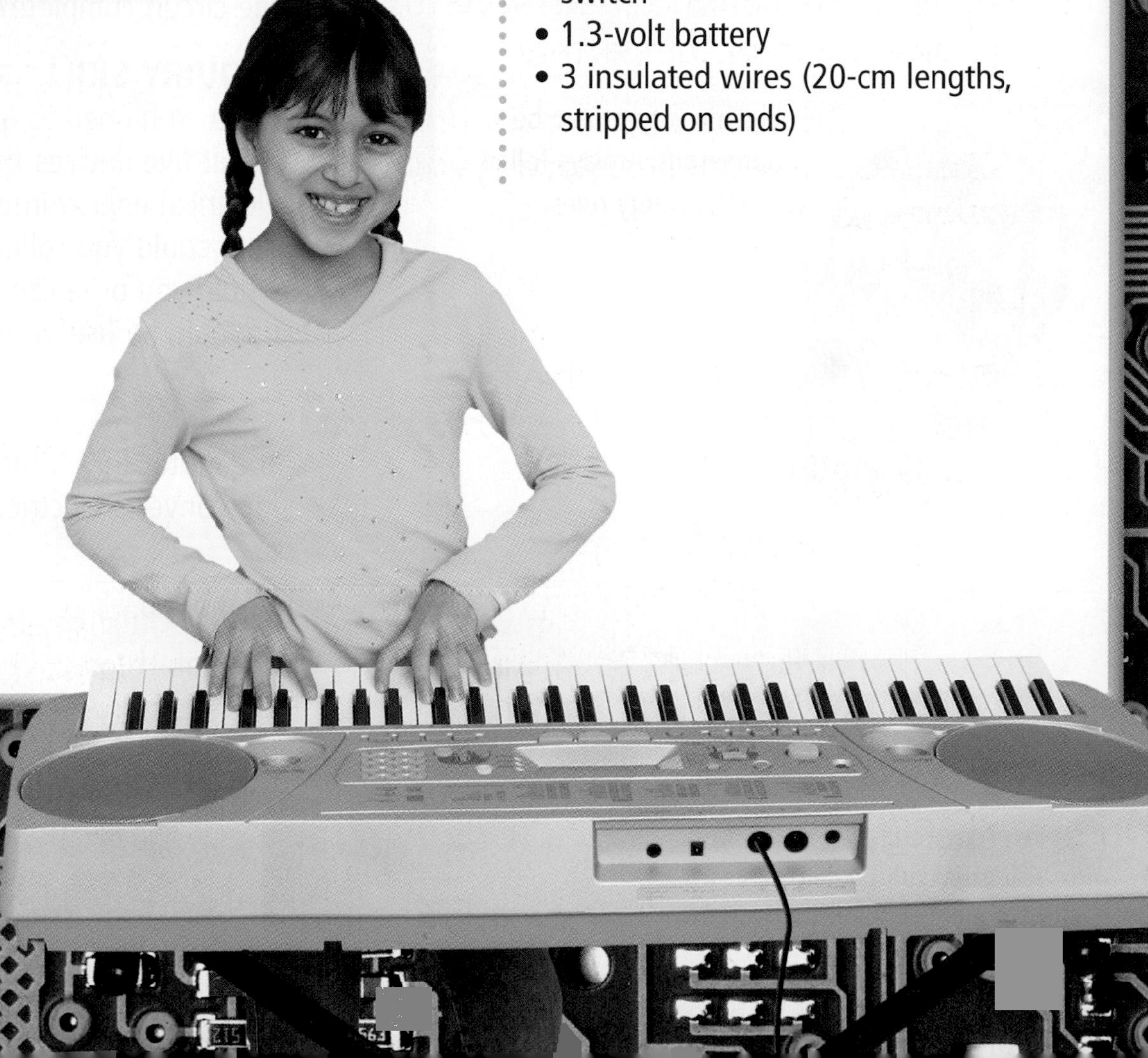

PREPARE TO INVESTIGATE

Inquiry Skill

Predict You explain your predictions by describing cause and effect relationships.

Materials

- plastic propeller
- motor
- switch
- 1.3-volt battery
- 3 insulated wires (20-cm lengths, stripped on ends)

Using Motors

Procedure

STEP 1

1. **Collaborate** Work in a small group. Attach a propeller to a motor as shown.

2. Make a circuit using a battery, a switch, the motor with attached propeller, and three wires as shown. Make sure the switch is in the "off" position.

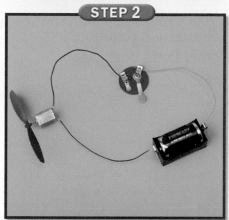

STEP 2

3. **Observe** Hold the motor so the propeller can turn. Turn the switch on. Observe the propeller. In your *Science Notebook*, record your observations.

4. **Experiment** Turn the switch off to stop the motor. Disconnect the wires from the battery. Reattach each wire to the opposite end of the battery.

5. **Observe** Turn the switch back on. Observe the propeller. Record your observations.

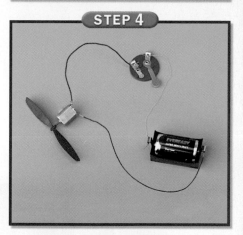

STEP 4

Conclusion

1. In step 3, what did you observe to be the response of the propeller when the switch was turned on?

2. **Compare** In step 5, what change did you notice in the response of the propeller?

3. **Predict** What would change if you reversed the order of the switch and the motor in the original circuit? Explain your answer.

Guided Inquiry

Ask Questions What else could be attached to the motor? Invent a device that is useful. Write a question that you would need to answer in order to test the device. **Hypothesize** the answer to your question.

Uses of Electricity

MAIN IDEA When people use electric current, they change the electrical energy to heat, light energy, and the energy of motion.

READING SKILL

Main Idea and Details
Use the graphic organizer to write details that support the main idea that electricity is converted into other forms of energy.

Electricity in Homes

Think about how you begin your day. You probably wake up to an alarm clock. You turn on the lights and the hot water in the bathroom. Maybe you or a family member cooks breakfast on the stove or in a microwave oven.

Your clock, water heater, and stove may, like your lights and microwave, be electrical devices. They get energy from electric current. You probably use electric current dozens of times a day, every day.

A television changes electrical energy to light energy and sound energy.

The car gets electrical energy from batteries. The electrical energy is changed to motion.

Each of these devices changes electrical energy to another form of energy. Electrical energy can be converted to almost any form of energy, including heat, light, motion, sound, and chemical energy. Radios and stereos convert electrical energy to the energy of sound. Rechargeable batteries use electrical energy to store chemical energy when they recharge.

Different electrical devices use different amounts of electric current. Keeping an electric clothes dryer on for one hour uses much more electric current than keeping a light bulb on for one hour. A **watt** is a unit of measure for electrical power. It is used to measure how fast electrical energy is being used.

Power companies use watts to measure how much electrical energy is used in a home. Then they send a bill to the home so that the people who live there can pay for the electricity they have used.

MAIN IDEA What forms of energy can electric current be converted into?

The children each have a remote-control device. The boy can adjust the sound and change the channels on the TV. The girl can use her device to make the model car move in different directions and at different speeds.

Express Lab

Activity Card 26
Observe the Uses of Electricity

Converting Electricity to Heat

Devices in your home produce heat. Toasters, electric ovens, electric stoves, water heaters, hair dryers, and other devices convert electrical energy to heat.

How do devices such as hair dryers work? In a hair dryer, electric current flows through a conductor, the cord, to a heating unit. The heating unit is made of a material that has a resistance to electric current. **Resistance** is the ability of a material to slow down or stop the flow of electric current.

As the current meets resistance, the material begins to heat up. The heat produced can be used to dry hair. In other devices, the heat is used to cook food, dry clothes, or warm houses.

Heating units in electrical devices can get very hot. They can stay hot for several minutes after the electric current has been turned off.

▲ The coils of an electric stove resist electric current. This causes the coils to become hot enough to cook food.

Electricity flows through metal coils in the hair dryer. Resistance causes the coils to become hot. Electricity also turns a fan that blows air. ▶

fan

heating coil

electric wire

Converting Electricity to Light

Electrical energy can also be converted to light. Some devices that change electrical energy to light include light bulbs, computer monitors, televisions, and lasers.

The way a light bulb creates light is similar to the way that a heating unit creates heat. Electric current passes through a material that has resistance. The resistance causes the material to heat up and glow brightly.

In a fluorescent light bulb, electric current passes through a gas. In other types of light bulbs, electric current passes through a wire. A fluorescent light bulb produces more light and less heat than other types of light bulbs.

MAIN IDEA How does a light bulb use resistance to produce light?

Computer monitor
Computer monitors and television screens change electrical energy to light energy. Flat-panel screens are more energy-efficient than regular screens.

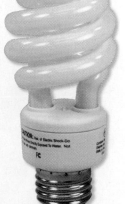

Energy-saving bulb
Regular bulbs use 40 to 60 watts of electricity to produce the same amount of light that a 15-watt compact fluorescent lamp (CFL) produces.

Converting Electricity to Motion

Electrical devices can also convert electricity to motion. This motion is useful for doing many kinds of work.

The motor in a power tool converts electrical energy to motion. In a power drill, the spinning motor turns a drill bit. In a power saw, the motor turns a sharp blade.

Many vehicles also convert electrical energy to motion. Some wheelchairs, scooters, and even some cars use electrical energy to turn wheels.

A hybrid car uses both a gas engine and an electric motor and batteries. Because of the electric motor and batteries, the gas engine in a hybrid car can be smaller. The car runs more efficiently and generally uses less gasoline for the same distance than does a non-hybrid car.

MAIN IDEA A blender converts electrical energy to what kind of energy?

▲ Power tools convert electricity to motion.

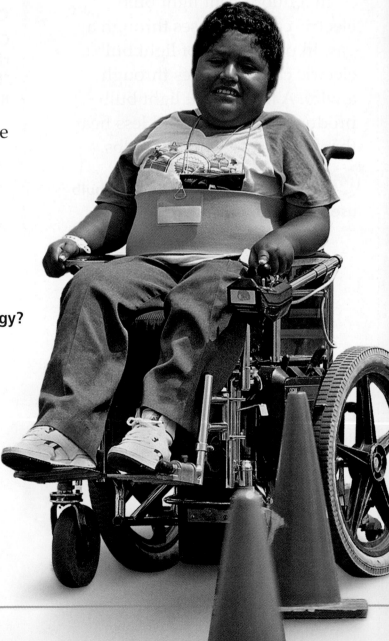

A large battery provides electricity for this wheelchair. ▶

Visual Summary

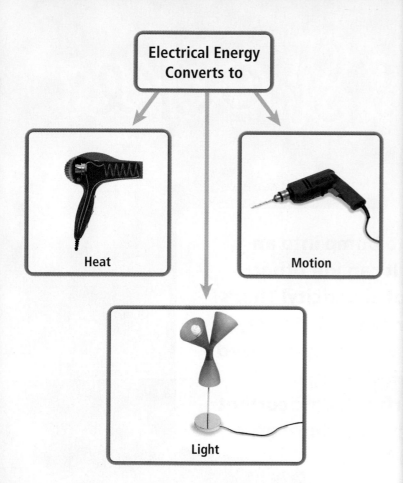

Electrical Energy Converts to

Heat

Motion

Light

Reading Review

1 **MAIN IDEA** A light bulb converts electrical energy to what two forms of energy?

2 **VOCABULARY** Write a sentence using the term *resistance* as it is used in this lesson.

3 **READING SKILL** What are three examples that support the idea that devices can convert electrical energy into heat?

Main Idea

Detail   Detail

4 **CRITICAL THINKING:** **Synthesize** Which would produce more heat: a typical light bulb, or a fluorescent light bulb?

5 **INQUIRY SKILL:** **Predict** Suppose a material that is a good conductor of electricity is used in making an electric heating unit. Predict whether the unit would work properly. Give reasons for your prediction.

✓ TEST PRACTICE

Electrical energy is measured in _____.

A. time.   **C.** watts.

B. kilograms.   **D.** degrees.

Technology
Visit **www.eduplace.com/cascp** to learn more about using electricity.

Nature's Shocker

Yow! You wouldn't want to bump into an electric eel while swimming. It can jolt other animals with over 600 volts of electricity! That's more than enough to stun or even kill its prey.

The electric eel uses thousands of specialized muscles to produce its electrical charge. These muscles cause a powerful electric current to flow from the eel's body through the water. The water and the eel's head and tail form a circuit. The circuit might also include any animal the eel wants to zap!

Shocker! Electric eels use their electrical power to hunt small fish, shrimp, frogs, and water birds.

The long tail is the negative pole of the eel's "battery."

The head of the eel is the positive pole.

"Wow! It would take about 400 flashlight batteries to produce the same charge as an adult electric eel!"

1.5V

Writing Journal

Do research to find out if other animals use electricity to hunt or for self-defense. In your writing journal, compare these animals to the electric eel.

299

MATH Analyze Data

The total amount of electricity an appliance uses over time can be measured in watt-hours. If a 50-watt light bulb is on for one hour, it uses 50 watt-hours of electricity. If it's on for two hours, it uses 100 watt-hours. This chart shows the number of watts different appliances use when they run for one hour. Use the chart to answer the following questions.

1. Which appliance uses the most electricity in one hour?

2. If a computer runs for 6 hours, how many watt-hours will it use?

3. Which uses more electricity: a clothes dryer that runs for two hours, or a television that is left on for 10 hours?

Electricity Use in Your Home	
Device	**Watts**
Water heater	3,800
Refrigerator	500
Microwave oven	1,500
Hair dryer	1,000
Computer with monitor	150
Clothes washer	500
Clothes dryer	5,000
Television	100
DVD player	40
Lamp (1 bulb)	60

WRITING Informative

Write instructions that describe how to build a circuit using a battery, wires, a switch, and a light bulb. Write your instructions for a reader who knows nothing about circuits and electric current. Be sure to use the correct vocabulary terms.

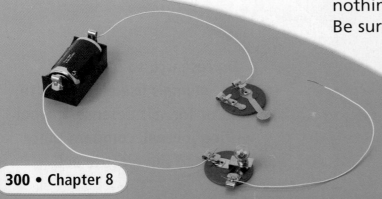

Robotics Engineer

Robots are used for everything from delivering medicine in hospitals to exploring other planets. Most robots are powered by electricity. Designing and producing robots is the job of a robotics engineer.

For many years, robots have been used to help build cars and handle dangerous materials. Today you can buy a robot to vacuum a rug and one to mow the lawn. Some robotics engineers are working on a technology to help robots make complex decisions.

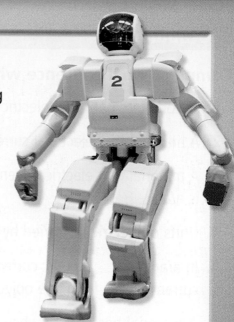

What It Takes!

- A degree in engineering
- Courses in computer science

Electrician

Electricians install wiring and electrical devices in homes, schools, and factories. An electrician must always make sure the systems they install meet safety codes. Electricians also rewire old buildings. Some work at power stations that supply electricity to cities.

What It Takes!

- High school diploma
- Apprentice in a training program
- In California, passing a licensing exam

Vocabulary

Complete each sentence with a term from the list.

1. A complete path that electric current can travel on is a/an _____.

2. A material that electrical current flows through easily is a/an _____.

3. A material that electric current does not flow through easily is a/an _____.

4. Units of electricity carried by tiny particles are called _____.

5. In a/an _____, electric current has only one path to follow. The current moves from one object to the next.

6. A material has _____ when it slows or stops an electric current.

7. A device that converts chemical energy into electrical energy is a/an _____.

8. The buildup of electric charges is called _____.

9. The movement of electric charges is called _____.

10. Electric current has more than one path to follow in a/an _____.

battery p. 286
conductor p. 283
electric charges p. 272
electric circuit p. 284
electric current p. 282
insulator p. 283
parallel circuit p. 285
resistance p. 294
series circuit p. 285
static electricity p. 274
watt p. 293

✓ Test Practice

Write the letter of the best answer choice.

11. What is a watt?

   A. A device that opens and closes a circuit
   B. A device that changes electrical energy to light energy
   C. A material that an electric current passes through easily
   D. A unit used to measure electric power

12. Two objects attract each other if they have opposite _____.

   A. static electricity.   C. electric circuits.
   B. electric charges.   D. electric currents.

13. An electric cord is made up of a wire that is _____.

   A. a conductor.
   B. an insulator.
   C. a conductor, wrapped in an insulator.
   D. in a parallel circuit.

14. The circuits in a house are usually _____.

   A. series circuits.
   B. simple circuits.
   C. static electricity.
   D. parallel circuits.

15. **Infer** Al creates a circuit that has one battery and two bulbs. When both bulbs are connected to the circuit, they are both lighted. When Al removes one of the bulbs from the circuit, the other bulb does not light. Based on this information, infer whether Al's circuit is a series circuit or a parallel circuit. Explain your answer.

16. Lang created a circuit using a battery, copper wire, and a bulb. The bulb lit. Then Lang replaced the copper wire with a glass rod. Glass is an insulator. Predict whether the bulb will light. Explain why it will or will not.

Map the Concept

Use the terms below to fill in the concept map.

conductor   **electric circuit**
battery   **switch**

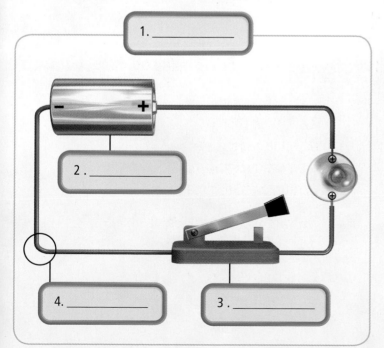

1. _____

2. _____

3. _____

4. _____

Critical Thinking

17. **Analyze** Explain why overloading an outlet is dangerous.

18. **Evaluate** A warning label on a hair dryer states that you should not use it while in the tub or the shower. Explain why this is a good warning.

19. **Synthesize** Suppose your home was wired entirely with series circuits. Describe some effects this might have on daily life in your home.

20. **Apply** You reach for a doorknob and receive a small shock. Use what you know about static electricity to explain why this happened.

Performance Assessment

Draw a Circuit
Draw a diagram of a parallel circuit that includes two light bulbs, a battery, and wires. Label your diagram.

Writing Journal

Review your answers to the questions on page 267. Change your answers, as needed, based on what you have learned.

Chapter 9

Magnetism and Electromagnets

Particles in Earth's magnetic field can glow, producing an aurora.

LESSON 1

Some materials attract other materials. What are magnets, and what do they attract?

LESSON 2

Compasses naturally point north. This is because of Earth's core. What effects does Earth's magnetized core have?

LESSON 3

Electromagnets combine electricity and magnetism. How are these two forces related? And how do people use electromagnets?

LESSON 4

Some ways of generating electricity use up resources. How can we generate energy so that we save resources?

Writing Journal

In your Writing Journal, show what you know by writing or drawing answers to each question.

Vocabulary Preview

Vocabulary

Glossary

English-Spanish p. H24

Vocabulary Skill

Word Parts

magnet

If you see the word *magnet* in a larger term, such as *magnetic, magnetism, electromagnet,* or *magnetic field,* you know that these terms deal with magnets.

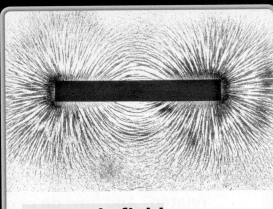

compass

An instrument that senses magnetic north using a free-moving magnet.

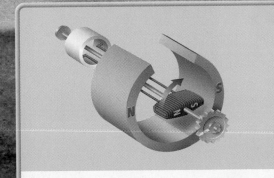

magnetic field

The area in which a magnet's force can act.

motor

A device that changes electrical energy to energy of motion.

aurora

A display of lights caused by particles from the Sun interacting with Earth's magnetic field and atmosphere.

Start with Your Standards

Standard Set 1. Physical Sciences

1.b. *Students know* how to build a simple compass and use it to detect magnetic effects, including Earth's magnetic field.

1.c. *Students know* electric currents produce magnetic fields and know how to build a simple electromagnet.

1.d. *Students know* the role of electromagnets in the construction of electric motors, electric generators, and simple devices, such as doorbells and earphones.

1.f. *Students know* that magnets have two poles (north and south) and that like poles repel each other while unlike poles attract each other.

1.g. *Students know* electrical energy can be converted to heat, light, and motion.

Standard Set 6. Investigation and Experimentation covered in this chapter: 6.a., 6.d., 6.e.

Lesson 1

How Do Magnets Behave?

Building Background

Magnets are used every day. They can be found in tools, motors, and even in art—such as this magnetic animal sculpture. Magnets have a north pole and a south pole. Opposite poles attract one another. Like poles repel one another.

PREPARE TO INVESTIGATE

Inquiry Skill

Infer When you infer, you use facts you know and observations you have made to draw a conclusion.

Materials

- 2 bar magnets with ends labeled
- 5 ring magnets
- pencil
- horseshoe magnet

Magnetic Poles

Procedure

STEP 1

1. **Observe** Bring the north end of one bar magnet near the south end of another bar magnet. Record what you observe. Repeat by bringing the north poles near each other. Then bring the south poles near each other.

2. **Experiment** Use one of the bar magnets to test each of five ring magnets to find which side is its north pole. As you do this, place each ring magnet on the work table with its north pole facing up.

STEP 2

3. **Observe** Place the ring magnets onto a pencil. Arrange them so each north pole faces a north pole and each south pole faces a south pole. Record what you observe in your *Science Notebook*.

4. **Experiment** Remove the top ring magnet from the pencil, flip it over, and put it back onto the pencil. Record your observations in your *Science Notebook*.

STEP 3

Conclusion

1. **Infer** From your observations, what can you infer about how like poles react? What can you infer about how unlike poles react?

2. **Predict** What result would you predict from placing all the ring magnets on the pencil so that every south pole was facing a north pole on the next magnet?

Guided Inquiry

Experiment Use a bar magnet to identify the north and south poles of other magnets. Try this on a compass needle. **Observe** what happens and record your results.

READING SKILL

Main Idea and Details

As you read, use charts like the one shown to record the main idea and details of each section.

If the particles making up an object line up, the object is a magnet.

Magnets

MAIN IDEA Magnets are objects that attract certain materials such as iron. Magnets have magnetic poles and magnetic fields where the magnetic force acts.

Properties of Magnets

If you place a magnet (MAG niht) on a refrigerator door, it will stay there. A **magnet** is an object that attracts certain metals, mainly iron. This property of attracting iron and certain other metals, such as nickel and cobalt, is called magnetism.

Magnets stick to most refrigerators because the doors are made of steel, which contains iron. Magnets do not attract most other metals or materials such as plastic, wood, and rubber.

The force of magnetism on objects decreases as the distance from the magnet increases. If you hold a magnet close to the refrigerator, the magnet and the steel will be very strongly attracted. If you move the magnet farther away, the magnet and the steel will not be as strongly attracted.

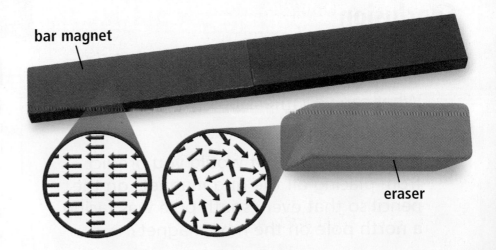

bar magnet

eraser

A **permanent magnet** is an object that keeps its magnetism for a long time. A **temporary magnet** loses its magnetism after a short time. You can magnetize some objects to make them temporary magnets. For example, you can stroke an iron nail with a permanent magnet to make it a temporary magnet. Increasing the number of strokes makes a temporary magnet stronger.

The areas on a magnet where the force of a magnet is greatest are called the **magnetic poles**. On a bar magnet and a horseshoe magnet, the magnetic poles are at the ends. On a ring magnet, the poles are on the top and bottom faces.

When a bar magnet is allowed to swing freely, one end always points toward the north. This end of the magnet is the north-seeking pole, or north pole. The other end of the magnet always points south. This end is the magnet's south-seeking pole, or south pole.

Recall what you learned about electric charges. Unlike charges attract or pull toward each other. Like charges repel or push away from each other. Magnets act in a similar way. The unlike poles of two magnets attract each other. The like poles of two magnets repel each other.

horseshoe magnet

bar magnet

ring magnets

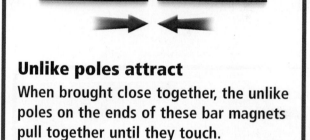

Unlike poles attract
When brought close together, the unlike poles on the ends of these bar magnets pull together until they touch.

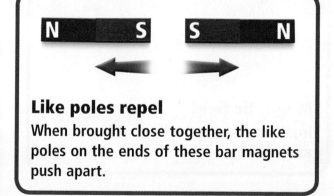

Like poles repel
When brought close together, the like poles on the ends of these bar magnets push apart.

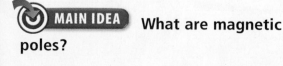 **MAIN IDEA** What are magnetic poles?

 **Express Lab**

Activity Card 27
Showing Magnetic Fields

Magnetic Fields

The space in which the force of a magnet can act is called its **magnetic field** (MAG neh tik feeld). In the picture below at the left, you can see the magnetic field in the pattern made by iron filings around a bar magnet.

Notice that the iron filings in the picture are thicker and closer together at the poles at each end of the magnet. They are also thicker closer to the magnet than they are farther away. The magnetic force is stronger close to the magnet and near the poles than it is farther away.

A magnet can attract any iron object that comes within its magnetic field. If the object is outside the magnetic field, the magnet will not act on it. A magnetic field can also cause an object to become a temporary magnet.

Magnetic force can act through air, water, and solid materials. This is why a magnet can hold a picture on a refrigerator. The magnetic force passes through the paper.

MAIN IDEA What happens to a piece of iron inside a magnetic field?

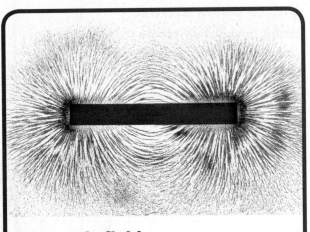

Magnetic field
Iron filings show the lines of force around the magnet.

A magnet can hold a note on a metal refrigerator door because a magnetic force can act through paper. ▶

Visual Summary

A magnet is an object that attracts objects made of iron, steel, and other metals.

Magnets have a north pole and a south pole. Unlike poles attract each other, and like poles repel each other.

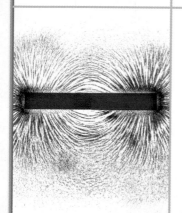

The force of a magnet can act within the magnetic field. The magnetic field surrounds a magnet and is strongest at its poles.

Technology
Visit **www.eduplace.com/cascp** to find out more about magnets.

Reading Review

❶ MAIN IDEA Why don't magnets attract wooden objects?

❷ VOCABULARY Use the terms *magnetic field* and *magnetic poles* in a sentence.

❸ READING SKILL When two bar magnets are placed end to end, they repel each other. Explain why the magnets behave this way.

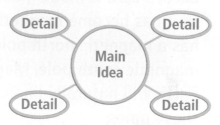

❹ CRITICAL THINKING:
Analyze A magnet can hold a piece of paper to the refrigerator. But the same magnet cannot hold an entire package of paper to the refrigerator. Why?

❺ INQUIRY SKILL: Infer
Suppose you use a magnetic iron nail to pick up several paper clips. Several hours later, the iron nail will not pick up the paper clips. Infer what happened.

✓ **TEST PRACTICE**
Magnets do not attract objects made of _____.

A. cobalt.   **C.** iron.

B. nickel.   **D.** plastic.

What Is Earth's Magnetic Field?

Building Background

Earth acts like a giant magnet. Earth's core is made mainly of iron that has become magnetized. Earth has a magnetic north pole and a magnetic south pole. Magnets on Earth will naturally line up with these poles.

PREPARE TO INVESTIGATE

Inquiry Skill

Experiment Do many trials, or repeat an experiment many times, before drawing a conclusion.

Materials

- goggles
- plastic-foam ball
- plastic bowl filled with water
- bar magnet
- steel craft needle

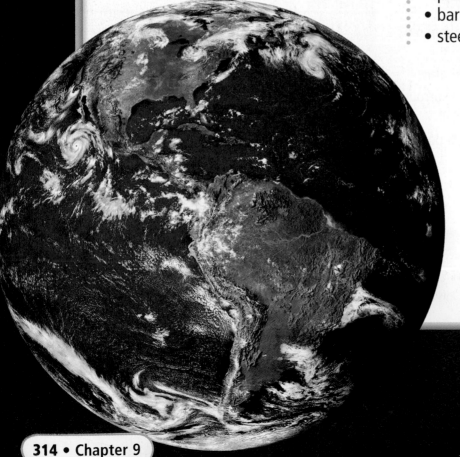

Detecting Earth's Magnetism

Procedure

1. **Collaborate** Work with a partner. Hold the eye of a steel craft needle so the tip points downward. Stroke a bar magnet down the needle 35 times. Use the north end of the magnet. Be sure to stroke in only one direction, not back and forth.

2. Slowly push the needle through the center of a small plastic-foam ball as shown in the picture. **Safety:** Wear goggles. The needle is sharp. Be careful when using it.

3. **Experiment** Place the ball in the center of a plastic bowl of water. Remove the ball and set it back in the water again several times. In your *Science Notebook*, record your observations each time.

4. **Compare** Observe your classmates' bowls and compare your results.

5. Bring the magnet's south end near the needle's point. Repeat with the magnet's north end. Record your observations.

STEP 1

STEP 2

STEP 4

Conclusion

1. **Infer** How do your observations help you infer whether the needle was magnetized?

2. **Hypothesize** What might explain the behavior of the needle in your bowl? How is this explanation supported by the behavior of the needles in your classmates' bowls?

Guided Inquiry

Ask Questions What question could you ask to decide if a suspended magnet is accurately indicating which direction is north? **Communicate** with a classmate by exchanging questions.

Magnetic Earth

VOCABULARY

compass   p. 317
aurora   p. 318

READING SKILL

Cause and Effect
Use the chart below to
record the effects that
Earth's magnetic field has
on objects.

MAIN IDEA Earth acts like a giant magnet, with
a magnetic field and magnetic poles. This allows
compasses to work and causes many effects on and
around Earth.

Earth's Magnetic Field

Today, scientists know that Earth acts like a
giant magnet. Earth's center is made up mostly
of molten iron. As Earth spins, the iron particles
line up, producing Earth's magnetic field. As a
result, Earth behaves like a giant bar magnet with
two magnetic poles. Like all magnets, Earth is
surrounded by a magnetic field with lines of force.

A compass works because
Earth has a magnetic field.

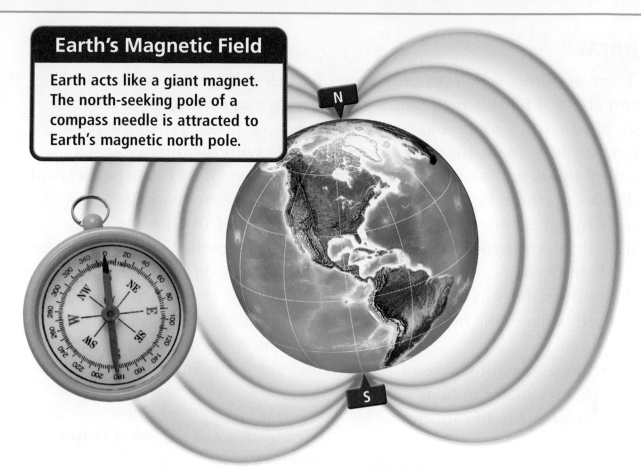

Earth's Magnetic Field

Earth acts like a giant magnet. The north-seeking pole of a compass needle is attracted to Earth's magnetic north pole.

How a Compass Works

Before scientists knew about Earth's magnetic field, people used compasses. A **compass** is an instrument that senses magnetic north, using a free-moving magnet.

Thousands of years ago, Chinese sailors floated small pieces of magnetic rock called lodestone on top of straw in a bowl of water. The lodestone would show the sailors the directions magnetic north and south. Today's sailors still use compasses as well as other equipment, such as radar and satellites.

The needle of a magnetic compass is a permanent magnet. The needle is set so it can turn freely. The north-seeking pole of the compass needle

will turn until it points toward the magnetic north pole of the Earth.

The magnetic north pole is not exactly over Earth's geographic North Pole. The geographic North Pole is the northernmost point at which Earth turns on its axis. Because Earth's core is spinning, the magnetic north pole moves. But it is close enough to the geographic pole for people to use it to find north.

You can make a compass by first changing a needle into a temporary magnet. Then float a small cork in water and place the needle on the cork.

 **CAUSE AND EFFECT** Why does a compass needle point north?

Auroras

There are times when people can see an effect of Earth's magnetic field. Near Earth's north and south magnetic poles, there are sometimes beautiful lights in the night sky.

These "northern lights" or "southern lights" are auroras (uh-ROHR uhz). An **aurora** is a display of lights in the sky caused by particles from the Sun interacting with Earth's magnetic field and atmosphere.

The Sun sends out waves of tiny particles called the solar wind. Earth's magnetic field captures some of these particles. The particles are pulled toward the strong magnetic force at Earth's magnetic poles. When the particles collide with the top of Earth's atmosphere, they cause particles in the atmosphere to glow.

Particles from the Sun and Earth's magnetic field can produce other effects. When the solar wind is very strong, it may affect satellites, telephones, and electricity. You will learn more about how magnetism and electricity interact in the next lesson.

 **What causes auroras?**

Auroras are most often visible near the north and south magnetic poles.

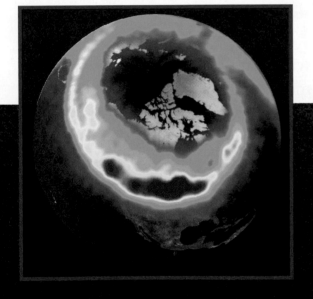

Express Lab

Activity Card 28
Find the Poles of a Magnet

Lesson Wrap-Up

Visual Summary

Earth acts like a giant magnet; it has a magnetic field and magnetic poles. It is caused by Earth's iron core, which is magnetized.

The north-seeking poles of a compass needle and other magnets on Earth are attracted to Earth's north magnetic pole.

When particles from the Sun are pulled toward Earth's magnetic poles, they may collide with particles in Earth's atmosphere, causing a glow called an aurora.

Technology
Visit **www.eduplace.com/cascp** to learn more about Earth's magnetic field.

Reading Review

1 MAIN IDEA What causes Earth's magnetic field?

2 VOCABULARY Explain what a compass does.

3 READING SKILL What evidence is there that Earth has a magnetic field?

4 CRITICAL THINKING: Apply The first Chinese compasses pointed south rather than north. Did these compasses work differently from compasses that point north? Explain.

5 INQUIRY SKILL: Experiment Suppose you have an unlabeled magnet. How could you use a piece of string to help you figure out which is the north-seeking pole and which is the south-seeking pole?

TEST PRACTICE
Auroras are most visible _____.

A. near Earth's north and south magnetic poles.

B. near the Equator.

C. in the tropics.

D. during the daytime.

SUN BLASTS

Did someone say BIG? The Sun is so big and powerful that the biggest explosion on Earth is *tiny* in comparison. So when the Sun erupts with a sudden blast of energy, you know it's going to be *extreme.*

This picture shows what is called an eruptive prominence. It is one of several types of solar bursts that can affect Earth. When one occurs, a huge portion of the Sun is literally blasted into outer space. The speed of these eruptions can reach millions of kilometers an hour!

When the particles of a solar eruption reach Earth, Earth's magnetic field pulls them in toward the magnetic poles. As the particles interact with the upper atmosphere, colorful auroras appear. Solar eruptions can create electrical effects as well. The most powerful solar eruptions can create electrical surges in power networks, causing blackouts for millions of people.

◄ Solar eruptions are so big, they can be measured in terms of Earth itself. How many Earths long is this eruption?

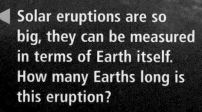

Writing Journal

In your writing journal, describe the effects of a power outage on people's lives.

How Are Electromagnets Used?

Building Background

Magnetism and electricity work together in electromagnets. You may never have seen electromagnets, but you depend on them every day.

Electromagnets run many common appliances and machines, such as fans, refrigerators, and the generators that make electricity.

PREPARE TO INVESTIGATE

Inquiry Skill

Record Data When you keep records that are accurate, they can be understood at a later time.

Materials

- insulated wire (stripped on ends, 125 cm)
- metric ruler
- iron or steel nail
- 20 metal paper clips
- 1.3-volt battery
- battery holder

Stick To It!

Procedure

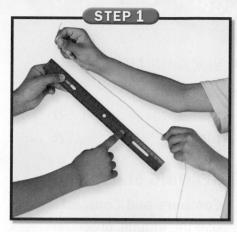
STEP 1

1. **Measure** Measure about 20 cm from one end of a 125-cm length of insulated wire. **Safety:** Wire may be sharp.

2. Starting at the 20-cm point, wrap 25 turns of the wire around a nail. Leave a length of free wire at both ends of the nail.

STEP 2

3. **Observe** Attach each end of the wire to a different end of a battery. Bring the tip of the nail near a small pile of 20 paper clips. Observe what happens.

4. **Use Numbers** In your *Science Notebook*, record the number of paper clips that stick to the nail when you lift it away from the pile.

5. **Use Variables** Repeat steps 2 and 3 with 5, 15, 35, and 45 turns of wire. Record the number of paper clips you can lift with the nail each time.

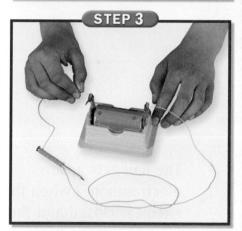
STEP 3

6. **Record Data** Use the data from your observations to create a bar graph that shows the relationship between the number of turns of wire and the number of paper clips that stick to the nail.

Conclusion

1. **Infer** How did electric current flowing through the wire affect the nail?

2. **Analyze Data** What does your graph tell you about how the number of turns of wire affects the force of the magnet you built?

Guided Inquiry

Experiment Repeat the experiment with at least three other objects, such as a pencil or a drinking straw. **Classify** the objects according to whether they became magnetized or not.

VOCABULARY

electromagnet	p. 324
generator	p. 327
motor	p. 326

READING SKILL

Compare and Contrast
Use the graphic organizer to compare and contrast permanent magnets and electromagnets.

Compare	Contrast

Electromagnetism

MAIN IDEA Electricity can produce magnetism, and magnetism can produce electricity.

Using Electromagnets

Whenever you play a video or turn on a hair dryer, you are putting electromagnets (ih lehk troh MAG nihts) to work. You have learned that you can make a weak temporary magnet by stroking a piece of iron with a permanent magnet. You can make a strong temporary magnet by using electricity to produce magnetism. An **electromagnet** is a strong temporary magnet that uses electricity to produce magnetism.

How does electricity produce magnetism? When electric current passes through a wire, the current produces a weak magnetic field around the wire. If the wire is wrapped around a piece of iron, the magnetic field becomes stronger, and the iron becomes magnetized.

The nail acts as an electromagnet when the circuit is closed and the electric current flows through the wire. ▶

Express Lab

Activity Card 29
Make a Magnetic Field

Like other magnets, electromagnets attract materials made of iron. They are also surrounded by magnetic fields.

The magnetic force of an electromagnet can be controlled. Increasing the number of wire coils or increasing the amount of current moving through the coils will increase the strength of the electromagnet. An electromagnet can be quite strong and still be small enough to fit in your hand.

An electromagnet can be turned on and off. It acts like a magnet only while electric current moves through the wire. As soon as the electric current is turned off, the electromagnet loses its magnetism.

To see how electromagnets can be useful, look at the picture of the crane. Cranes with very strong electromagnets are used to pick up cars and other heavy objects that contain iron.

Many objects in your home have electromagnets in them. Small electromagnets are located inside such devices as blenders, computer disk drives, and doorbells.

COMPARE AND CONTRAST How are a bar magnet and an electromagnet alike? How are they different?

1 The electromagnet attracts scrap metal and moves it.

electromagnet

2 When the current is turned off, the crane is no longer magnetized and the metal drops into the pile.

How a Motor Works

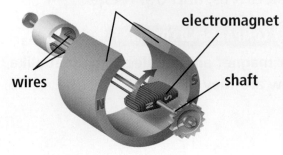

permanent magnet

electromagnet

wires

shaft

1 In a motor, an electric current passes through an electromagnet. The direction of household current keeps reversing.

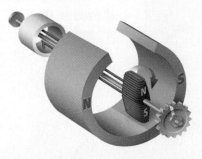

2 As the current changes direction, the poles of the electromagnet keep reversing. The permanent magnet repels and attracts the electromagnet, turning the shaft of the motor.

3 As the shaft turns, electrical energy changes to energy of motion.

Motors

What do refrigerators, mixers, and ceiling fans have in common? They all have an electric motor. An electric **motor** is a device that changes electrical energy to energy of motion.

How does an electric motor work? All electric motors contain electromagnets and permanent magnets. Recall that an electromagnet is formed when a conductor is wrapped around an iron core and electric current runs through the conductor.

Now recall how magnetic fields interact with each other. Like poles repel, and unlike poles attract. When a motor is turned on, electric current passes through a wire that is wrapped around an iron core. The magnetic field of this electromagnet interacts with the magnetic field of a permanent magnet. The like poles of each magnet repel each other and the unlike poles attract each other, producing motion.

Generating Electricity

You have learned that an electric motor uses magnetism to convert electrical energy into energy of motion. A generator does the opposite. A **generator** (JEHN-uh ray tuhr) is a device that uses magnetism to convert energy of motion into electrical energy.

Giant generators produce the electricity that lights up cities and runs machinery. These generators have powerful permanent magnets and huge coils of wire. Electric current is produced in the wires when the coils move across the magnetic field of the permanent magnet.

There are two ways to increase the amount of electricity a generator produces. One way is to use stronger permanent magnets. A second way is to increase the number of coils of wire.

Where does the energy to move the coils of a generator come from? In many power plants, energy released by nuclear fuels or by burning coal or oil heats water to produce steam. The pressure of the steam moves the coils. Energy to move the coils can also come from falling water or wind.

COMPARE AND CONTRAST How are electric motors and generators different?

From Generator to Customer

Energy source Energy from falling water or burning fuels turns generator coils, producing electricity.

Electric power lines Power lines carry electricity to customers.

Homes and businesses Although generated far away, electricity is as close as the nearest light switch.

The Cost of Using Electricity

Using electricity costs money. Your monthly electric bill is based on the total amount of electricity used in your home each month.

The cost of using an electric device depends on the amount of time it is used and the amount of electrical energy it needs to run. Some devices, such as fans and washing machines, use electricity only part of the time. Others, such as refrigerators and clocks, use electricity 24 hours a day.

Some electric devices use electricity even when the devices are not in use. If a computer were left on "standby" or "sleep" mode for an entire year, it would use about $40 worth of electricity. Some appliances, such as DVD players and stereos, have built-in clocks. The clocks run on electricity even when the appliance is turned off.

Not all the electricity that people pay for is used to run devices. Some electricity is lost each time electricity passes from one conductor to the next. All electric wires have a little bit of resistance, which blocks some of the current. Also, appliances that use electricity often waste some of it as heat.

Many appliances are being built that use electricity very efficiently. These appliances cost less to run.

COMPARE AND CONTRAST How do a clock and fan use electricity differently?

◀ A computer uses electricity even when it is in standby mode or turned off.

Visual Summary

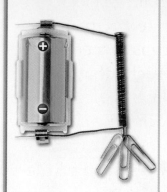

An electromagnet is a temporary magnet formed when an electric current travels around a magnetic material such as iron.

Motors use electromagnets and permanent magnets to change electricity into the energy of motion.

Generators turn motion into electricity by spinning magnets around wires.

Reading Review

❶ **MAIN IDEA** How do electromagnets and permanent magnets differ? How are they similar?

❷ **VOCABULARY** Write a sentence using the term *generator*.

❸ **READING SKILL** How do electric motors and generators use magnetism?

Compare	Contrast

❹ **CRITICAL THINKING: Synthesize** Use what you know about electromagnets and magnetism to explain how recycling centers use electromagnets to separate discarded materials.

❺ **INQUIRY SKILL: Record Data** Make a chart to record these data: an electromagnet with 25 turns of wire picks up 5 paper clips; one with 35 turns picks up 7 paper clips; one with 45 turns picks up 9 paper clips.

✓ **TEST PRACTICE**
Electric motors are *not* found in a _____.

A. ceiling fan.　　**C.** power drill.

B. light bulb.　　**D.** refrigerator.

Technology
Visit www.eduplace.com/cascp to learn more about electromagnets.

The "Father of Broadcasting"

A hundred years ago, few people had radios. That changed when educator and inventor Charles Herrold began broadcasting in San Jose, California.

After the 1906 San Francisco earthquake, Herrold started experimenting with radios. He invented an improved radio transmitter and began to send signals out to anyone who wanted to listen. His microphone, transmitter, and radio speakers used electromagnets to either convert sound energy into electric current, or electric current into sound energy.

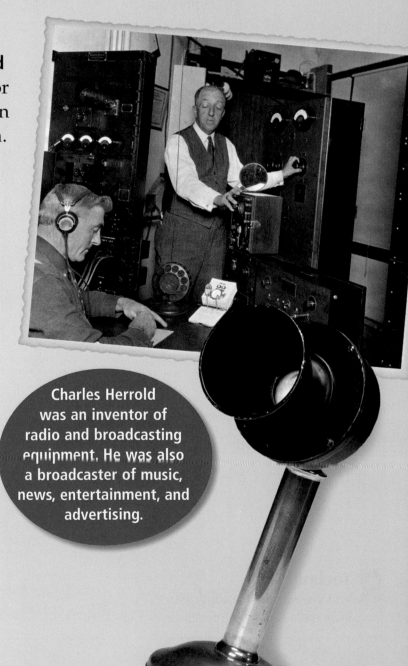

Charles Herrold was an inventor of radio and broadcasting equipment. He was also a broadcaster of music, news, entertainment, and advertising.

How Radios Work

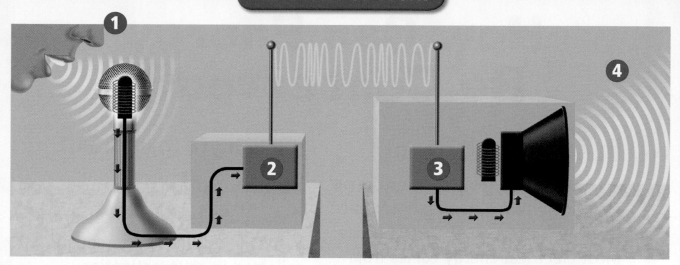

1 **Microphone** A microphone picks up the vibrations made by music or other sounds. The vibrations move tiny magnets, which produce a small electric current in a wire inside the microphone.

2 **Transmitter** A radio transmitter turns the electric current into radio waves. These invisible waves move through the air in all directions.

3 **Receiver** A radio receiver uses an antenna to detect radio waves. It changes the radio waves back into an electric current.

4 **Speaker** A speaker works like a microphone in reverse. It uses electric current to power an electromagnet. The electromagnet interacts with a permanent magnet inside the speaker, causing it to vibrate. These vibrations are heard as sound.

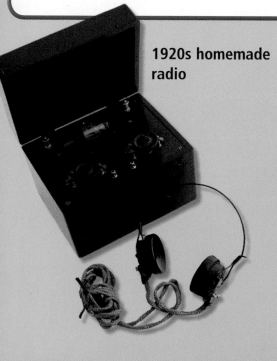

1920s homemade radio

Sharing Ideas

1. **READING CHECK** In what devices did Charles Herrold use electromagnets?

2. **WRITE ABOUT IT** Summarize how radios work, from microphone to speaker. Include the equipment, its parts, and the energy changes that occur.

3. **TALK ABOUT IT** Discuss what kinds of things might happen if the electromagnet in a speaker was replaced with a permanent magnet.

How Can Energy Be Conserved?

Building Background

A fan in a hat could easily run on electricity from a small battery, but this one is powered by solar energy. Most electrical energy comes from converting the chemical energy of fuels. There is a limited supply of these fuels, and their use can cause pollution. So it makes sense for people to conserve, or use less, electricity.

PREPARE TO INVESTIGATE

Inquiry Skill

Communicate You can construct graphs to display measurements collected in an investigation.

Materials

- Electricity Use Support Master
- 2 sheets of graph paper

Science and Math Toolbox

For step 4, review **Making a Bar Graph** on page H3.

Electricity Use

Procedure

1. **Analyze Data** Your teacher will give you an Electricity Use chart like the one shown. The chart gives information about the electricity used by a household in one day.

2. **Communicate** Use one sheet of graph paper to construct a bar graph of the number of hours that each device was used. Use the graph to predict which device used the most total electricity and which used the least.

3. **Use Numbers** Multiply the watts by the hours each device was used. Write the product in the last column of the chart.

4. **Communicate** Use your results and a second sheet of graph paper to construct a bar graph of the total electricity used by each device.

5. **Compare** Compare the two graphs to see if your prediction was correct.

Conclusion

1. **Analyze Data** Which uses more electricity: a low-power device that runs for many hours, or a high-power device that runs for only a few hours?

2. **Draw Conclusions** What would be the best way to reduce total electricity used in the household?

STEP 1

Electricity Use Chart

Device	Watts	Hours Used	Total Electricity Used
Computer	150	4	
Stereo	30	2	
Television	100	3	
Microwave	1,500	1	
Fan	25	6	
Clothes Dryer	5,000	2	
Air Conditioner	1,400	8	
Lamp	60	5	
Refrigerator	500	24	

STEP 2

STEP 3

Guided Inquiry

Experiment Change the number of hours used for three devices on the Electricity Use chart. **Use numbers** to recalculate the total amount of electricity used by each device.

READING SKILL

Main Idea and Details
As you read, use charts like the one below to record the main idea and details for each section of the lesson.

Conserving Electricity

MAIN IDEA Electricity uses natural resources. Conserving electricity helps save natural resources. Finding alternate sources of electrical energy can also prevent pollution.

Reasons to Conserve

Generators create electric current by moving magnets near coils of wire. It takes energy to move those magnets. Different generators get this energy from different sources. Most power plants in the United States get this energy by burning **fossil fuels**, which are coal, oil, and natural gas. Heat from burning fuels is used to produce steam, which turns turbines in generators.

But the supply of fossil fuels on Earth is limited. And once they are gone, there are no more. Burning fossil fuels also creates pollution. It adds soot, smoke, and poisonous gases to the air.

Smog is a form of air pollution. Many cities have smog from burning fossil fuels.

Alternate Energy Sources

Other sources of energy can be used to produce electricity besides fossil fuels. One source is hydroelectric (HY droh ee LEHK-trihk) power. Hydroelectric power plants use moving water to run generators. This energy source produces minimal pollution.

Wind power is becoming more popular. Wind turbines are giant blades that the wind turns. The turning blades power a generator.

Geothermal (JEE oh thuhrm uhl) energy is energy from heat within the Earth. This heat can be used to produce steam that powers a generator.

Solar energy, or energy from the Sun, can also be used to generate electric current. Solar cells do not use magnets. They change solar energy directly into electrical energy.

MAIN IDEA **What are two ways to get power to generate electric current?**

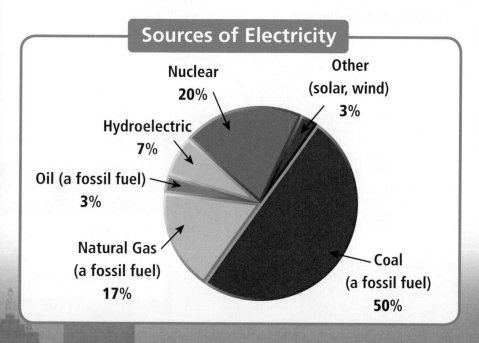

Sources of Electricity

- Nuclear 20%
- Other (solar, wind) 3%
- Hydroelectric 7%
- Oil (a fossil fuel) 3%
- Natural Gas (a fossil fuel) 17%
- Coal (a fossil fuel) 50%

The United States gets most of its electricity by burning fossil fuels. Which source does the United States use the least?

Express Lab

Activity Card 30
Use Solar Energy

What You Can Do

One of the best ways to reduce pollution and save natural resources is to conserve electricity. If you use less electricity, then less needs to be generated, and fewer natural resources need to be used.

Don't leave the refrigerator door open any longer than you need to. Decide what you need before you open it.

Turn off the lights when you leave a room.

Use cold water whenever possible. Heating water uses electricity.

Turn off TVs, radios, and stereos when no one is using them.

It takes the same amount of electricity to run an empty washer as it does to run a full washer—but you get more things clean for the same amount of electricity when it's full.

Visual Summary

Most electricity in the United States is generated using fossil fuels. Fossil fuels are limited resources, and they can cause pollution. Other energy sources are better for the environment.

Other sources of energy include hydroelectric power, wind power, and solar power.

You can conserve electricity by turning off devices when they are not in use and following other tips.

 Technology
Visit **www.eduplace.com/cascp** to find out more about conserving electricity.

Reading Review

❶ MAIN IDEA What are two ways to reduce the pollution caused by generating electricity?

❷ VOCABULARY What is hydroelectric power?

❸ READING SKILL What are four tips you can follow to help conserve electricity?

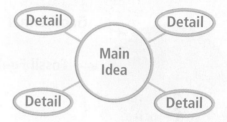

❹ CRITICAL THINKING:
Evaluate A classmate says you don't need to conserve electricity because your local power plant does not produce pollution. Are there other reasons to conserve electricity? Explain.

❺ INQUIRY SKILL:
Communicate Shawna recorded her family's electricity bills for six months: $58, $47, $42, $39, $39, $36. What would a line graph of her data look like?

 TEST PRACTICE
The United States generates most of its electricity using ___.

A. fossil fuels.

B. hydroelectric power.

C. wind power.

D. solar power.

MATH Energy Use Profiles

These two graphs show how Iceland and the United States generate electricity. Use the graphs to answer the questions.

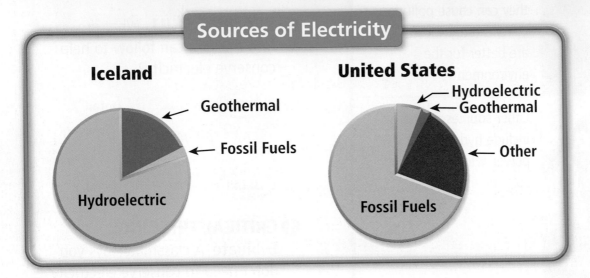

Sources of Electricity

Iceland
- Geothermal
- Fossil Fuels
- Hydroelectric

United States
- Hydroelectric
- Geothermal
- Other
- Fossil Fuels

1. Which country depends more on fossil fuels, the United States or Iceland?

2. Estimate the percentage of Iceland's power plants that do not create pollution. Remember, the entire circle represents 100 percent. One quarter of the circle represents 25 percent.

WRITING Narrative

Suppose it is 100 years in the future and most of Earth's fossil fuels have run out. Write a story in which you describe how people get their electricity from other sources.

OUT OF GAS

Dr. John Clarke

On Earth, auroras form when charged particles from the Sun are pulled by Earth's magnetic field and collide with particles in the atmosphere. As Dr. John Clarke could tell you, auroras form in a similar way on other planets.

Dr. Clarke is a professor at Boston University. He has worked with NASA's Jet Propulsion Laboratory in Pasadena, California. Over the past few years, NASA telescopes and spacecraft have captured many images of auroras on Jupiter and Saturn. Some of the information gathered has surprised scientists.

"We've just begun to study the data," Dr. Clarke said. "We're seeing bright auroras in places we've never seen them before."

Auroras of Saturn

Vocabulary

Complete each sentence with a term from the list.

1. An object that is magnetized for a short time is a/an _____.

2. Coal, oil, and natural gas are _____ that can provide energy to run a generator.

3. In an electric power plant, a giant _____ uses magnetism to convert energy of motion to electricity.

4. The two ends of a magnet are called the_____.

5. An object that keeps its magnetism for a long time is a/an _____.

6. A magnet created by wrapping an electric current around a piece of iron is a/an _____.

7. A device that changes electrical energy to energy of motion is a/an _____.

8. A display of lights caused by particles from the Sun interacting with Earth's magnetic field is a/an _____.

9. The space in which the force of a magnet can act is a/an _____.

10. An instrument that senses magnetic north is a/an _____.

aurora p. 318
compass p. 317
electromagnet p. 324
fossil fuels p. 334
generator p. 327
magnet p. 310
magnetic field p. 312
magnetic poles p. 311
motor p. 326
permanent magnet p. 311
temporary magnet p. 311

Test Practice

Write the letter of the best answer choice.

11. A fan uses a/an _____ to create motion from electric current.

   A. generator   **C.** motor
   B. aurora   **D.** compass

12. Which of the following objects will a magnet probably *not* attract?

   A. a copper penny
   B. a motor-powered toy
   C. an iron nail
   D. a steel wool pad

13. Earth can be considered a/an _____.

   A. electromagnet.   **C.** temporary magnet.
   B. permanent magnet.   **D.** generator.

14. The north pole of a magnet will repel _____.

   A. objects made of iron.
   B. the south pole of another magnet.
   C. objects made of wood or plastic.
   D. the north pole of another magnet.

15. Experiment Suppose you have a box of bar magnets. The poles are labeled on only one of the magnets. You want to label the poles on the other magnets. Explain how you would do this.

16. You do an experiment to test a prediction you have made. Why is it a good idea to try the experiment several times before you draw a conclusion based on your results?

Map the Concept

Use the chart to classify each object on the list.

iron nail
steel knife
plastic spoon
wooden pencil

Attracted to a Magnet	Not Attracted to a Magnet

Critical Thinking

17. Analyze Suppose an astronaut on the moon looks at a compass. The compass does not point in only one direction. Explain why.

18. Evaluate Suppose you are hiking, and you stop for a rest under some large power lines. Your hiking buddy wants to use the map and the compass to decide which way to go next. Evaluate this idea.

19. Synthesize Use what you know about how magnetism affects electricity to explain why the charged particles that cause auroras can cause electric blackouts.

20. Apply Which would be more useful for moving heavy iron objects in industry: an electromagnet or a permanent magnet? Explain.

Performance Assessment

Diagram the Flow of Electricity
Draw a diagram that shows how energy flows from burning fossil fuels to a spinning fan in your home. Remember to include magnets, motors, and generators in your diagram.

Writing Journal

Review the answers you wrote in your journal before you read the chapter. Change your answers, as needed, based on what you learned.

Write the letter of the best answer choice.

1. What is an electric current made up of?
   A. simple circuits
   B. watts
   C. magnets
   D. moving electric charges

2. Which two balloons will attract each other?

A.

B.

C.

D.

3. Which material will provide the most resistance?
   A. a superconductor
   B. a good conductor
   C. a good insulator
   D. a poor insulator

4. If you magnetize an iron nail using a permanent magnet, you have created a _____.
   A. permanent magnet.
   B. electromagnet.
   C. compass.
   D. temporary magnet.

5. Which type of circuit is shown below?

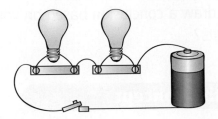

   A. simple circuit
   B. parallel circuit
   C. series circuit with a switch
   D. simple circuit with a switch

6. Which device converts electrical energy to energy of motion?
   A. battery
   B. electric motor
   C. electromagnet
   D. generator

7. What is lightning?

   A. a discharge of static electricity

   B. an effect of Earth's magnetic field

   C. an electric current in a circuit

   D. an aurora

8. Which change could make this magnet more powerful?

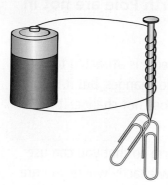

   A. Use a shorter nail.

   B. Add more coils of wire.

   C. Wrap the wire around two nails.

   D. Connect the wires to the center of the nail.

Answer the following in complete sentences.

9. Explain how the cord on an electric device uses insulators and conductors to control electric current.

10. The diagram shows Earth's magnetic field. Explain how this magnetic field affects the way a magnetic compass works.

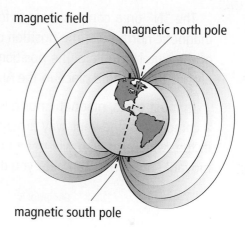

magnetic field

magnetic north pole

magnetic south pole

You Can...

Discover More

Why doesn't a compass needle always point to Earth's true north, that is, toward the geographic North Pole? A compass needle points to Earth's magnetic north pole. But the magnetic north pole and Earth's geographic, or true, North Pole are not in the same place.

The "N" on a compass stands for "north." A compass needle is attracted to Earth's magnetic north pole. The position of the magnetic north pole changes, but it is south of the true North Pole. The position of the true North Pole does not change. It is always in the same place in the Arctic Ocean.

In most cases, magnetic north is close enough to true north so that you can use a compass to find your way around. But if you need to know exactly where you are in the wilderness, you will need to calculate where true north is. A compass with a movable outer ring can help you do this.

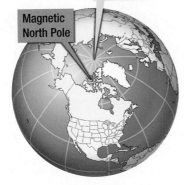

The true North Pole is in the Arctic Ocean. The magnetic north pole is south of the true North Pole. The angle of the difference between the two poles depends on where you are.

This compass has an outer ring that can move to match a number on your map. The pointer will then show you true north.

 Simulations Visit **www.eduplace.com/cascp** to discover more about magnets and their uses.

Science and Math Toolbox

Using a Hand Lens

A hand lens is a tool that magnifies objects, or makes objects appear larger. This makes it possible for you to see details of an object that would be hard to see without the hand lens.

Look at a Coin or a Stamp

1. Place an object such as a coin or a stamp on a table or other flat surface.

STEP 1

2. Hold the hand lens just above the object. As you look through the lens, slowly move the lens away from the object. Notice that the object appears to get larger and a little blurry.

STEP 2

3. Move the hand lens a little closer to the object until the object is once again in sharp focus.

STEP 3

Making a Bar Graph

A bar graph helps you organize and compare data.

Make a Bar Graph of Animal Heights

Animals come in all different shapes and sizes. You can use the information in this table to make a bar graph of animal heights.

Heights of Animals

Animal	Height (cm)
Bear	240
Elephant	315
Cow	150
Giraffe	570
Camel	210
Horse	165

1. Draw the side and the bottom of the graph. Label the side of the graph as shown. The numbers will show the height of the animals in centimeters.

2. Label the bottom of the graph. Write the names of the animals at the bottom so that there is room to draw the bars.

3. Choose a title for your graph. Your title should describe the subject of the graph.

4. Draw bars to show the height of each animal. Some heights are between two numbers.

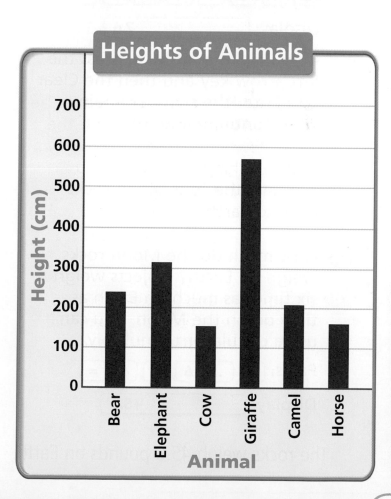

Heights of Animals

H3

Using a Calculator

After you've made measurements, a calculator can help you analyze your data.

Add and Multiply Decimals

Suppose you're an astronaut. You may take 8 pounds of Moon rocks back to Earth. Can you take all the rocks in the table? Use a calculator to find out.

	Weight of Moon Rocks	
Moon Rock	**Weight of Rock on Moon (lb)**	
Rock 1	1.7	
Rock 2	1.8	
Rock 3	2.6	
Rock 4	1.5	

1. To add, press:

   [1] [.] [7] [+] [1] [.] [8] [+]
   [2] [.] [6] [+] [1] [.] [5] [=]

   Display: [7.6]

2. If you make a mistake, press the left arrow key and then the Clear key. Enter the number again. Then continue adding.

3. Your total is 7.6 pounds. You can take the four Moon rocks back to Earth.

4. How much do the Moon rocks weigh on Earth? Objects weigh six times as much on Earth as they do on the Moon. You can use a calculator to multiply.

   Press: [7] [.] [6] [×] [6] [=]

   Display: [45.6]

The rocks weigh 45.6 pounds on Earth.

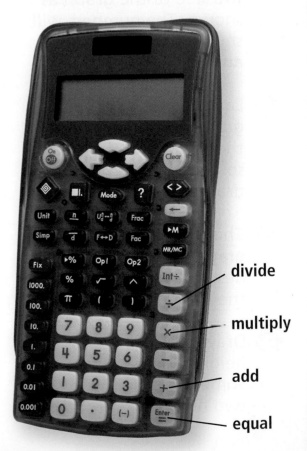

divide

multiply

add

equal

Finding an Average

An average is a way to describe a group of numbers. For example, after you have made a series of measurements, you can find the average. This can help you analyze your data.

Add and Divide to Find the Average

The table shows the amount of rain that fell each month for the first six months of the year. What was the average rainfall per month?

1 Add the numbers in the list.

$$
\left.\begin{array}{r} 102 \\ 75 \\ 46 \\ 126 \\ 51 \\ +\ 32 \\ \hline 432 \end{array}\right\} \text{6 addends}
$$

2 Divide the sum (432) by the number of addends (6).

$$
\begin{array}{r}
72 \\
6\overline{)432} \\
-\ 42 \\
\hline
12 \\
-\ 12 \\
\hline
0
\end{array}
$$

Rainfall	
Month	**Rain (mm)**
January	102
February	75
March	46
April	126
May	51
June	32

The average rainfall per month for the first six months was 72 mm of rain.

Using a Tape Measure or Ruler

Tape measures and rulers are tools for measuring the length of objects and distances. Scientists most often use units such as meters, centimeters, and millimeters when making length measurements.

Use a Tape Measure

1. Measure the distance around a jar. Wrap the tape around the jar.

2. Find the line where the tape begins to wrap over itself.

3. Record the distance around the jar to the nearest centimeter.

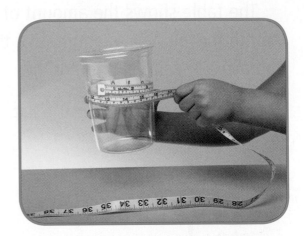

Use a Metric Ruler

1. Measure the length of your shoe. Place the ruler or the meterstick on the floor. Line up the end of the ruler with the heel of your shoe.

2. Notice where the other end of your shoe lines up with the ruler.

3. Look at the scale on the ruler. Record the length of your shoe to the nearest centimeter and to the nearest millimeter.

Measuring Volume

beaker, a measuring cup, and a graduated cylinder are used to measure volume. Volume is the amount of space something takes up. Most of the containers that scientists use to measure volume have a scale marked in milliliters (mL).

Beaker
50 mL

Measuring cup
50 mL

Graduated cylinder
50 mL

Measure the Volume of a Liquid

1 Measure the volume of juice. Pour some juice into a measuring container.

2 Move your head so that your eyes are level with the top of the juice. Read the scale line that is closest to the surface of the juice. If the surface of the juice is curved up on the sides, look at the lowest point of the curve.

3 Read the measurement on the scale. You can estimate the value between two lines on the scale.

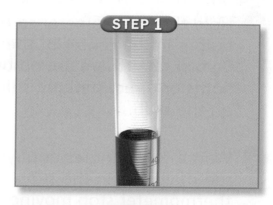

STEP 1

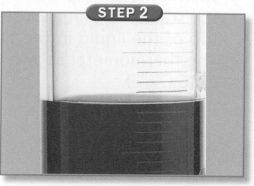

STEP 2

cience and Math Toolbox

Using a Thermometer

A thermometer is used to measure temperature. When the liquid in the tube of a thermometer gets warmer, it expands and moves farther up the tube. Different scales can be used to measure temperature, but scientists usually use the Celsius scale.

Measure the Temperature of a Liquid

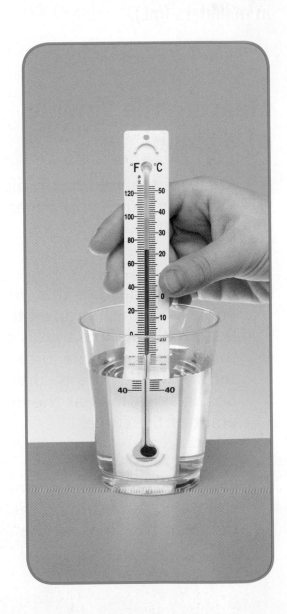

1. Half fill a cup with warm tap water.

2. Hold the thermometer so that the bulb is in the center of the liquid. Be sure that there are no bright lights or direct sunlight shining on the bulb.

3. Wait a few minutes until you see the liquid in the tube of the thermometer stop moving. Read the scale line that is closest to the top of the liquid in the tube. The thermometer shown reads 22°C (72°F).

Using a Balance

A balance is used to measure mass. Mass is the amount of matter in an object. To find the mass of an object, place it in the left pan of the balance. Place standard masses in the right pan.

Measure the Mass of a Ball

1 Check that the empty pans are balanced, or level with each other. When balanced, the pointer on the base should be at the middle mark. If it needs to be adjusted, move the slider on the back of the balance a little to the left or right.

2 Place a ball on the left pan. Then add standard masses, one at a time, to the right pan. When the pointer is at the middle mark again, each pan holds the same amount of matter and has the same mass.

3 Add the numbers marked on the masses in the pan. The total is the mass of the ball in grams.

Making a Chart to Organize Data

A chart can help you keep track of information. When you organize information, or data, it is easier to read, compare, or classify it.

Classifying Animals

Suppose you want to organize this data about animal characteristics. You could base the chart on the two characteristics listed—the number of wings and the number of legs.

1 Give the chart a title that describes the data in it.

2 Name categories, or groups, that describe the data you have collected.

3 Make sure the information is recorded correctly in each column.

Next, you could make another chart to show animal classification based on number of legs only.

My Data

Fleas have no wings. Fleas have six legs.

Snakes have no wings or legs.

A bee has four wings. It has six legs.

Spiders never have wings. They have eight legs.

A dog has no wings. It has four legs.

Birds have two wings and two legs.

A cow has no wings. It has four legs.

A butterfly has four wings. It has six legs.

Animals–Number of Wings and Legs

Animal	Number of Wings	Number of Legs
Flea	0	6
Snake	0	0
Bee	4	6
Spider	0	8
Dog	0	4
Bird	2	2
Butterfly	4	6

Reading a Circle Graph

A circle graph shows a whole divided into parts. You can use a circle graph to compare the parts to each other. You can also use it to compare the parts to the whole.

A Circle Graph of Fuel Use

This circle graph shows fuel use in the United States. The graph has 10 equal parts, or sections. Each section equals $\frac{1}{10}$ of the whole. One whole equals $\frac{10}{10}$.

Oil Of all the fuel used in the United States, 4 out of 10 parts, or $\frac{4}{10}$, is oil.

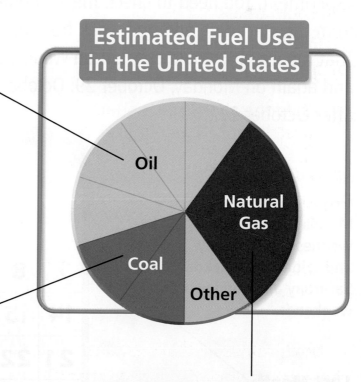

Estimated Fuel Use in the United States

Oil

Natural Gas

Coal

Other

Coal Of all the fuel used in the United States, 2 out of 10 parts, or $\frac{2}{10}$, is coal.

Natural Gas Of all the fuel used in the United States, 3 out of 10 parts, or $\frac{3}{10}$, is natural gas.

Measuring Elapsed Time

A calendar can help you find out how much time has passed, or elapsed, in days or weeks. A clock can help you see how much time has elapsed in hours and minutes. A clock with a second hand or a stopwatch can help you find out how many seconds have elapsed.

Using a Calendar to Find Elapsed Days

This is a calendar for the month of October. October has 31 days. Suppose it is October 22 and you begin an experiment. You need to check the experiment two days from the start date and one week from the start date. That means you would check it on Wednesday, October 24, and again on Monday, October 29. October 29 is 7 days after October 22.

Days of the Week
Monday, Tuesday, Wednesday, Thursday, and Friday are weekdays. Saturday and Sunday are weekends.

Last Month
Last month ended on Sunday, September 30.

October

Sunday	Monday	Tuesday	Wednesday	Thursday	Friday	Saturday
	1	2	3	4	5	6
7	8	9	10	11	12	13
14	15	16	17	18	19	20
21	22	23	24	25	26	27
28	29	30	31			

Next Month
Next month begins on Thursday, November 1.

Using a Clock or a Stopwatch to Find Elapsed Time

You need to time an experiment for 20 minutes.

It is 1:30 P.M.   **Stop at 1:50 P.M.**

You need to time an experiment for 15 seconds. You can use the second hand of a clock or watch.

Start the experiment when the second hand is on number 6.

Stop when 15 seconds have passed and the second hand is on the 9.

You can use a stopwatch to time 15 seconds.

Press the reset button on a stopwatch so that you see 0:00₀₀.

Press the start button. When you see 0:15₀₀, press the stop button.

Measurements

Volume

1 L of sports drink is a little more than 1 qt.

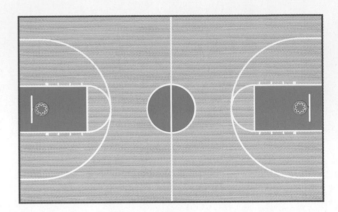

Area

A basketball court covers about 4,700 ft². It covers about 435 m².

Metric Measures

Temperature

- Ice melts at 0 degrees Celsius (°C)
- Water freezes at 0°C
- Water boils at 100°C

Length and Distance

- 1,000 meters (m) = 1 kilometer (km)
- 100 centimeters (cm) = 1 m
- 10 millimeters (mm) = 1 cm

Force

- 1 newton (N) =
  1 kilogram × 1 (meter/second)
  per second

Volume

- 1 cubic meter (m³) = 1 m × 1 m × 1 m
- 1 cubic centimeter (cm³) =
  1 cm × 1 cm × 1 cm
- 1 liter (L) = 1,000 milliliters (mL)
- 1 cm³ = 1 mL

Area

- 1 square kilometer (km²) =
  1 km × 1 km
- 1 hectare = 10,000 m²

Mass

- 1,000 grams (g) = 1 kilogram (kg)
- 1,000 milligrams (mg) = 1 g

Temperature

The temperature at an indoor basketball game might be 27°C, which is 80°F.

Length and Distance

A basketball rim is about 10 ft high, or a little more than 3 m from the floor.

Customary Measures

Temperature
- Ice melts at 32 degrees Fahrenheit (°F)
- Water freezes at 32°F
- Water boils at 212°F

Length and Distance
- 12 inches (in.) = 1 foot (ft)
- 3 ft = 1 yard (yd)
- 5,280 ft = 1 mile (mi)

Weight
- 16 ounces (oz) = 1 pound (lb)
- 2,000 pounds = 1 ton (T)

Volume of Fluids
- 8 fluid ounces (fl oz) = 1 cup (c)
- 2 c = 1 pint (pt)
- 2 pt = 1 quart (qt)
- 4 qt = 1 gallon (gal)

Metric and Customary Rates
km/h = kilometers per hour
m/s = meters per second
mph = miles per hour

Health and Fitness Handbook

Being healthy means that all parts of your body and mind work well together. To keep your body healthy,

- know how to take care of your body systems.
- use safe behaviors when you play.
- choose the right amounts of healthful foods.
- get physical activity every day.
- use behaviors that keep you well.

This handbook will help you learn ways to keep yourself healthy and safe. What will *you* do to stay healthy?

The Nervous System

Central Nervous System

Brain The brain is the control center for the body.

Spinal Cord The spinal cord is a bundle of nerves that extends down your back.

- Messages to and from the brain travel through the spinal cord.
- Sometimes the spinal cord sends messages directly to other nerves without sending them to the brain first.

brain

spinal cord

Peripheral Nervous System

Peripheral means "on the outside." Peripheral nerves connect the brain and spinal cord to the rest of the body. There are two kinds of peripheral nerves.

Sensory Nerves These nerves carry messages *to* the central nervous system.

Motor Nerves These nerves carry messages *from* the central nervous system.

The nervous system carries millions of messages every minute. These messages tell you:

- what you see, hear, taste, smell, and touch.
- what you think and how you feel.
- how your body is working.

A Nerve Cell

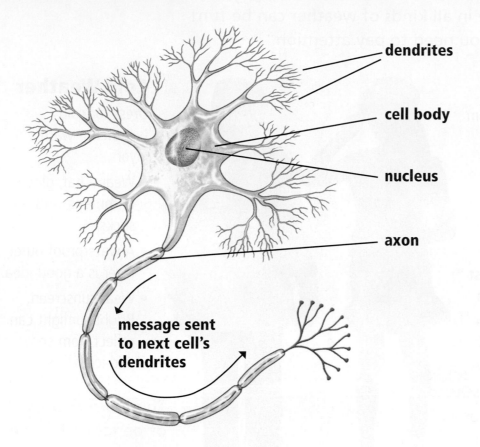

dendrites

cell body

nucleus

axon

message sent
to next cell's
dendrites

Nerve cells are called *neurons*. They carry messages to and from the brain and spinal cord. You are born with almost all the neurons your body will ever form. Here's an example of how neurons work.

1 You touch something hot. Cells in your fingertips send a warning message.

2 Dendrites in cells in your sensory nerves pick up the message. They send it to other neurons through their axons.

3 The message reaches the spinal cord.

4 The spinal cord sends messages to motor nerves. The messages cause the muscles in your hand to move away from the hot object.

All of this happens in less time than it takes you to blink!

Safety in Every Season

Being outside in all kinds of weather can be fun! But to be safe, you need to pay attention.

Hot Weather

Protect your skin from the harmful rays of the Sun.

- Always wear sunscreen with a SPF of at least 15.
- Wear sunglasses that protect against UVA and UVB rays.
- Loose-fitting clothes keep you cool and protect your skin. A hat helps, too!
- Drink plenty of water.

Cold Weather

Dress for cold weather in warm layers.

- Wear a hat, gloves or mittens, and socks.
- A waterproof outer layer is a good idea.
- Wear sunscreen. Bright sunlight can reflect from snow and ice.

Water Safety

When swimming:
- always have a buddy.
- know your limits.
- rest often.

Ice Safety

When walking on ice:
- tilt your body forward.
- set your feet down flat.
- take short steps.

Poisonous Plants

If you touch a poisonous plant, rinse the area with rubbing alcohol or water. If a red, itchy rash appears, soak the area with cold water for 10 minutes three times a day. Do not break any blisters.

Stinging Insects

Remove the insect's stinger by scraping it with something stiff, like a credit card. Make a paste of baking soda and water. Apply it to the place where the stinger was. Use a cold pack to help reduce itching and swelling.

The Exercise Cycle

Physical activity is important for good health. It makes your heart, lungs, and muscles strong. It helps you keep a healthful weight, too. It's best to get physical activity every day. When you exercise, include a warm-up, exercise, and a cool-down.

① Warm-up Begin with five minutes of gentle activity. Walking is a good way to warm up your body. Also stretch your muscles gently. This helps prevent injury.

② Exercise Exercise at a steady level for 20 minutes. You should feel your heart beating faster. You should also be breathing hard, but not so hard that you couldn't talk to a friend at the same time.

③ Cool-down Exercise at a lower level for about five minutes. Your heart rate and breathing should slow down. Then spend five more minutes stretching your muscles again.

Tips

✔ Drink extra water before, during, and after exercise. This replaces water your body loses when you sweat.

✔ If you are injured or an exercise hurts when you do it, stop right away and tell an adult.

Servings for Good Nutrition

Food gives you energy. It also provides materials your body needs to grow and develop. It's important to eat the right kinds of food in the right amounts and to get physical activity. Together, these will help you maintain a healthful weight.

Food Group	Daily Amount	Examples
Grains	3–6 oz.	bread cereal cooked rice or pasta
Vegetables	2–4 cups	leafy vegetables chopped vegetables, cooked or raw vegetable juice
Fruits	1–2 cups	apple, banana, or orange chopped, cooked, or canned fruit
Milk	2–3 cups	milk or yogurt natural cheese processed cheese
Meat and Beans	$5\frac{1}{2}$ oz.	cooked lean meat, poultry, or fish beans nuts

Stop Diseases From Spreading

Sometimes when you're ill, you have a contagious disease. *Contagious* means that you can spread the illness to others. These diseases are caused by harmful bacteria or viruses that enter the body.

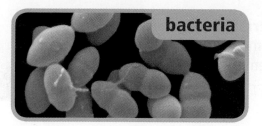
bacteria

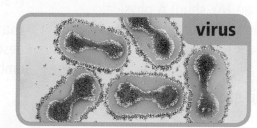
virus

Bacteria cause...
- tetanus
- food poisoning
- strep throat

Viruses cause...
- the common cold
- the flu
- measles
- mumps
- chicken pox

To help stop the spread of these diseases, stay home when you are ill. Also do these things:
- Cover your mouth and nose when you sneeze or cough.
- Throw away tissues after you use them.
- Wash your hands often during the day.
- Keep wounds clean and covered.

❖ **The Best Recipe for Disease Prevention** ❖

Eat healthful foods and handle food safely.

Exercise every day.

Get plenty of sleep.

Keep your body clean.

Have regular check-ups with your doctor and dentist.

Glossary

English-Spanish Glossary

adaptation (ad ap TAY shun) A physical feature or a behavior that helps a plant or animal survive. (56)

adaptación Rasgo físico o comportamiento que ayuda a sobrevivir a una planta o a un animal.

aurora (uh ROHR uh) A display of lights in the sky caused by particles from the Sun interacting with Earth's magnetic field and atmosphere. (318)

aurora Luces del cielo causadas por partículas procedentes del Sol que interactúan con el campo magnético y la atmósfera terrestre.

bacteria (bak TEER ee uh) Microorganisms found in all living organisms and everywhere on Earth. (104)

bacteria Microorganismos que se hallan en todos los organismos vivos y en todos los lugares de la Tierra.

battery (ba tur REE) A device that converts chemical energy to electrical energy. (286)

batería Dispositivo que convierte la energía química en energía eléctrica.

bay (bay) A body of water that is partly enclosed by land and has a wide opening. (239)

bahía Masa de agua limitada por tierra y con una gran entrada al mar.

biodegradable material (by oh dee GRAYD ah buhl muh TEER ee uhl) Matter that breaks down easily in the environment. (136)

material biodegradable Material que se descompone con facilidad en el medio ambiente.

camouflage (KAM uh flahzh) The coloring, marking, or other physical appearance of an animal that helps it blend in with its surroundings. (58)

camuflaje La coloración, marcas u otra apariencia física de un animal, que le ayudan a esconderse en sus alrededores.

carnivore (KAHR nuh vawr) An animal that eats only other animals. (90)

carnívoro Animal que sólo se alimenta de otros animales.

cell (sehl) The basic unit that makes up all living things. (104)

célula Unidad básica de la que se componen todos los seres vivos.

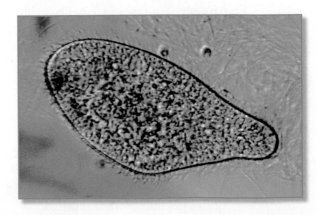

chaparral (shap ur AL) An ecosystem with wet and mild winters and extremely hot and dry summer. (25)

chaparral Ecosistema con inviernos templados y húmedos y veranos muy cálidos y secos.

cleavage (KLEE vedj) The tendency of a mineral to split easily along flat surfaces. (163)

fisura Tendencia de un mineral a partirse fácilmente formando superficies lisas.

community (kuh MYOO nih tee) All the organisms in an ecosystem. (16)

comunidad Todos los organismos que componen un ecosistema.

compass (KUHM puhs) An instrument that senses magnetic north using a free-moving magnet. (317)

brújula Instrumento que localiza el norte magnético por medio de un imán en movimiento.

compost (KAHM pohst) Decayed material from once-living things that is used to enrich the soil. (124)

abono orgánico Material de desecho de lo que fueron seres vivos, que se usa para enriquecer la tierra.

conductor (kuhn DUHK tuhr) A material through which charged particles flow easily. (283)

conductor Material a través del cual circulan fácilmente las partículas con carga.

consumer (kuhn SOO mur) An animal that gets energy by eating plants, or by eating other animals that eat plants. (50)

consumidor Animal que obtiene energía alimentándose de plantas, o alimentándose de otros animales que comen plantas.

coral reef (KOR uhl reef) An ecosystem found in warm, tropical saltwater and built on a structure of coral deposits. (33)

arrecife de coral Ecosistema que se encuentra en las aguas marinas tropicales y sobre una estructura de depósitos de coral.

creep (kreep) Slow movement of land along a fault. (201)

arrastre Movimiento lento de tierra a lo largo de una falla.

decay (dih KAY) To break down into simpler materials. (122)

descomponerse Separarse en materiales más simples.

decomposer (dee kuhm POH zur) A living thing that breaks down the remains of dead organisms. (122)

desintegrador Ser vivo que descompone los restos de los organismos muertos.

delta (DEHL tah) A large mass of sediment deposited at the mouth of a river. (240)

delta Gran masa de sedimentos depositados en la boca de un río.

deposition (dehp uh ZIHSH uhn) The dropping of sediment moved by water, wind, and ice. (238)

sedimentación Caída de sedimento arrastrado por el agua, el viento o el hielo.

desert (DEH zurt) A dry ecosystem with sandy soil. (24)

desierto Ecosistema seco con suelo arenoso.

earthquake (URTH kwayk) A sudden movement of part of Earth's crust. (200)

terremoto Movimiento repentino de la corteza terrestre.

ecosystem (EE koh sihs tuhm) All the living and nonliving things that interact in an area. (8)

ecosistema Todos los seres vivos y las cosas sin vida que interactúan en una misma zona.

ecotourism (ee koh TUR ihz uhm) Travel to natural habitats that avoids harming and helps preserve these areas and the organisms that live there. (139)

ecoturismo Viajes por los hábitat naturales, en los que se evitan los daños y se ayuda a preservar estas zonas y a los organismos que viven en ellas.

electric charges (ih LEHK trihk CHAHR juhz) Units of electricity. (272)

carga eléctrica Unidades de electricidad.

electric circuit (ih lehk trihk SUR kiht) The pathway that electric current follows. (284)

circuito eléctrico Recorrido que sigue la corriente eléctrica.

electric current (ih lehk trihk KUR uhnt) Continuous flow of electric charges. (282)

corriente eléctrica Fluido continuo de cargas eléctricas.

electromagnet (ih lehk troh MAG niht) A strong temporary magnet that uses electricity to produce magnetism. (324)

electroimán Imán potente que funciona con electricidad para producir magnetismo.

energy (EHN ur jee) The ability to cause change. (14)

energía Capacidad de causar cambios.

environment (ehn VY ruhn muhnt) Everything that surrounds and affects an organism. (16)

medio ambiente Todo lo que rodea y afecta a un organismo.

epicenter (EHP ih sehn tur) Where an earthquake is felt most strongly or has its greatest intensity. (203)

epicentro Lugar donde un terremoto se siente con más fuerza o intensidad.

erosion (ih ROH zhuhn) The movement of rock material from one place to another. (234)

erosión Desplazamiento de material de roca de un lugar a otro.

erratic (ih RAH tihk) A single large boulder moved by a glacier and deposited when the glacier melts. (251)

roca errática Gran canto rodado movido por un glaciar y depositado en el lugar donde el glaciar se descongela.

extinction (ihk STIHNK shun) When all the members of a species die out. (62)

extinción Cuando mueren todos los miembros de una especie.

fault (fawlt) A crack in Earth's crust. (201)

falla Grieta en la corteza terrestre.

focus (FOH kuhs) The point underground where an earthquake starts. (202)

foco Punto bajo la superficie de la Tierra donde comienza un terremoto.

food chain (food chayn) The path of food energy in an ecosystem from plants to animals. (90)

cadena alimenticia Recorrido que en un ecosistema sigue la energía de la comida, desde las plantas a los animales.

food web (food web) The overlap of two or more food chains. (96)

red alimenticia Superposición de dos o más cadenas alimenticias.

fossil fuels (FAHS uhl FYOO uhlz) Natural fuels such as coal, oil, or natural gas. (334)

combustibles fósiles Combustibles naturales, como el carbón, el petróleo o el gas natural.

generator (JEHN uh ray tuhr) A device that uses magnetism to convert energy of motion into electrical energy. (327)

generador Dispositivo que funciona con magnetismo para convertir la energía cinética en energía eléctrica.

glacier (GLAY shur) A large mass of slow-moving ice. (234)

glaciar Gran masa de hielo que se mueve lentamente.

habitat (HAB ih tat) The place where a plant or animal lives. (56)

hábitat Lugar donde viven las plantas o los animales.

hardness (HAHRD nihs) A measure of how easily a mineral can be scratched. (162)

dureza Resistencia que tiene un mineral a ser rayado.

hazardous waste (HAZ ur duhs WAYST) Waste that can pollute the environment even when it occurs in very small amounts. (132)

desechos peligrosos Desechos que incluso en pequeñas cantidades pueden contaminar el medio ambiente.

headland (HED land) A point of land, usually high, that extends out into the water. (239)

cabo Punta de tierra, generalmente elevada, que se extiende hacia el mar.

herbivore (HUR buh vawr) An animal that eats only plants. (90)

herbívoro Animal que sólo come plantas.

hibernate (HY bur nayt) Go into a deep sleep during which very little energy is used. (59)

hibernar Entrar en un sueño profundo, durante el cual se gasta muy poca energía.

igneous rock (IHG nee uhs rahk) Rock that forms when melted, or molten, rock from deep below the Earth's surface cools and hardens. (178)

roca ígnea Roca que se forma cuando la roca fundida del interior de la Tierra sale a la superficie y se endurece.

insulator (IHN suh lay tuhr) A material that electric charges do not flow through easily. (283)

aislante Material a través del cual las partículas eléctricas no circulan fácilmente.

landslide (LAND slyd) The sudden movement of loose rock and soil down a steep slope. (218)

deslizamiento de tierra Movimiento repentino de rocas sueltas y suelo en una pendiente.

lava (LAH vuh) Molten rock that reaches Earth's surface. (210)

lava Roca fundida que sale a la superficie de la Tierra.

litter (LIHT uhr) Trash that is not disposed of in a way that prevents harm to ecosystems. (131)

basura Desechos que se tiran sin prevenir daños al ecosistema.

luster (LUH stehr) The way a mineral shines, or reflects light. (160)

brillo Luz que emite o refleja un mineral.

magma (MAG muh) The molten rock beneath Earth's surface. (210)

magma Roca fundida que hay bajo la superficie de la Tierra.

magnet (MAG niht) An object that attracts certain metals. (310)

imán Objeto que atrae ciertos metales.

magnetic field (mag NEHT ihk feeld) The space in which the force of a magnet can act. (312)

campo magnético Espacio en el que actúa la fuerza de un imán.

Glossary

Glossary

H28 • Glossary

magnetic poles (mag NEHT ihk pohlz) Two areas where the force of a magnet is at its greatest. (311)

polos magnéticos Las dos zonas donde es más potente la fuerza de un imán.

metallic mineral (MEH tahl ihk MIHN ur uhl) A mineral that is shiny like metal. (169)

mineral metálico Mineral que brilla como el metal.

metamorphic rock (meht uh MAWR fihk rawk) New rock that forms when existing rocks are changed by heat, pressure, or chemicals beneath Earth's surface. (180)

roca metamórfica Roca nueva que se forma cuando las rocas ya existentes son modificadas por el calor, la presión o los compuestos químicos bajo la superficie de la Tierra.

microorganism (my kroh AWR guh nihz uhm) An organism that cannot be seen without the help of a microscope. (104)

microorganismo Organismo que no se puede ver sin la ayuda de un microscopio.

mimicry (MIHM ih kree) An adaptation that allows an animal to protect itself by looking like another kind of animal or like a plant. (58)

mimetismo Adaptación que protege a un animal por el parecido de éste con otra planta o animal.

mineral (MIHN ur uhl) A nonliving solid material that has a definite chemical makeup and is found in Earth's outermost layer. (160)

mineral Material sólido sin vida que tiene una composición química definida y se encuentra en la capa exterior de la Tierra.

moraine (muh RAYN) The long ridge formed by boulders, rocks, and soil carried and deposited by a glacier. (251)

morrena Estructura alargada formada por cantos rodados, rocas y suelo transportados y depositados por un glaciar.

motor (MOH tuhr) A device that changes electrical energy to energy of motion. (326)

motor Dispositivo que convierte la energía eléctrica en energía cinética.

nonmetallic mineral (NOHN meh tahl ihk MIHN ur uhl) A mineral that is dull or glassy. (168)

mineral no metálico Mineral que es opaco o vidrioso.

nutrient recycling (NOO tree uhnt ree SY kuh ling) The process of breaking down materials into a different form that can be used again. (123)

reciclaje de nutrientes Proceso que sirve para descomponer materiales de forma que se puedan usar de nuevo.

H29

O

omnivore (AHM nuh vawr) An animal that eats both plants and animals. (90)

omnívoro Animal que se alimenta de otros animales y plantas.

organism (AWR guh nihz uhm) A living thing. (14)

organismo Ser vivo.

oxygen (AHK sih juhn) A gas most living things need to survive. (14)

oxígeno El gas que necesitan la mayoría de los animales para sobrevivir.

P

parallel circuit (PAR uh lehl SUR kiht) A circuit in which the parts are connected so that electric current passes along more than one pathway. (285)

circuito paralelo Circuito cuyas partes están conectadas de modo tal que la corriente eléctrica hace más de un recorrido.

permanent magnet (PUR muh nuhnt MAG niht) An object that keeps its magnetism for a long time. (311)

imán permanente Un objeto que mantiene su magnetismo durante mucho tiempo.

photosynthesis (foh toh SIHN thih sihs) The process through which plants make their own food. (88)

fotosíntesis Proceso por el cual las plantas fabrican su propio alimento.

plankton (PLANK tuhn) Microorganisms that exist in the water and form the beginning of most aquatic food chains. (106)

plancton Microorganismos que existen en el agua y que forman el primer eslabón de la mayoría de las cadenas alimenticias acuáticas.

pollinator (PAHL uh nay tur) An animal that helps plants make seeds by moving pollen. (52)

polinizador Animal que transporta el polen de un sitio a otro ayudando a las plantas a fabricar semillas.

pollutant (pah LOOT uhnt) A material that causes pollution. (131)

contaminante Material que produce contaminación.

pollution (pah LOO shun) The addition of harmful materials to the environment. (131)

contaminación La liberación de materiales perjudiciales en el medio ambiente.

population (pahp yuh LAY shun) All the members of one kind of plant or animal in a community. (16)

población Todos los miembros del mismo tipo de plantas o animales que viven en una comunidad.

predator (PREH deh tur) An animal that hunts other animals for food. (56)

depredador Animales que cazan a otros animales para alimentarse.

prey (PRAY) Any animal that is hunted for food by a predator. (56)

presa Cualquier animal que un depredador caza para alimentarse.

producer (pruh DOO sur) An organism that makes its own food. (50)

productor Organismo que produce su propio alimento.

rainforest (RAYN fawr ihst) An ecosystem where it rains a lot. (22)

bosque tropical Ecosistema donde llueve mucho.

reproduce (ree pruh DOOS) To make more organisms of their own kind. (15)

reproducir Cuando un ser vivo crea más organismos del mismo tipo.

resistance (ree ZIH stans) The ability of a material to slow down or stop electric current. (294)

resistencia Capacidad de un material para desacelerar o detener la corriente eléctrica.

resource (REE sors) Something found in nature that is useful to organisms. (68)

recurso Algo que se encuentra en la naturaleza y que es útil para los organismos.

river system (RIH vur sys tehm) The largest river and all the waterways that drain into it. (240)

sistema fluvial Un río grande y todos sus afluentes.

rock (rahk) A solid material made up of one or more minerals. (176)

roca Material sólido que está compuesto de uno o más minerales.

rock cycle (rahk SY kuhl) The continuous series of changes that rocks undergo. (186)

ciclo de las rocas Serie continua de cambios producidos en las rocas.

sand dune (SAND doon) A hill or pile of sand that was formed by the wind. (254)

duna de arena Colina de arena formada por el viento.

scavenger (SKAV uhn jur) An animal that feeds on the remains or wastes of dead animals. (120)

carroñero Animal que se alimenta de los restos o desechos de animales muertos.

sediment (SEHD uh muhnt) Sand, particles of rock, bits of soil, and remains of once-living things. (179)

sedimento Arena, partículas de roca, trocitos de suelo y restos de lo que fueron seres vivos.

sedimentary rock (sehd uh MEHN tuh ree rahk) Rock that forms when sand, particles of rock, bits of soil, and bits of once-living things are pressed together and harden. (179)

roca sedimentaria Roca que se forma cuando arena, partículas de roca y restos de seres vivos se compactan y endurecen.

seed dispersal (SEED dih SPUR suhl) The scattering or carrying away of seeds from the plant that produced them. (52)

dispersión de semillas Esparcimiento de las semillas lejos de la planta que las produjo.

seismology (syz MAHL uh jee) The study of earthquakes. (202)

sismología Estudio de los terremotos.

series circuit (seer EEZ SUHR kiht) A circuit in which the parts are connected so that electric current passes through each part, one after another, along a single pathway. (285)

circuito en serie Circuito en el que las partes están conectadas de modo que la corriente eléctrica pasa por cada parte, una tras otra, a lo largo de un solo recorrido.

species (SPEE sheez) A group of organisms that produces organisms of the same kind. (56)

especie Grupo de organismos que producen organismos del mismo tipo.

static electricity (STAT ihk ih lehk TRIHS ih tee) A built-up electric charge. (274)

electricidad estática Carga eléctrica contenida.

streak (streek) The color of a mineral when it is ground to a powder. (161)

raspadura El color de un mineral cuando se muele hasta convertirlo en polvo.

taiga (TY guh) A fairly dry ecosystem with very cold, long winters and short, cool summers. (26)

taiga Ecosistema seco con inviernos muy largos y fríos y veranos cortos y frescos.

temperate zone (TEHM pur iht zohn) An area of Earth where the temperature rarely gets very hot or very cold. (16)

zona templada Zona de la Tierra donde la temperatura rara vez es muy cálida o muy fría.

temporary magnet (TEHM puhr ayr ee MAG niht) An object that loses its magnetism after a short time. (311)

imán temporal Un objeto que mantiene su magnetismo por poco tiempo.

tsunami (tsoo NAH mee) A very large ocean wave caused by an earthquake that occurs on the ocean floor. (202)

maremoto Ola gigantesca de mar causada por un terremoto que tiene lugar en el suelo del océano.

volcano (vahl KAY noh) An opening in Earth's crust through which hot ash, gases, and molten rock escape from deep within Earth. (210)

volcán Apertura en la corteza terrestre por la que escapan cenizas calientes, gases y roca fundida del interior de la Tierra.

watt (waht) A unit of measure of electrical power. (293)

vatio Unidad que mide la energía eléctrica.

weathering (WETH ur ihng) The slow wearing away of rock into smaller pieces. (232)

desgaste Erosión lenta de la roca al deshacerse en trozos más pequeños.

Index

Permission Acknowledgments

Excerpt from *The Secret World of Spiders,* by Theresa Greenaway, illustrated by Tim Hayward and Stuart Lafford. Copyright © 2001 Steck-Vaughn Company. Reprinted by permission of Steck-Vaughn Company, an imprint of Harcourt Education International. Excerpt from "Arachne the Spider" from the *Orchard Book of Greek Myths,* retold by Geraldine McCaughrean, illustrated by Emma Chichester Clark. First published in the U.K. by Orchard Books in 1992. Text copyright © 1992 by Geraldine McCaughrean. Illustrations copyright © 1992 by Emma Chichester Clark. Reprinted by permission of The Watts Publishing Group and Margaret K. McElderry Books, an imprint of Simon & Schuster Children's Publishing Division. Excerpt from "The Alligator" from *The Florida Water Story: From Raindrops to the Sea,* by Peggy Sias Lantz and Wendy A. Hale. Copyright © 1998 by Peggy Sias Lantz and Wendy A. Hale. Reprinted by permission of Pineapple Press, Inc. Excerpt from *Animals in Danger: Florida Manatee,* by Rod Theodorou. Copyright © 2001 by Reed Educational & Professional Publishing. Reprinted by permission of Harcourt Education. Excerpt from "The Search" from *The Midnight Fox,* by Betsy Byars, illustrated by Ann Grifalconi. Copyright © 1968 by Betsy Byars. Reprinted by permission of Viking Penguin, A Division of Penguin Young Readers Group, A Member of Penguin Group (USA) Inc., 345 Hudson Street, New York, NY 10014. All rights reserved. Excerpt from *Crafty Canines: Coyotes, Foxes, and Wolves,* by Phyllis J. Perry. Copyright © 1999 by Franklin Watts. All rights reserved. Reprinted by permission of Franklin Watts, an imprint of Scholastic Library Publishing. Excerpt from "First Snow: A Native American Myth" from *The Golden Hoard: Myths and Legends of the World* by Geraldine McCaughrean, illustrated by Bee Willey. Text copyright © 1995 by Geraldine McCaughrean. Illustrations copyright © 1995 by Bee Willey. Reprinted by permission of Orion Children's Books and Margaret K. McElderry Books, an imprint of Simon & Schuster Children's Publishing Division. Excerpt from *Crafty Canines: Coyotes, Foxes, and Wolves*, by Phyllis J. Perry. Copyright © 1999 by Franklin Watts. All rights reserved. Reprinted by permission of Franklin Watts, an imprint of Scholastic Library Publishing. Excerpt from *The Search* from *The Midnight Fox*, by Betsy Byars, illustrated by Ann Grifalconi. Copyright © 1968 by Betsy Byars. Reprinted by permission of Viking Penguin, A Division of Penguin Young Readers Group, A Member of Penguin Group (USA) Inc., 345 Hudson Street, New York, NY 10014. All rights reserved.

Cover and Title Page

Front cover (black bear cub) © Royalty-Free/CORBIS. (forest) © Lester Lefkowitz/CORBIS. (ferns) © Theo Allofs/CORBIS. Back cover (climbing cub) Daniel Dempster Photography/Alamy. (forest) © Lester Lefkowitz/CORBIS. Spine © Royalty-Free/CORBIS. Title page © Royalty-Free/CORBIS. End Paper (t) Bill Lea/Dembinsky Photo Assoc. (b) Photodisc/Getty Images.

Photography

iv Joe McDonald/Corbis. **v** Terry Donnelly/Dembinsky Photo Assoc. **vi** Craig Lovell/Eagle Visions Photography/Alamy. **vii** Jeremy Woodhouse/Pixelchrome.com. **ix** George Ranalli/Photo Researchers, Inc. **x** David Young-Wolff/Photo Edit, Inc. **xi** Cosmo Condina/Tips Images. CA Standards (bl) Roger Ressmeyer/Corbis. (l–bkgrd) Roger Ressmeyer/Corbis. (c–bkgrd) Tom Bean/DRK Photo. (rt) Tom Bean/DRK Photo. (rb) Gibson Stock Photography. (rc) Chiaki Tsukumo/Associated Press. **S1** Gibson Stock Photography. **S3** © David Aubrey/Corbis. **S4** © Charles Krebs/CORBIS. **S5** Gerry Ellis/Minden Pictures. Unit A Opener: © Phillip Colla/OceanLight. CA Field Trip: (bkgrd) Julie Mowbray/Alamy Images. (tr) Phil Schermeister/National Geographic/ Getty Images. (br) © Stephen J. Krasemann/DRK Images. **1** © Phillip Colla/OceanLight. **2–3** J. Schultz/T. Souce/AlaskaStock.com. **3** (tr) Geroge Ranalli/Photo Researchers, Inc. (cr) Tom Brakefield/Corbis.(bl) © Tom Velzo/Minden Pictures. (cl) Charles O'Rear/Corbis. **4** (t) Dan Suzio/Photo Researchers, Inc. (c) Richard Hamilton Smith/Dembinsky Photo Assoc. (b) Francois Gohier Nature Photography. **4–5** (bkgrd) Terry Donnelly/Dembinsky Photo Assoc. **6** (bl) Photonica. **6–7** (bkgrd) Terry W. Eggers/Corbis. **9** John Anderson/Animals Animals. **10** (t) RGK Photography/Stone/Getty Images. (b) Jeff Foott/Bruce Coleman, Inc. **11** (t) Photonica. (c) John Anderson/Animals Animals. (b) RGK Photography/Stone/Getty Images. **12** (bl) Dennis Flaherty/Photo Researchers, Inc. **12–13** (bkgrd) Marc Moritsch/National Geographic Image Collection. **14** (bl) Jeff L. Lepore/Photo Researchers, Inc. **15** (t) Francois Gohier/Photo Researchers, Inc. (1 down from t) John Beedle/Alamy. (2 down from t) © Jose Fuste Raga/Zefa/Corbis. (2 up from b) M. T. Frazier/Photo Researchers, Inc. (1 up from b) Bud Lehnhausen/Photo Researchers, Inc. (b) Gail M. Shumway/Bruce Coleman, Inc. **16** (br) Stan Osolinski/Corbis. **16–17** John Anderson/Animals Animals. **17** (tr) Danita Delimont/Alamy. (br) Garry Black/Masterfile. (cl) franzfoto.com/Alamy. **19** (t) Jeff L. Lepore/Photo Researchers, Inc. (c) John Anderson/Animals Animals. **20** Lynda Richardson/Corbis. **20–21** (bkgrd) Michael Fogden/DRK Photo. **24** (tl) Joe McDonald/Corbis. (tr) Norbert Wu/Minden Pictures. (bkgd) Terry Donnelly/Dembinsky Photo Assoc. **25** (br) Joe McDonald/Corbis. (cl) Joe McDonald/Corbis. (bkgrd) Dan Suzio/Photo Researchers, Inc. **26** (inset) Michael S. Bisceglie/Animals Animals. (bkgrd) Richard Hamilton Smith/Dembinsky Photo Assoc. **27** (c) Terry Donnelly/Dembinsky Photo Assoc. (b) Joe McDonald/Corbis **29** (inset) Tom and Pat Leeson/Photo Researchers, Inc. (bkgrd) Galen Rowell/Corbis. **30** Georgette Douwma/The Image Bank/Getty Images. **30–31** (bkgrd) Photodisc Green/Getty Images. **32** (bl) Stuart Westmorland/Corbis. (br) Corbis. **33** (cr) KLEIN/Peter Arnold, Inc. (br) Norbert Wu/Minden Pictures. (bl) Corbis. **34** (inset) Corbis. (bkgrd) Michio Hoshino/Minden Pictures. **35** (t) Stuart Westmorland/Corbis. (c) Norbert Wu/Minden Pictures. (b) Michio Hoshino/Minden Pictures. **39** (tr) David Young-Wolff/Photo Edit, Inc. (bl) Paul A. Souders/Corbis. **42–43** (bkgrd) Ahup Shah/DRK Photo. **43** (tl) Jim Steinberg/Photo Researchers, Inc. (cr) William Ervin/Photo Researchers, Inc. (bl) Corbis. **44** (t) © E.R. Degginger/Color-Pic, Inc. (c) David Aubrey/Corbis. (b) Gregory K. Scott/Photo Researchers, Inc. **44–45** (bkgrd) Johnny Johnson/DRK Photo. **46** Michael Fogden/DRK Photo. **46–47** (bkgrd) J. A. Kraulis/Masterfile. **48** P. Sharpe/OSF/Animals Animals. **49** (cl) Norbert Wu/DRK Photo. (br) Warren Photographic. **50** (tr) Robert Pickett/Papilio/Alamy. (br) Jim Zuckerman/Corbis. **50–51** Chuck Place/ Alamy. **51** (cl) Michael Habicht/Animals Animals. (tl) Francois Gohier/Photo Researchers, Inc. **52** (bl) © E.R. Degginger/Color-Pic, Inc. (br) Gregory K. Scott/Photo Researchers, Inc. **53** (t) P. Sharpe/OSF/Animals Animals. **53** (c) Jim Zuckerman/Corbis. (b)© E. R. Degginger/Color-Pic, Inc. **54** (bl) Anne DuPont. **54–55** (bkgrd) Brandon D. Cole/Corbis. **56** Sharon Cummings/Dembinsky Photo Assoc. **57** (tl) Nigel j. Dennis/Gallo Images/Corbis, (tr) Michael Fogden/DRK Photo, (br) John Eastcott/YVA Momatiuk/Photo Researchers, Inc. (bl) C.K. Lorenz/Photo Researchers, Inc. **58** (cr) Buddy Mays/Corbis. (br) Benelux Press/Taxi/Getty Images, (bl) © E.R. Degginger/Color-Pic, Inc. **59** (br) Stephen Dalton/Photo Researchers, Inc. (cl) Bob and Clara Calhoun/Bruce Coleman, Inc. **60** Galen Rowell/Corbis. **60–61** Keren Su/Taxi/Getty Images. **61** Mark J. Thomas/Dembinsky Photo Assoc. **62** (tl) © Steven Holt/Vireo. (tc) Don & Pat Valenti/DRK Photo. (br) Tom McHugh/Photo Researchers, Inc. **63** (t) Buddy Mays/Corbis. (tc) Benelux Press/Taxi/Getty Images. (bc) Keren Su/Taxi/Getty Images. (b) Don & Pat Valenti/DRK Photo. **66** (bl) Galen Rowell/Corbis. **66–67** (bkgrd) Mattias Klum/National Geographic Image Collection. **68** (cl) Joe McDonald/Corbis. (c) Corbis. (cr) Kevin Schafer/Corbis. (b) © David Aubrey/Corbis. **68–69** (b) Gary Cralle/The Image Bank/Getty Images. **69** (tr) Dean Kildaw /USFWS. **70** Eastcott Momatiuk/National Geographic/Getty Images. **71** (t) David Aubrey/Corbis. (c) Dean Kildaw /USFW, (b) Eastcott Momatiuk/National Geographic/Getty Images. **72–73** (inset) Chris Adami. (bkgrd) Killer Stock, Inc./Corbis. **73** (tl), (tcl), (trc), (tr) Chris Adami. **74** (tr) S. J. Krasemann/Peter Arnold, Inc. **75** (inset) Courtesy Alejandro Acevedo/Western Washington University. (bkgrd) Flip Nicklin/Minden Pictures. Unit B Opener: Muench Photography Inc. CA Field Trip: (bkgrd) Dennis Flaherty. (tr) Craig Lovell/Eagle Visions Photography/Alamy. (br) Bill Leaman/Dembinsky Photo Assoc. **81** Charles Krebs/Corbis. **82–83** (bkgrd) Norbert Wu. **83** (tr) © Arthur Morris/CORBIS (br) Wim van Egmond/Visuals Unlimited/Getty Images. (cl) George Grall/National Geographic/Getty Images. **84** (t) Jeremy Woodhouse/Pixelchrome.com. (c) Konrad Wothe/Minden Pictures. (b) S Lowry/Univ Ulster/Stone/Getty Images. **84–85** (bkgrd) Art Wolfe, Inc. **86–87** J. Borris/Zefa/Masterfile **88** (inset) Michael P. Gadomski/Photo Researchers, Inc. **88–89** (b) Frank Krahmen/Zefa/Corbis. **89** (bl) Michiel Schaap/Foto Natura/Minden Pictures. (br) Stephen J. Krasemann/DRK Photo. **90** (tl) © E.R. Degginger/ Color-Pic, Inc. (tr) Paul Sterry/Worldwide Picture Library/Alamy. **91** (tl) Konrad Wothe/Minden Pictures. (tr) Jeremy Woodhouse/Pixelchrome.com. **92** (t) © hunziker-photo/Alamy (c) John Cancalosi/Peter Arnold, Inc. (b) Yva Momatiuk & John Eastcott/Photo Researchers, Inc. **93** (t-bkgrd) Frank Krahmen/Zefa/Corbis. (t-inset) Michiel Schaap/Foto Natura/Minden Pictures. (c) Paul Sterry/ Worldwide Picture Library/Alamy. (b) hunzikerphoto.com/Alamy. **94** (bl) Mike Hill/Taxi/Getty Images. **94–95** (bkgrd) Art Wolfe, Inc. **96** (br) © Lighttrace Studio / Alamy **96–97** (bkgrd) Corbis. **97** (tl) Mark Moffett/Minden Pictures, (tr) Tom Vezo/Minden Pictures. (tc) Darrell Gulin/Dembinsky Photo Assoc. (bc) © Joe McDonald/Animals Animals (br) Joe McDonald/Corbis. **98** (tl) © Sinclair Stammers/Science Photo Library (tcr) Stuart Westmorland/Corbis. (tr) Fred Hazelhoff/Foto Natura/Minden Pictures. (bl) Flip Nicklin/Minden Photo Obtained Under N.M.F.S. Permit #987/Minden Pictures. (cl) David Tipling/Getty Images. (bcr) Ken Lucas/Ardea. (br) David Fleetham/Alamy. (bkgrd) Robert George Young/Masterfile. **99** (t) Art Wolfe, Inc. (c–tl) Mark Moffett/Minden Pictures. (c–r) Darrell Gulin/Dembinsky Photo Assoc. (c–bl) Tom Vezo/Minden Pictures. (b–tl) Stuart Westmorland/Corbis. (b–r) Ken Lucas/Ardea. (b–bl) David Fleetham/Alamy. **100** (tc) Photo 24/Brand X Pictures/PictureQuest. (cr) The New York Public Library/Art Resource, NY. **101** (inset) Courtesy of The Sierra Club. (bkgrd) Library of Congress/Science Photo Library. **102** (inset) VVG/Science Photo Library/Photo Researchers, Inc. **102–103** (bkgrd) Brandon D. Cole/Corbis. **104** (bl) E. R. Degginger/Earthscenes/Animals Animals. (br) S Lowry/Univ Ulster/Stone/Getty Images. **105** SciMAT/Photo Researchers, Inc. **106** (l) © E.R.Degginger/Dembinsky Photo Assoc. (br) © Dennis Kunkel Microscopy, Inc. **107** (t) S. Lowry/Univ Ulster/Stone/Getty Images. (c) SciMAT/Photo Researchers, Inc. (bl) © Dennis Kunkel Microscopy, Inc. **111** (tr) © Micheal Newman/Photo Edit, Inc. (br) © A Ramey/Photo Edit, Inc. **114–115** Don & Pat Valenti/DRK Photo. **115** (t) Inga Spence/Index Stock (c) © David Jay Zimmerman/Corbis (bl) PhotoDisc Blue/Getty Images. **116** (t) Phillip Wallick/Corbis. (c) © Oliver Strewe/Getty Images (b) Kenneth W. Fink/Photo Researchers, Inc. **116–117** (bkgrd) Macduff Everton/The Image Bank/Getty Images. **118–119** (bkgrd) Mike Lane/Photo Researchers, Inc. **120** Jack Wilburn/Animals Animals. **121** (t) Kenneth W. Fink/Photo Researchers, Inc. (b) Nigel J Dennis/NHPA. **123** Donald Specker/Animals Animals. **124** © Oliver Strewe/Getty Images **125** (t) Mike Lane/Photo Researchers, Inc. (b) © Oliver Strewe/Getty Images **128–129** (bkgrd) Frits Hoffmann/The Image Works. **130** Joel W. Rogers/Corbis. **131** Phillip Wallick/Corbis. **132** Joe Mcdonald/Bruce Coleman, Inc. **133** (t) Joel W. Rogers/Corbis. (c) Phillip Wallick/Corbis. (b) Joe Mcdonald/Bruce Coleman, Inc. **134** (bl) Stephen J. Krasemann/DRK Photo. **134–135** (bkgrd) Gordon Whitten/Corbis. **136** © HMCo. **137** IEV Mercier/Wallis/Photri, Inc. **138** Frans Lanting/Minden Pictures. **139** Macduff Everton/The Image Bank/Getty Images. **140–141** (bkgrd) Raymond German/ National Geographic Image Collection. **141** (inset) David Cavagnaro/DRK Photo. **142** (l) Jose Azel/Aurora Photos. **143** (t) © HMCo. (c) David Cavagnaro/DRK Photo. (b) IEV Mercier/Wallis/Photri, Inc. **144** (bl) Corbis. (br) Morton Beebe/Corbis. **144–145** (bkgrd) Darrell Gulin/Stone/Getty Images. **145** (bl) Martha Cooper/Viesti. **147** Dana Bolles. Unit C Opener: Fritz Polking/Visuals Unlimited. CA Field Trip: (bkgrd) Carlos Adolfo Sastoque N./Superstock. (tr) David Boyle/Animals Animals- Earth Scenes. (br) Michael T. Sedam/Corbis. **153** Tom Bean/Stone/Getty Images. **154–55** (bkgrd) Gerry Ellis/Minden Pictures. **155** (tr) PHOTOTAKE Inc./Alamy. (cl) Wayne Scherr/Photo Researchers, Inc. (cr) Bio Associates/Photo Researchers, Inc. (bl) © Jim Sugar/Corbis. **156** (t) ©